Social Justice in the Ancient Near East
and the People of the Bible

Social Justice
in the Ancient Near East
and the People of
the Bible

Léon Epzstein

SCM PRESS LTD

Translated by John Bowden from the French
*La Justice Sociale dans le Proche-Orient ancien et le
Peuple de la Bible,*
published 1983 by Les Editions du Cerf, Paris

British Library Cataloguing in Publication Data

Epzstein, Léon
Social justice in the Ancient Near East
and the people of the Bible.
1. Social justice——History   2. Near
East——History——To 622   3. Near East
——Social policy
I. Title   II. La justice sociale dans le
Proche-Orient ancien et le peuple de la
Bible. *English*
323.4′0939   HN656.A8

ISBN 0–334–0233–4–3

First British edition 1986
published by SCM Press Ltd
26-30 Tottenham Road, London N1

Phototypeset by Input Typesetting Ltd
and printed in Great Britain by
Richard Clay (The Chaucer Press Ltd),
Bungay, Suffolk

To the memory of my great-uncle
Abraham Epstein
historian and Hebrew scholar
– a just and wise man
(1841-1918)

CONTENTS

PREFACE

On the completion of this work I would like to express a debt of gratitude to a number of people.

First of all I must thank M.Henri Cazelles. The conversations which he had with me were a great source of encouragement. Moreover, he was very ready to follow the progress of the book while I was writing it and was lavish with extremely valuable advice. I am delighted to have been able to profit from his great skills. M.André Caquot drew my attention to the dangers presented by a subject like the present one: his comments, which went to the very heart of the problem, were extremely useful and I am much in debt to him. M.Guillaume Cardascia kindly read the chapter on Mesopotamia and Mme Bernadette Menu that on Egypt, while M.Melèze-Modrzejewski showed me many kindnesses and I have benefited immensely from his erudition. I feel deeply grateful to all of these.

I benefited from the help of my old colleagues of the Centre National de la Recherche Scientifique, Mme Mireille Dreisine and MM.Rolland Chollet, Daniel Louÿs and Benoit Zawisza, who must also be given warm thanks; and I am indebted to Mlle Monique Roman for her valuable help in preparing the typescript for production. I would also like to use this opportunity to thank all those nameless people who have contributed to the production of this work, especially those at the Bibliothèque Oecuménique et Scientifique d'Etudes Bibliques, the excellent organization of which made my work very much easier.

INTRODUCTION

I am afraid that my decision to embark on such a vast and difficult subject might suggest a lack of modesty on my part. However, that is not at all the case. My choice has been dictated by a feeling of curiosity, of involvement, of recognition, related to a group of traditions and values which come to us from a remote distance but which seem still to be extremely topical.

Having worked on a book about the relationships between economics and morality in modern times,[1] I felt the need to go back to the sources. Given the very keen concern with social questions in our day, it seemed to me to be interesting to investigate one of the principal legacies from the world of the Bible, and to examine from a historical and sociological perspective the main elements of this great complex from the heart of which modern social justice has grown and matured.

The topic has already been the object of a variety of researches, but it has usually been treated in monographs by specialists. In order to gain an overall view and bring out its essential features, and to answer a number of burning questions, I thought that it would be useful to examine the subject on a sufficiently broad scale to see it as a complex within which everything holds together. A work of this kind, a comparative study, runs great risks, above all when it relates to a somewhat intangible abstract phenomenon. However, even if others have reservations about my work and criticisms of it, I hope that it will stimulate and help further reasearch.

The rule of justice is one of the essential objectives of all moral systems which have reach a certain stage of development. This generalization seems to apply in a quite special way to Judaism which, as we know, attaches prime importance to social justice. One of the great rabbis of former days, Simon Gamaliel, stressed that justice is the first of the three pillars (alongside truth and peace) which ensure the continuity of human society (Lehmann 1963, I, 129). According to Albert Einstein, in Judaism the concern to give each person his or her due, the love of justice, comes close to fanaticism (Runes 1959, 397). The American economist and sociologist Louis Wallis, whose work I shall be discussing later, declared that the history of the Jewish people is to a large degree a series of reactions against economic injustice (Wallis 1953). According to Emmanuel Levinas (1963, 38), the state of mind which it is convenient to call Jewish messianism consists in 'the subordination of all possible relations between God and man – redemption, revelation and creation – to the inauguration of a society in which justice is strong enough to extend to all members and become a reality instead of remaining an inspiration of individual piety'.

The problem I shall be discussing is of enormous interest and has many aspects. So that we do not get lost in such a vast and complicated subject, I shall concentrate on the period between the settlement of the Hebrews in Canaan and the exile, taking account above all of the period represented by the eighth and seventh centuries BC. This was the time when the new forms of economic and social life began to attack the roots of the old tribal organization and undermine the foundations of traditional morality (Kapelrud 1966, 197).

My choice has been dictated by the feeling that it was at this stage, at the time of the first great writing prophets, that the problem of social justice was raised with unparalleled strength and keenness, and that it prefigured what was going to come next in the history of the Jewish people.

At the gateway to three continents, at the meeting point of the great trade routes (Rathjens 1962, 124), almost equidistant from the pillars of Hercules and the Persian Gulf (Steinmann 1959, 22), Israel was an important junction in the then known world. However, it was surrounded by powerful and formidable neighbours whose predominance could be felt in almost every sphere (Albright 1968, 207). This quite special geographical and political situation (Wright 1946, 6: Glueck 1946) clearly demands our attention, and it seems natural that we should begin by looking at the state of affairs in the neighbouring regions, in Mesopotamia and Egypt: in the basin of the Tigris and the Euphrates (Boyer 1938, 66) on the one hand and in the Nile valley on the other (Bonneau 1964, 11). Here, thanks to irrigation and the fertile alluvial deposits brought by the river 'there came into being, if not the first civilizations, at least the first states' (Wittfogel 1964, 9).

PART ONE

Social Justice among the Neighbours of Ancient Israel

1

The Mesopotamian Laws

In the prehistoric period at the beginning of the third millennium, before a centralized and autocratic government became established (Jacobsen 1943, 172), the small human communities were scattered over the countryside and separated by marshes or desert regions (Jacobsen 1957, 98). As the Sumerian epic poem *Gilgamesh and Agga* describes them (Malamat 1963, 250) they seem to have enjoyed the prerogatives of the *vox populi* (Kramer 1964b, 148-56; Jacobsen 1964, 157f.; Artzi 1964, 159-66) and to have profited from the advantages of a democratic régime in the classical (rather than the modern) sense of the word (Jacobsen 1943, 159), i.e. from a form of government based on a council of elders, though its ultimate authority was vested in a general assembly comprising all the members, or rather all the adult free men, of which the community was composed (Jacobsen 1943, 172; Speiser 1954, 8-15; Evans 1958, 11).

This embryonic social morality, this quest for equality and this need for equity which appear so soon in the evidence of how people lived, was manifested in an even more explicit way in religious thought and the law.

The main deities which make up the Mesopotamian pantheon are exalted, as being enamoured of all that is good and just (Kramer 1964b, 129). One of the most important and longest hymns in Sumerian literature is dedicated to Utu, the sun-god and god of justice, who governs the order of the universe (Kramer 1961, 255). Another deity, the Lagashite goddess Nanshe, is described in one of the hymns as she who is sensitive to the oppression of one man by another, who acts as mother to the orphan, is concerned for the fate of the widow, seeks justice for the poor and is a refuge for the weak (Kramer 1964b, 126).

A passage from the great hymn to Shamash (the Assyro-Babylonian equivalent of the Sumerian god Utu, Deshayes 1969, 610) makes a clear distinction between the bad judge who accepts jars of wine and the good one who does not become corrupt, who protects the weak and prolongs life. He is protected by Shamash, and the royal palace is his dwelling place (Seux 1976, 58). In the two main Babylonian sanctuaries dedicated to this god, at Sippar and at Larsa, the worshippers of the sun counted among the children of Shamash two personifications of justice, Kittu and Mêsharu (the two names derive from the Akkadian roots *kânu* and *eshêru* which denote 'be true' and 'be just' respectively, Rosenberg 1965, 161).

Among the very ancient religious texts discovered by J.P.Peters and J.H.Haynes between 1889 and 1900 (Kramer 1964b, 22), a hymn celebrates Dungi, the deified king of Ur, not only as a warrior and hunter, but also as guardian of the city, who brings justice, protects the weak and helps the worker (Peters 1921, 140; Barton 1918, 27-9). It is also said in this same hymn that the perversion of justice brings the country to ruin (Barton 1918, 31).

As proof that Sumerian social life was steeped in a need for justice and a respect for the law, S.N.Kramer cites the famous judgment (pronounced about 1850 BC) acquitting the 'silent wife', Nin-dada, who was to be executed for not having told the authorities about the assassination of her husband. The members of the tribunal finally came round to the view of the defence by declaring that the woman had reasons for keeping silent and concluded that the punishment of the actual criminals should suffice. According to Kramer, the fact that two copies of the same account of the trial have been found shows that the decree of the Nippur assembly on the 'silent wife' was known in all the legal circles of Sumer and that it served as jurisprudence (Kramer 1961a, 101).

We obviously find the largest number of elements relating to our subject in the series of legislative texts which belong to the 'common Mesopotamian source, a source which could be called Sumero-Akkadian' (Szlechter 1957, 192), and which represents 'the earliest legal archives that we possess' (Cuq 1929, V). These texts, as we know, go back to a very distant past, but they have only been rediscovered and deciphered during the course of the last century.

In the present state of our knowledge, mention must first be made of the 'reforms' of Urukagina, now read Uruinimgina (Lambert 1970, 419), the prince-pontiff (Kramer 1961a, 89) of Lagash, a city-state in the south-east of Sumer which played a very important role in the political history of Sumer between about 2450 and 2300 (Kramer 1964, 52), but which was in a pitiful state both socially and politically when Urukagina appeared (Kramer 1961a, 92f.). The inscriptions inspired by the person who is with some degree of justification considered as the first reformer in history (Deshayes 1969, 74) are for Mesopotamia 'the earliest collect of coherent texts which report other facts than wars won and give other listings than those of sanctuaries built' (Lambert 1956, 169). Some scholars put the reign and the 'reforms' of Urukagina between 2850 and 2650 (Deimel 1931, 72), but according to more recent research they would seem to come from a much later date: towards 2400 according to some (*Reallexikon der Assyriologie*, 246) or according to others in the middle of the twenty-fourth century (Yeivin 1962, I, 439).

The 'reforms' of Urukagina comprise two parts which contrast with each other yet correspond point for point: the first lists the 'abuses' preceding his reign and the second gives an account of the edicts promulgated in order to remedy them (Lambert 1956, 169). In fact this second part consists of a series of measures aimed at eliminating the injustices committed by the officials of the palace or the temple and by the rich with regard to the shepherds, the builders, the peasants, the debtors and their families (Szlechter 1957, 81). There is a section about reducing the dues claimed by the clergy on a number of occasions, notably those connected with funerals (Deshayes 1969, 75); or it is said that if a poor man makes a catch, his fish should not be taken from him. And in the conclusion we read that Urukagina 'cleansed the homes of the inhabitants of Lagash of usury, of hoarding, of famine, of theft and of attacks and instituted their liberty'. He 'had this declaration sealed by Ningirsu that he would not deliver the widow and the orphan to the rich' (Lambert 1956, 183).

Something similar to this also appears in connection with another 'ensi' of Lagash, the famous Gudea, represented by several dozen statues the majority of which now adorn the museum of the Louvre (Parrot 1960, 347). Stepson of the founder of a new dynasty, in power at a time (towards the first half of the twenty-first century, *Realexikon der Assyriologie*, 246) when Lagash played a dominant role among the other cities in the south of Sumer, Gudea had commercial relationships with almost all the then 'civilized' world. And as he also had considerable success in military matters, he served as the inspiration for an important work (Kramer 1964, 66) in which it is said that he was chosen to 'be the good shepherd in the country' (Thureau-Dangin 1905, 107), that he 'gave his attention to the laws of Nina and of Ningirsu' and saw to it that the rich and powerful man did not do any ill to the orphan or the widow (ibid. 1905, 113). We also know that among his instructions given to the people, some are aimed at protecting slaves (Szlechter 1957, 81; Kramer 1964, 139).[1]

After the 'reforms' of Urukagina and Gudea come legislative acts in the strict sense, some of which are assimilated to codes.

According to our present knowledge, the earliest legislative archive of Lower Mesopotamia is represented by the Sumerian code of Ur-Nammu (Szlechter 1957, 74), whose reign began about 2112 (*ANET.S*, 523). He was the founder of the Third Dynasty of Ur (Fish 1938, 160-74; Oppenheim 1954, 6-17; Lambert 1964, 89-109; Schmökel 1966, 143-7), capital of the Sumerian empire, which at that time was even more glorious than Lagash (Woolley 1950, 112-47). Although the code of Ur-Nammu was discovered more than half a century ago (Klima 1967, 125), it was only deciphered, translated and published much later (Korošec 1961, 12, by S.N.Kramer in 1952, cf. Kramer 1961a, 94). It is considered to be a link between the 'reforms' of Urukagina and Gudea on the one hand and the codes of Eshnunna, Lipit-Ishtar and Hammurabi on the other. The dispositions of the prologue recall what we find in the 'reforms' of the two 'princes' of Lagash (Szlechter 1953, 6).

Ur-Nammu, designated by the will of the gods to ascend the throne of Ur, declares that with the help of the god Nanna he has re-established equity and justice in the country. He fixed stable relationships between various monetary units (of bronze and silver) by weight. He did away with the cheats and tricksters who appropriated the oxen, the sheep and the asses of the citizens. He saw to it that the man with a shekel did not become the prey of the man with a mina (a mina was worth sixty shekels, Kramer 1961a, 98). He took effective steps to protect the orphans, the widows and the poor (Szlechter 1955, 174). But the 'most effective feature of the code of Ur-Nammu', according to Szlechter (1957, 75), 'is the adoption of the system of legal composition as the basis of penal law. Thus we see that four centuries before Hammurabi, whose code is based on the *lex talionis*,[2] legal composition was already known in the Mesopotamian basin.' We should recall that the *lex talionis*, which consisted in giving the same treatment (from the Latin *talis*) to the offender, is a mode of punishment which represents a step forward from vengeance by virtue of which the punishment given is much more serious than the evil suffered. However, Cruveilhier (1938, 196 notes) writes, 'the *lex talionis* is a brutal and unintelligent sanction. It satisfies the victim's instinct for vengeance without bringing him any compensation. The modern codes impose on the offender a loss proportionate to the damage.'

Still, we should note that this way of looking at things is by no means universal: G.Cardascia, developing the views summarized by A.S.Diamond (1957, 151-5), stresses that by contrast it is the system of legal composition which represents an earlier stage than the *lex talionis*: the latter has a superior ethical value because it affords better protection to the life and integrity of the human person (Cardascia 1979, 176).

The second Sumerian legislative text is the code of Lipit-Ishtar, the fifth king of the dynasty of Isin which reigned during the first half of the nineteenth century (Szlechter 1957, 92). He succeeded his father Ismedagan who was depicted in the literary works of the time as a propagator of law and justice (Edzard 1957, 80). The Code of Lipit-Ishtar is about two centuries later than the Code of Ur-Nammu and about a century earlier than that of Hammurabi. Excavated at the beginning of this century but only identified and translated in 1947-48 by F.Steele (Kramer 1961a, 95), as we now have it the Code of Lipit-Ishtar is composed of nine tablets forming forty-three articles with a prologue and epilogue (Szlechter 1957, 57). Both codes enunciate the general principles relating to the origin of the royal power and its exercise (ibid. 1957, 117). In the prologue it is said that 'Lipit-Ishtar, the obedient pastor, has been called by Nunamnir to establish justice in the land, to blot out corruption by "the word", to break "by force" evil doing and ill will' (61).

In the first part of the Code an important section is devoted to slaves. There we find regulations about 1. the flight of slaves; 2. disputes over the state of slavery; 3. the marriage of a female slave; 4. the freeing of children born from intercourse between the master and his slave concubine. Among other things it is said that 'while considering the slave as a patrimonial possession', 'nevertheless he is to be recognized as having the right to go to court in processes relating to his freedom' (180-2).

Round about a century after the Code of Lipit-Ishtar we have the first of the Akkadian codes, the one that comes from Eshnunna (Yaron 1969). Eshnunna was a city state situated in the valley of the Diyala, a tributary of the Tigris, north of Baghdad; the city is now called Tell Ashmar (Szlechter 1954, 12; Deshayes 1969, 541). The Laws of Eshnunna seem to go back to the beginnings of this principality, perhaps in the period between the fall of the Third Dynasty of Ur at the end of the third millennium and the time when it was conquered by Hammurabi (Boyer 1965, 243). They are now placed towards 1790, that is to say only some decades before the Code of Hammurabi according to the middle chronology of the reign of Hammurabi (1792-1750) which, as we shall see, is the one most generally followed today. Their origin is attributed to Bilalama, king of Eshnunna, but according to Szlechter (1978, 109), they probably date from the reign of Ipiq Addad II or his son Dadusha.

Discovered successively in 1935 and 1947 at Tell Harmal on the territory which at one time formed part of the principality of Eshnunna (Szlechter 1978, 12), and consisting of a prologue and sixty articles, the Laws of Eshnunna comprise certain elements which appear sometimes in Sumerian law (Code of Ur-Nammu, Code of Lipit-Ishtar) and sometimes in Assyrian (Kultepe, Assyrian laws) or Babylonian law (Code of Hammurabi, ibid. 1978, 12).

Parallel to what we shall rediscover in the Code of Hammurabi, the Laws of Eshnunna distinguish three social classes: the *awilu* (patricians who enjoy freedom and full rights), the *mushkenu*, translated 'mesquins', 'mean', by G.Cardascia (a term that can be defined as plebeians who, while being free, are subject to certain limitations), and the *wardu* (slaves, Moscati 1955, 70).

The *mushkenu* were inferior to the *awilu* from a political and social point of view; nevertheless they enjoyed special protection from the palace. Article 35 allows the *mushkenu* to adopt a child of a palace slave in return for compensation paid to the palace. But, in a more characteristic way, article 50 indicates that the palace could pursue outside the frontiers of Eshnunna fugitive slaves and stray animals belonging to the palace, to the *awilu* or the *mushkenu*, though the *mushkenu* could not be associated directly with the palace either as servants or as officials paid by the palace. Coming from different origins (freed slaves, foreigners), the *mushkenu* were independent from the *awilu* and completely free *vis-à-vis* them (Szlechter 1954, 42).

The Laws of Eshnunna fix the price of basic goods, the wages of workers, the loading of boats and chariots; they establish a stable relationship between money (silver by weight) and merchandise used as money (barley) (Szlechter 1954, 65); they regulate the mode for repayment of certain debts (Rosen 1977, 35-8). The penal régime of the Laws of Eshnunna, as in the Code of Ur-Nammu, is based essentially on the principle of legal composition: anyone responsible for an infringement must pay the victim or those who have rights over him an indemnity fixed by the legislator. The level of the legal composition is related to the infringement committed and the legal and social status of the victim (Szlechter 1954, 197).

We owe the most famous code of Mesopotamia to the illustrious representative of the Amorite dynasty, king Hammurabi, who did away with one of his rivals (Finet 1973, 9) and made Babylon the political, religious, economic and intellectual capital of Asia Minor (Boyer 1965, 271). The dates given for his reign vary depending on whether one chooses the high (1848-1806), middle (1792-1750) or low chronology (1782-1686); at present there seems to be general agreement in favour of the medium chronology (1792-1750; Garelli 1969, 229). The stele of laws in the form in which we know it was composed in the last years of his reign. The diffusion of this code was so important (Cardascia 1960, 43) in the Near East that about forty copies and adaptations have come down to us. However, by far the most complete text remains that of the stele kept in the Louvre, discovered in December-January 1901-1902 and transcribed, translated and edited in the same year by Père V.Scheil (Finet 1973, 11).

The fame of this code is explained not only by the fact that it was discovered relatively early and in an almost complete form (Deshayes 1969, 414), but also by its contents. The more recent discoveries of codes which I have just surveyed have changed scholarly views about the originality of the Code of Hammurabi (Moscati 1955, 69). We now know that Hammurabi was not the first to have had the idea of a systematic redaction of the law, but he went further than his predecessors (Parrot 1960, 305). His code 'remains the most important monument of Babylonian law by virtue of the number of dispositions which it contains and by the extent and scope of the prologue and epilogue, which amount to a real treatise on public law' (Szlechter, 1957, 77). It is not a code in the modern sense of the word: Hammurabi collected into a single whole a series of edicts which he had either promulgated himself or taken from tradition or from his predecessors. The code as a whole has not been perfectly unified, but despite the joins, the lacunae and the contradictions, the code nevertheless remains one of the great classics of Babylonian literature (Finet 1973, 11). In parallel to the political unification of the region this code, written in Akkadian, collected and unified the Sumerian and Semitic traditions (Moscati 1955, 70). It was not composed of entirely new laws, but took up old laws revised and made to apply to the whole kingdom (Powis Smith 1931, 11).

In this book we clearly cannot go into the complex of problems raised by the Code of Hammurabi and which are discussed in what is already a vast series of works; I simply want to recall the essential details relevant to us.

The stele on which the code is engraved represents Hammurabi paying homage and receiving the insignia of power from Shamash, sun god and god of justice (Driver and Miles 1952-55, I, 28). From the beginning of the prologue we learn that the vocation of Hammurabi consists in 'establishing justice over Babylon and the vassal regions', 'destroying the wicked and the evil', 'that the strong might not oppress the weak' (Cruveilhier 1938, 3-5). The 'first among kings' (29), he has 'concern for his people in famine' (31); he has 'set justice and equity in the mouth of the people' (41).

In the epilogue, Hammurabi declares himself to be the 'shepherd bringing salvation' (255), legislator 'to bring the orphan and the widow their rights' (257). He addresses 'the oppressed man who has a cause' and recommends him to come into the presence of the image of the king to read the text of the stele so that 'he can understand his cause (the decision in his case)' and 'his mind may be set at ease' (261). In addressing his successors, Hammurabi 'exalts the merits of those who respect the laws inscribed on the stele and utters imprecations against any who may modify or abolish them. While affirming that he is the author of the laws that he has decreed, Hammurabi does not fail to invoke the authority of the gods in support of the legitimacy of his action; the source of legislative power is of divine origin and it is for the king to exercise it' (Szlechter 1977, 182).

In order to protect the people against the exactions of the great, some dispositions of the code are aimed at averting the corruption of judges or abuses practiced by officials. To improve the lot of those who are discriminated against, Hammurabi commends the distribution of plots of land not only to nomads but also to the inhabitants of lower rank, the *mushkenu*. He also tried to improve the situation of tenants by regulating building works (Deshayes 1969, 183); he introduced a degree of liberalization (as compared with the laws of Eshnunna) in favour of debtors for the repayment of debts (Rosen 1977, 182).

However, as I have already said in connection with the Laws of Eshnunna, the Code of Hammurabi also institutes the division of society into three classes (*awilu, mushkenu, wardu*), and the individuals who make them up are far from enjoying the same rights. Contrary to the Code of Ur-Nammu and the Laws of Eshnunna, the Code of Hammurabi applies the *lex talionis*, but only in relationships between the privileged:

§196. If a free man has put out the eye of the son of a free man, his eye shall be put out.

§197. If he has broken the bone of a free man, his bone shall be broken.

As to damage caused to the *mushkenu* and the slaves, the Code of Hammurabi imposes on the person causing the damage a fine proportional to the damage.

§198. If a free man has put out the eye of a *mushkenum* or has broken the bone of a *mushkenum* he shall pay one mina of silver.

§199. If he has put out the eye of the slave of a free man or broken the bone of a slave of a free man he shall pay half of his value.

§204. If a *mushkenum* has struck the head (cheek, jaw) of a *mushkenum*, he shall pay ten shekels of silver (Cruveilhier 1938, 196-9).

It should be noted, however, that no compensation is provided for the owner in the case of damage done by the free man to the slave of a plebeian.

Although from a formal point of view the slaves were included in the section of the code devoted to people and not to things (Falkenstein 1956, 86), in practice it was quite otherwise. The one advantage of this situation lay in the protection that the master offered to his slaves (Moscati 1955, 71).

If we compare the Code of Hammurabi and the Old Testament, it must be recalled that according to the former a slave may be set at liberty at the end of three years as opposed to six years in the Covenant Code and Deuteronomy. However, the latter do not make any distinction of class (Deshayes 1969, 210), provided that a Hebrew is involved, whereas the clause in the Code of Hammurabi (§117) only applies to a patrician (who for example has been sold by an indebted member of his family, Van Leeuwen 1955, 84).

Among the Mesopotamian laws the Code of Hammurabi holds a mean between the Sumerian, which is the most lenient, and the Assyrian, which is the most cruel (Moscati 1955, 75; Cardascia 1969, 84).

The Laws of Eshnunna (§31) simply prohibit a slave from going out by the great gate of Eshnunna, without providing for any sanction against the transgressor. By contrast, the Code of Hammurabi (§15) ordains the death penalty for anyone who aids the escape of a slave belonging to the palace or a *mushkenum*. Anyone who harboured a fugitive slave at Babylon was subject to the death penalty (§§16,19), while acording to the Code of Lipit-Ishtar (art.121) he lost his own slave or in default paid his price in money; at Eshnunna he also lost his slave (§49), or he was even considered to be a thief (§50, Korošec 1961, 20).

In Babylon, the death penalty was often pronounced for such crimes as theft, plunder, receiving of stolen goods and false witness, and the penal law was also applied to the representatives of certain professions who had not had good fortune in the practice of their work. Thus the Code of Hammurabi demands punishment or recompense for surgeons depending on the result of their operations, while making a distinction depending on the condition of the patient (§§215-20, Moscati 1955, 75).

Among the legislative texts later than Hammurabi (Cazelles 1966, 753), after the edict of his son Samsu-iluna (a collection of social provisions aimed at removing or at least relieving difficulties primarily of an economic kind, Klima 1967, 127), attention ought to be paid particularly to the edict of the king of Babylon, Ammisaduqa, the fourth successor of Hammurabi, who reigned a century after he did, perhaps at the end of the first half of the second millennium before our era (about 1646-1624, Bottéro 1961, 114; Hentschke 1965, 115).

The edict of king Ammisaduqa, discovered more than half a century ago, but not at all well known, was published with a commentary by F.R.Kraus in a very important work which appeared in 1958 (*Ein Edikt des Königs Ammi-tsaduqa von Babylon*, see Finkelstein 1961, 81-104). Of a maximum total of about 230 lines which will have made up the intact original, F.R.Kraus has succeeded in making almost 180 legible (Bottéro 1961, 113).

The main aim of this edict is to remedy a dangerously disorganized economic situation (ibid., 154). The disorder came about above all because the majority of citizens, the workers, did not earn enough to live on: this drove them disastrously into debt and made them dependent on a minority of people with possessions (161). Moreover, this state of things paralysed their productive work or at least did not encourage them enough for their performance to reach the level of the needs of the whole country (154).

To cope with this critical state, this edict decreed, among other things:

1. An amnesty or cancellation of arrears of rents (143: these arrears, which had accumulated from one redemption date to the next, made the unfortunate debtors virtually insolvent and reduced them to working simply in order to pay off their debts, 153).

2. An amnesty on certain repayments, namely those called 'loans of necessity' (143: understood as the result of a deficit which there is no means of remedying, produced by the burdensome pressure of levies and taxes which the great majority of workers had found extremely difficult to pay off, 152).

The problem of ownership of land and the means of production is not touched on in this edict. It apparently sought only a temporary remedy for the noxious effects of the system without modifying it in the least (161).

This present chapter is clearly far from being exhaustive. New excavations and researches will certainly produce further interesting information in the future (Klima 1967, 120). At present, it is still often very difficult to make straightforward statements about certain important problems relating to the nature and significance of the Mesopotamian laws. For example, in the present state of our knowledge it seems impossible to give a firm answer to one question which is of great interest to us, namely whether the development of a particular collection of laws is governed primarily by customary right or the personal views of the sovereign (Finkelstein 1970, 256). According to R.de Vaux, the collections which Mesopotamia has bequeathed to us were collections of customary law rather than laws of state promulgated by the sovereign (de Vaux 1961, 145). In speaking of the law in ancient Mesopotamia, Szlechter 'stresses the fact that people would not have neglected the importance of customary law and custom, the source of law'. According to him, 'the legal prescriptions are often aimed only at modifying or abrogating a customary rule, producing solutions to particular cases or more complex cases, or specifying certain rules which have given rise to a divergent jurisprudence' (Szlechter 1965, 75). However, other scholars adopt a more hesitant, if not a more qualified, approach (Leemans 1968, 108; Finkelstein 1970, 256); the former seems even to lean towards the interpretation according to which the views of the sovereign prevailed over customary law, in which case the law would present more the character of a reform than of a codification.

What I have just said on the subject of the role played by the Mesopotamian sovereigns leads us to consider the motives which lay behind their actions. It is not always easy to pronounce on the intentions of others, since there are imponderables and intangible features. It is particularly difficult to do so in this precise case because we have no evidence for getting to the bottom of things. However, it seems impossible entirely to avoid this question. The whole moral dimension of the phenomenon at issue cannot leave us indifferent, and we must at least recall what has been written on this subject by certain specialists.

For example, Urukagina seems to have been a usurper who was very badly received by the upper classes (Stephens 1955, 129); to provide himself with a better defence against his dangerous enemies, he sought the sympathy and support of the people. However, according to Deimel (1931, 77; cf. Hruška 1974, 160), what acted principally in favour of the reforms were the military needs which compelled the sovereign to secure the support of the peasants, the fishermen and the shepherds who were the main components of the army. Diakonoff (1953, 12), by contrast, does not think that the 'reforms' of Urukagina can be explained by the struggle between Lagash and Girsu; it is rather the hostility of the clergy and the aristocracy which will have led the prince to reinforce his economic and political position by confiscating the goods belonging to the temple. On the matter of the edict of king Ammisaduqa, Bottéro (1962, 159; cf. Jacobsen 1943, 128) asks whether the proclamation of a cancellation of debts and an amnesty on taxes was not, if not obligatory, at least usually expected at the beginning of a reign. Perhaps there will have been a 'theological' reason for it: the new king found himself in some way confronted with a chaos from which he had to make a cosmos. But there was above all a more down-to-earth reason: the sovereign who was interested in reconciling himself with the people had first of all to settle the accounts of his predecessors. Since he saw better than the previous ruler the failings of the administration, it was easier for the new ruler to combat disorder and 're-establish equity for the country' (Bottéro 1961, 159).

In a communication of the Académie des Inscriptions et Belles-Lettres specifically devoted to the laws of Hammurabi, Klima (1972, 308) seems to sum up very well the problem of the motives and intentions of all the Mesopotamian rulers. He draws attention to the fact that the intention of implementing public law which appears with Hammurabi was already evoked in a very similar way by King Ur-Nammu in the twenty-second century and by King Lipit-Ishtar in the nineteenth. If we add to that yet other analogies, as for example the principle of the protection of widows, the fatherless, the poor, 'this very striking resemblance suggests that we should conjecture a practice established in the scribal schools from which the authors of the law codes came; a practice which had been adopted quite formally from one ruler to the next because it best expressed the intention of the sovereign unchanged over the centuries. The efforts of the sovereigns tended to reinforce their empire and their personal power; that is why they appreciated and exploited all the means which could serve this end.'

One of the most important problems of cuneiform law (Klima 1972, 316) is how far the law was binding and how it was applied in legal practice (Szlechter 1965, 64). For example, numerous Assyriologists refuse to accept that the Code of Hammurabi was ever applied, invoking 'the fact that hitherto no document of everyday legal practice has been discovered in which a specific disposition of the legislation of Hammurabi had been introduced' (Klima 1972, 308). This approach seems too intransigent, since 'the sovereign legislator of the ancient Near East did not demand that the sentences or the decisions of tribunals, the complaints of individuals, and so on should cite a specific law on which they are based' (308), and 'even in our day, one can find plenty of acts of legal practice which have not the slightest relationship to the basis of legislation' (316). Nor must it be forgotten that we are very far from having all the documents of ancient Babylonian legal practice, since the majority of these acts, buried in the earth, remain unknown (316). In fact, so far we know only two documents of economic and legal practice in which there is a formal relationship to the terms of the stele, but they do not specify what paragraph is concerned. However, if we take account of the whole of Mesopotamian jurisdiction and analyse all the records of the practice in question in a meticulous way (308), we find that numerous documents indicate that the law was binding and that it was in fact applied. This is true above all if we take account not only of the royal laws but also of the decisions of jurisprudence or rules of customary justice with the force of 'law' (Preiser 1969, 33; Szlechter 1965, 64).

Moreover, as far as the Code of Hammurabi is concerned, some scholars stress the fact that the king has shown his intention of introducing his laws vigorously and that 'with all his energy he seeks to institute a living legal order the norms of which will serve to unify the country' (Klima 1972, 316). We must also keep in mind the working hypothesis developed by G.Cardascia that the widespread circulation of the code either in foreign countries or in Babylonia down to a thousand years after the fall of Hammurabi's empire – for example the inclusion of numerous copies of the stele in the seventh century in the famous library of the Assyrian ruler Assurbanipal (669-627) – cannot be explained on purely scientific or scholarly grounds. There must have also been a practical interest: the code was copied not only to preserve a model of literary and linguistic value but because it contained positive law (Cardascia 1960, 47; Preiser 1969, 34).

It seems possible to make a similar observation about all the collections of Mesopotamian law: it would be wrong to believe that their authors simply sought to leave ceremonial steles which had great literary value but were unimportant for legal practice (Klima 1967b, 121).

However, as far as Hammurabi is concerned, we may note that his brilliant success which put Babylon at the centre of the Near Eastern world was short-lived (Cardascia 1956, 40). Moreover the final period of his reign was hardly peaceful (great military expeditions against countries which had not yet been pacified, and internal disturbances). I should also add that he seems to have published his code in the thirty-fourth year of his reign, so that at most he only had eight years to establish the law on his stele. The task was not easy, and one might ask whether he had the time and the means to realize his intention. Now according to Klima, alongside the documents in which the laws on the stele are indubitably applied (though these documents make no reference to the stele) we shall find – in an indisputably much larger number of cases – documents in which the laws on the stele were not applied (Klima 1972, 307-9).

If we return to the 'reforms' of Urukagina we discover that they do not seem to have established his power at Lagash. Undertaken two years before the prince's overthrow, they were soon blown away by the wind. Like many other reformers, Urukagina seems to have come 'too late with too little' (Kramer 1961, 94). As for the laws promulgated by king Ammisaduqa, J.Bottéro compares them with 'edicts of grace' coming from above which never succeeded in abolishing the evil because they attacked only external phenomena – consequences and not root causes (Bottéro 1962, 161).

If even the laws relating to specific phenomena which formed part of current practice proved so difficult to apply, the same thing will be true to an even greater degree in the more intangible area of social morality, which is situated midway between economics and morality. The principle of the protection of widows, orphans and the poor appears in different prologues of the Mesopotamian laws, but it is formulated in an almost stereotyped way, and probably served primarily for the propaganda of the sovereign, who sought to satisfy public opinion. This principle is presented as a prescription without any legal sanction and consequently the chances of its application in actual life would seem to have been very limited (Klima 1972, 308). W.Preiser (1969, 35), among others, shows himself less sceptical in this connection, but despite his approach, which seeks to be 'sociological', he does not seem to bring sufficiently specific convincing arguments to support his thesis.

2

Egyptian Maat

(i) The Old Empire

A great deal has already been written about Egyptian law, above all in recent decades, but its history is still largely unknown (Lurje 1971, 19). That is because the documentation relating to it is fragmentary in character (Theodorides 1967, 109); especially for the period preceding the New Empire (Menu 1977, 439) the original sources are scanty and inadequate (Seidl 1957, 61). Very few legal documents dating from the Old Empire have been preserved in their original form, i.e. on papyrus (Seidl 1942, 198). Moreover the rare strictly legal texts which have come down to us on stone or on papyrus are about specific cases, scattered in time and from very different places (*Dictionnaire de la civilisation égyptienne*, 91). An additional problem is posed by the vagueness of the vocabulary used by the Egyptians in legal texts (Theodorides 1967, 121).

Nevertheless, despite the opinion which has been widespread until recently it seems no longer possible to deny the existence of law (Allam 1978, 65) from the dawn of the Pharaonic dynasties, from the period of the unification of Upper and Lower Egypt under king Menes about 3100 (Theodorides 1974, 501). The legislative work of the kings of Egypt was clearly not achieved all at once nor did it remain uniform, but under the Old Empire and above all after the organization of justice under the Fifth Dynasty the country had its tribunals, its supreme court formed of professional magistrates, its legal archives (Pirenne and Theodorides 1966, 75) and its written procedure (Seidl 1957, 204).

However, unless new excavations change the picture given us by the present state of our knowledge (Seidl 1942, 198), for the moment we find almost nothing coming from Egypt which can compare with the Mesopotamian codes (Theodorides 1971, 291). We have to wait for that until Boccharis (who reigned about 715 BC and was the sole member of the Twenty-Fourth Dynasty).[1] And after that we wait until the 'Code of Hermopolis', which can be dated on palaeographical grounds to the reign of Ptolemy II Philadelphus.[2]

It seems difficult to relate the edict of Horemheb to Mesopotamian codes. As we shall see later, this is a document promulgated more in respect of specific cases, while the Mesopotamian laws were codifications which as a whole regulated the status of society without envisaging particular historical circumstances (Cazelles 1946, 164).[3]

This absence of Egyptian legal codes is attributed by some scholars to the fact that the order of the ruling king (*mdw, wd*) was considered to be the real law and no written law could exist outside it. However, this is only a hypothesis which is yet to be proved (Fensham 1962, 132).

But in the sphere in which we are interested the most original legacy, if not the main one, which comes to us from the banks of the Nile is Maat (Bolkestein 1939). In the ancient Egyptian pantheon the goddess Maat, the personification of values like order, justice and truth (Morenz 1977, 177), played a central role. She was intimately connected with the two chief gods (Re, the sun god, and Osiris, the god of the dead) and thus had close relationships with the king, who was the representative of divine order on earth (Westendorf 1966, 201).

Considered as being of similar importance to the Israelite *tsedaqa* (Cazelles 1963, 36) or the Greek *logos* (Ramlot 1972, 822), this essential notion of Egyptian wisdom seems to have been taught to the people from the middle of the third millennium (Moret 1940, 1) and down to the end of Egyptian civilization (Allam 1973, 18). Since it cannot be translated into other languages (Anthes 1952, 2), its exact meaning is not easy to discern. As we have already seen, it corresponds to several notions, the importance of which changed with time and circumstances. Its first meaning was cosmological (Schmid 1966, 17): Maat was primarily the world order instituted by God (Volten 1963, 98; Brunner 1963, 103). The idea of equilibrium symbolized by the balance was predominant in Egypt. Maat signified regularity (Theodorides 1975, 91), the harmonious relationship between different elements of the universe, their necessary cohesion, indispensable to the maintenance of created forms. Moreover, as we shall soon see, Maat was an ethic which 'consists in acting, in all circumstances, in accord with one's awareness of this universal order' (*Dictionnaire de la civilisation égyptienne*, 156).

During the most typically Egyptian period (Wilson 1956, 104), i.e. during the Old Empire, under the reign of the absolute monarchy (Seidl 1957, 199), the pharaoh, like the Chinese emperor, believed himself to be responsible for the cosmic order and the social order (Westermann 1974, 120). Maat was the main attribute of the king, who was charged with ensuring it for his reign through the law (Pirenne 1965, 41). The king was the sole legislator, but his power was not as arbitrary as it might seem to have been at first sight (Wilson 1954, 2). As son of the gods he was responsible for his acts before them (Theodorides 1967, 137). Although the unique source of the law, when promulgating laws at the moment of his enthronement he had to take into consideration what had been done by his predecessors; at least in specific circumstances his legislative work followed that of his predecessors (Theodorides 1967, 137).

The king was the centre and the soul of the state, but given the extent of the country and the new tasks which its prosperity called for (*DOTT*, 156), along with its political and cultural development, he was obliged to delegate part of his powers (for example to the judges, Pirenne 1965, 42) and to respect some local autonomy. The result of this was that the period of the development of the young empire, when royal absolutism was at its height, was at the same time a period of progressive decentralization (Wilson 1956, 69), with the appearance of a ruling class and the creation of a vast administration (Theodorides 1973, 53) and all the apparatus of bureaucracy. Thus from the Third Dynasty onwards we have the office of the vizier, who after the Fifth Dynasty no longer had to be of princely origin (Schmid 1966, 38). And this administrative head, whose functions are parallel to those of the king, lived as much as the latter from Maat since he had to try to realize it on earth; he who was second to the king, in all the expressive force of the term, had to have as his aim always doing Maat, to the point that the first secretary of the vizier was called the secretary of Maat, as if the vizier was Maat and Maat depended on the vizier (Theodorides 1973, 52f.). This role attributed to the vizier is formulated in an explicit way in the inscriptions to be found on the tomb of Rekhmire, descendant of the old nobility (Newberry 1900, 13), Vizier of Upper Egypt under Thutmosis III (1490-1436): on the occasion of his installation, the Pharaoh makes a speech in which he stresses the importance of justice and the role which falls in this respect on the vizier, who must be an impartial judge, available to all, comprehensive, not too severe (Lichtheim 1975, II, 22-4).[4]

For a long time sheltered from outward perils and internecine quarrels, the Old Empire encouraged the growth of a feeling of security, optimism and even pride, which went hand in hand with a pragmatic and materialist conception of life (Wilson 1956, 104). Above all, those who belonged to the upper strata of society (for example the high officials near to the court) believed in material success on earth, in the benefits and good foundation of the established order (Schmid 1966, 56). Their way of envisaging existence appeared in the *Instructions*, one of the first and main literary forms of the time, which well reflect their moral conceptions. Here Maat takes a somewhat utilitarian form (58).

The earliest of the *Instructions*, some fragments of which have been kept, is attributed to one of the sons of Cheops (in Egyptian Khufu, second king of the Fourth Dynasty, *Dictionnaire*, 50), the prince Hordedef. This wise man and scribe, who probably lived under the Fifth Dynasty and left an abiding memory in Egyptian literature (Posener 1952, 109), gave his son a series of practical recommendations about a family, a home and agricultural property. First of all he advised him to make a home and marry a strong woman who would bear him a male child.

At the time when Hordedef lived, the tomb was an assurance of immortality; it was the material guarantee of survival. Faced with human confusion over the antimony between life and death, this wise man recommended that his son should build a house and a tomb (Posener 1952, 113).

In comparison with the little that the *Instructions of Hordedef* offer us, we find much more in the *Instructions to Kagemni*. Kagemni was the vizier who served Huni, the last king of the Third Dynasty, and Snefru, the first king of the Fourth Dynasty. However, the *Instructions* seems to come from a later date, the time of the Sixth Dynasty. To explain this delay it must be recalled that contrary to all the other Egyptian literary works, which remain anonymous, the *Instructions* were always published as coming from one or other famous wise man, but that they were usually later than the figure whose name they bore. The result is that today there is no complete unanimity among scholars over the attributions and dating of certain works. The language of Hordedef seems sufficiently archaic for it to be considered as belonging to the Old Empire, without having undergone any important changes. On the other hand, the *Instructions to Kagemni* and the *Maxims of Ptahhotep*, which we shall be considering later, seem to have undergone profound alterations in the course of successive generations: the two, which are very close stylistically, reflect the eloquence of the inscriptions of the monuments of the Sixth Dynasty and correspond to the atmosphere at the end of the Old Empire, to the pragmatic wisdom of the code of behaviour proper to the aspirations of a high official of the court (Lichtheim 1975, I, 6f.; Schmid 1966, 45).

From the first line of the fragments of the last part of the *Instructions to Kagemni* which have come down to us, the work deals with the causal relationships between the application of a certain ethical code and success in one's life. The man worthy of respect is assured of living well and being happy. The wise man particularly stresses the specific advantages which are derived from a reserved attitude, from reticence in speech. Modesty attracts sympathy and even success; the silent person will find that the doors of the great open to him. Another thing that constitutes a real trump card in human relationships is inner discipline; for example, the way one behaves at table. The man who is friendly and even timid predisposes the hard man favourably towards him and prompts others to do him service (Lichtheim 1975 I, 59).

Preoccupations similar to those which I have just mentioned appear in the *Maxims of Ptahhotep*, the earliest ancient Egyptian literary text which has come down to us in its entirety without any gaps (Zaba 1956, 8). According to some scholars it contains parallels with the Old Testament book of Proverbs (Schulman 1971, 484). According to what the text itself tells us, the work was produced by Ptahhotep, vizier under Isesi, the next but last king of the Fifth Dynasty (about 2450 BC), but in reality it seems to date from the Sixth Dynasty. It is known from four different manuscripts, three of which are written on papyrus scrolls and the fourth on a wooden writing tablet covered with stucco (Zaba 1956, 7). The only complete version, which differs considerably from the three others, is that on the Prisse papyrus in the Bibliothèque nationale (Lichtheim 1975, 61), which dates from the Middle Empire (Eleventh to Twelfth Dynasties, about 2000 BC, Zaba 1956, 7). The two others which are in the British Museum are from the Middle and New Empire respectively. The wooden tablet, in Cairo, also comes from the New Empire.

Considered by G. Jéquier as the most difficult Egyptian literary text to translate, this work is composed of thirty-seven maxims (each comprising at least four and rarely more than twelve phrases or parts of phrases), preceded by a prologue and followed by an epilogue (Lichtheim 1975, 61). As in the *Instructions of Hordedef*, we again find the theme of the home (Posener 1952, 114) and, as in the *Instructions to Kagemni*, restraint in ways of speaking and eating is commended. The aging vizier also gives his successor a whole series of pieces of advice relating, for example, to relationships with superiors, the attitude to take towards one's host, women and children (Schmid 1966, 10).

What is particularly interesting is the appearance of the theme of justice. In the quest for immortality (Fecht 1958, 51), in order to validate the material preparation for survival (Posener 1952, 116), Ptahhotep turns towards justice, towards equity. 'If you are a leader commanding the affairs of the multitude, seek out for yourself every beneficial deed until your own affairs are without wrong. Justice is great and its appropriateness lasting; it has not been disturbed since the time of him who made it whereas there is punishment for him who passes over its laws. It is the right path before him who knows nothing. Wrongdoing has never brought its undertaking into port, though fraud often amasses riches.' According to Ptahhotep, the only thing which is indestructible and does not disappear with death is justice: 'When it is the end, justice lasts' (Zaba 1956, 74). The justice which Ptahhotep claims must go hand in hand with impartiality: 'If you are the son of a member of the legal body, an ambassador entrusted with calming the multitude, protect the impartiality (?) of justice(?). When you speak, do not lean to one side...' (Zaba 1956, 94).

However, in spite of these declarations, what seems to take the upper hand for this author, or at least play a very important role, is an individualism for which the moral values of social character seem to count less than personal advantage. Ptahhotep urges his son always to seek to elevate himself into first place. Every man who knows how to adapt himself to the administrative and social system, who satisfies the needs of thoroughness in work and honesty, will earn riches, and acquire esteem and honour. In some situations it is necessary to keep silence because people have much deference towards those who know how to keep silent (Wilson 1956, 92-4).

The young official desiring advancement is recommended to bow his back to his superior: 'Bow your back before your superior, your master at the royal palace; then your house will have a good foundation and your recompense will have its true place. It is bad for the one who opposes his superior – one lives as long as he is benevolent – when the arm destined to salute does not bend' (Zaba 1956, 96).

In this work we find a number of passages in favour of honesty in business, and these seem to indicate that what matters is honesty in the face of a policy 'destined to assure the favours of the king, the approval of others and good fortune' (Wilson 1961, 91).

Alongside the *Instructions*, the other main literary genre which spread during the Old Empire was that of inscriptions on tombs. The origins of these inscriptions go back to the beginnings of the dynastic period. They appear primarily in the form of *Lists of Offerings* and then, above all in the Sixth Dynasty, in the form of *Autobiographies* (Lichtheim 1975, 3). While the *Instructions* are given by high-ranking officials, the inscriptions often come from figures of a less elevated rank, and they are also addresed to the simple passer-by. According to Schmid (1966, 45), we find relatively more consideration of the neighbour, and more commiseration for the unfortunate, in them than in the *Instructions*.

Among other things, Nefer-Seshem Ra, surnamed Sheshi, called hereditary prince, to whom a whole series of titles is given (chief of the priests of the pyramid of Teti, judge supreme, vizier, chief scribe of the royal documents...), declared in the panegyric engraved on his tomb at Sakkarah: 'I have spoken the truth, I have done the truth, I have spoken the good, I have repeated it, ...I have been the arbiter between adversaries to pacify them. I have saved the wretched from the hand of the violent, ..I have given bread to the hungry, clothing (to the naked)... I have buried him who had no son (to pay the last respects to him). I have been the barque of him who had none' (Capart 1907, 17).

Uni, whose long career lies between the successive reigns of three kings of the Sixth Dynasty (Teti, Pepi I and Mernere), and who became governor, though he began from a lowly post, proclaims in his *Autobiography* that thanks to his sense of equity, when he was in power no one attacked his neighbour, no one deprived the traveller of his bread or his sandals, and no one stole a goat from his neighbour (Lichtheim 1975, 20).

The most famous of the *Autobiographies* of the officials of the Old Empire is that of Hirkhuf (Yoyotte 1953, 173), who served kings Mernere and Pepi II, and like Uni became governor of Upper Egypt. It not only describes his warlike exploits but takes stock of his spirit of charity (Lichtheim 1975, 23f.).

As we shall see in due course, in connection with the *Book of the Dead*, the main aim of these panegyrics is to ensure immortality; they corresponded to sentiments which were not entirely disinterested.

Alongside those who, like Sheshi, Uni or Hirkhuf, could make their own eulogy, and alongside the representatives of the upper classes, there was the inarticulate mass which remained dumb (Cotterell 1955, 136) and was composed of workers (artisans, peasants and workers). Some categories of workers were less unfortunate than one might have supposed (Della Monica 1975, 76). However, all in all, their living conditions were very wretched. Unfortunately the documentation of economic and social history, especially that of the Old Empire, is very incomplete, and it is extremely difficult, if not impossible, to get any more or less precise idea about the state of things. In this chapter, which serves as an introduction to our main subject, we shall therefore limit ourselves to what seem to be the main characteristics.

In this predominantly agricultural country, what was and still remains essential was the fertile inundation of the Nile. Here we should not forget that the Nile demanded a heavy return for its gifts (Wilson 1956, 9). The building of barrages and canals, and the flattening of the soil of arable ground, were beyond the capabilities of individual peasants or even groups within a village or a community (Seidl 1957, 16). If it was to be done in time, sometimes between two inundations, all this work called for a collective and well co-ordinated effort which could only be made by a strong central power extending all down the valley of the Nile (Vercoutter 1979, 121; Wittfogel 1964, 78). Hence conscription (Helck 1975, 226), forced labour (Bakir 1953, 4), great masses of manual labour and important concentrations of workers who inevitably called for a discipline which often resorted to violence (Seidl 1957, 4).

It should be noted that nowadays the theory that there is a connection between the great irrigation works and the birth of a central despotic power is contested by some scholars, above all in connection with the Old Empire; at that stage, in their view, artificial irrigation will not yet have been applied (Schenkel 1978, 73; Endelsfelder 1979, 51). However, in all probability the last word on this much-debated problem has yet to be spoken; it is interesting to recall that, for example, those responsible for the work of cleaning the canals and strengthening the dykes were threatened with the death penalty if everything had not been done. The study on which I have based these comments relates to a period which runs from 332 BC to AD 641. However, the author writes that the performance of these works dates from time immemorial and that the organization followed by the Ptolemies was not their creation (Bonneau 1964, 53).

There is a parallel to my comments on these irrigation works in the construction of the pyramids, which were intended to contain the embalmed body of the pharaoh and assure him a passage to the beyond. Down to the beginning of the Third Dynasty there seems to have been no essential difference in conception between the royal tomb and that of a noble or a high official, but from this period on, for centuries the latter were to continue to be buried in mastabas, while the kings had their pyramids (*Dictionnaire*, 237).

The pyramids of the Third and Fourth Dynasties eclipse by far those which were to come after them in the perfection of the technology used to build them (Wilson 1956, 55). The first and most enduring of the seven wonders of the ancient world (Mumford 1966, 4), the pyramid of Cheops, the so-called Great Pyramid, which dates from the beginning of the Fourth Dynasty, and was built about five miles west of Gizeh, marks the culmination of this type of building. Composed of some 2,300,000 blocks each weighing on average 2.5 tons (Edwards 1961, 87), its construction over twenty years with the participation of about 100,000 men (Helck 1975, 99), including specialist manual workers, assisted by an army of more or less skilled workers, took priority every three months over agricultural work. The whole of the work was done without any other help than that of simple machines based on classical mechanics (inclined plane and lever); the great stones were dragged on sledges across the desert sands, on a surface of mud, by battalions of men (Mumford 1966, 5). Enjoined to the strictest obedience, simply carrying out the orders that came from the king through a whole bureaucratic hierarchy, deprived for the duration of their work of all semblance of autonomy or initiative, the workers were rivetted like slaves to the execution of their task. According to Mumford, absolute submission was required of them, and any disobedience was punished by torture, mutilation or death (7).[5] This assessment is probably exaggerated. The work to which the labourers were conscripted does not seem to have been done in such terrifying conditions as has often been claimed, but they were far from being idyllic (Goyon 1977, 45-7). According to some scholars, the 'pyramids were not built under constraint and fear but as an act of faith and love' (Della Monica 1975, 20). However, according to others this work cannot be considered an exceptional achievement, 'carried out in the fever and enthusiasm of a whole people in action' (Goyon 1977, 18). In any case, according to Herodotus the Egyptians of his time still detested Cheops and Chephren to the point of avoiding pronouncing their names; they accused them of having oppressed the people by forcing them to build the royal pyramids (Posener 1956, 10).

When one analyses the other categories of abuse or injustice, those which are more particularly linked with the formation of a whole bureaucratic apparatus, it must be remembered that to begin with, work in the royal service was a duty and that in exchange the officials were fed and their needs were seen to. In time, the king began to recompense them by means of gifts. As a consequence of the import- ance accorded to survival, which was believed to be calculated on the basis of life on earth, the king began not only to offer favoured officials money for their burial, but to bestow on them land the revenue of which was to serve to ensure the funerary cult for a long period of time. These donations were sometimes considerable, and the lands seem to have been exempt from taxes or at least from an important number of charges (Drioton and Vandier 1938, 181). Some officials of the Old Empire were thus transformed into great landowners, and their descendants enjoyed great advantages without necessarily performing any function or having to do public service (Meyer 1914, 197; Kanawati 1978, 78). This favouritism was exercised in a way which was perhaps particularly calculated to benefit the priests. The domains belonging to the temples grew, thanks to donations and foundations (Dykmans 1936-37, III, 171); moreover they were exempt from charges like taxes or forced labour (Meyer 1914, 199). Under the Fifth Dynasty the royal priesthood became a hereditary nobility whose 'benefice', first money then land, was also hereditary (Pirenne 1938, 20).

This formation of an oligarchy was accompanied by the development of private law. The 'benefices', indivisible and inalienable, could not be shared among the children as the right of succession might require, and as they did not cease to grow from the fourth to the sixth dynasty, riches and property increasingly became concentrated in the hands of the nobility. The seigneurial régime stagnated in total immobility and the country was covered with estates (Pirenne 1938, 21).

This favouritism and inequality was further aggravated by 'the decadence of the old judicial, imperial and homogenous adminis- tration', which was not without its danger for the security of people and goods. The advent of multiple feudal justiciaries destroyed the unitary jurisprudence of former days, which though rigorous and with strict procedures, had been sure (Dykmans 1936-37, III, 243). Those who had to see to it that the laws were respected behaved in a way which went against the elementary principles of justice. The tribunal cheated instead of helping the poor (*ANET*, 380). High officials behaved like looters. As the *Story of the Man from the Oasis* will put it, 'The one who has to repress evil himself commits iniquity, and he who has to show the way of the laws commands theft' (Lefebvre 1949, 54).

(ii) The First Intermediate Period: The Middle Empire

The state of affairs that I have just outlined, the social abuses, seems to have played a very important, if not decisive, role in the collapse of the Old Empire (Spiegel 1950, 7). With the exception of immigration movements (Wilson 1956, 119), foreign invasions, that of the Bedouins at the end of the long reign of Pepi II (Drioton and Vandier 1938, 214), all the factors which contributed to the fall of the Old Empire seem to have been of internal origin. It was not a contamination but an organic sickness (Wilson 1956, 110) which already began under the Old Empire (Posener 1956, 8) and which ate away at the very foundations of the edifice (Yoyotte 1960, 144).

The excesses of the abuses, injustice in the incidence of financial levies, the brutality of the tax collectors, and so on, produced a discontent (Della Monica 1975, 21) which ended in a violent revolution at the end of the reign of Pepi II or under one of his successors. The repercussions of what is considered to be the first social revolution in antiquity made themselves felt throughout the country, but the popular uprising seems to have broken out around Memphis and Heliopolis, a region with a strong urban concentration, where the priests and the artisans had gained in strength and dignity. The 'little ones' swept along the 'poor' and attacked the rich and the administration (Yoyotte 1960, 144f.). The old social hierarchy collapsed and the masses came to power (Drioton and Vandier 1938, 214). The nobles and the rich were attacked, dispossessed and executed, and their servants took their places. The lesser officials made common cause with the people and gave themselves over to the pillage of public offices; they destroyed the registers of the cadastre and of the civic state (Della Monica 1975, 21).

According to Spiegel (1950, 7), this revolutionary movement lasted about thirty years (2270-2240)[6] and had as its leader a person whom he calls 'Regent', but whose real name is unknown. The work on which Spiegel principally bases his argument, the *Admonitions of Ipuwer*, 'paint a magnificent picture of the tragic magnitude of the facts' (Yoyotte 1960, 145) relating to the revolution, but it has come down to us with a great many lacunae (Simpson 1972, 210), and the real name of the 'Regent' is possibly contained in the missing beginning (Spiegel 1950, 45). To cope with these inadequacies and fill the gaps, Spiegel draws on other works (the *Instructions to Merikare*, the *Dialogue of the Despairing Man with his Soul*). The author of the *Admonitions*, which voice the recriminations of the upper classes dispossessed after the fall of the Old Empire (Posener 1956, 43), proves very critical of the revolutionary movement, but it is precisely by taking the opposite attitude to Ipuwer that Spiegel defends the Regent. He considers him to be the first great 'Reformer'[7] known not only in Egypt but also in the history of humanity in general. He introduced the principle of equal rights for all and sought to apply it in practice, in the form of the absolute sharing of goods and the abolition of all class differences. His programme of social reform derived from his conception of life, entirely steeped in a universalist love of mankind. That prevented him from resorting to any form of violence in fulfilling his function of 'Regent'. His message of love for the neighbour, again according to Spiegel, was based on his faith in a benevolent God, who created the world, and all creatures, for love of humanity, whose needs he will never cease to satisfy. His faith was in Re, the sun god, and at the centre of his conception of the world lay justice, conceived of in a profoundly ethical sense (Spiegel 1950, 45). But the 'Regent' was not the sole spokesman of this new spirit.

The popular movement directed against the régime (Posener 1956, 9) put an end to the period of stability and prosperity; the collapse of the Old Empire marks the beginning of some five hunded years of difficult times, namely the First Intermediate Period, which is usually put about 2200-2050 (Wilson 1961, 318; Posener 1971, 9). The entry of the middle classes into political life (Yoyotte 1960, 153), the atmosphere of conflict and insecurity which characterized the First Intermediate Period, prompted people to rethink a number of questions in a deeper way (Daumas 1962, 170), to reflect on moral problems as they had never done before (*DOTT*, 156; Posener 1956, 9). The national ills would engender a form of piety lacking in the Old Empire (Wilson 1956, 110).

The break-up of the static order cleared the way for more open and dynamic conceptions (Lanczkowski 1960, 41), for a new interpretation of Maat, and for prophecy (ibid., 75). Whereas in earlier times Maat was almost exclusively the symbol of unchangeable cosmic order, with the break-up of the Old Empire it came more to signify right (Schmid 1968, 61), and became an ideal of justice and humanitarianism (Wilson 1956, 110).

The work which seems to reflect this change well and to move one step forward from the *Instructions* of the Old Empire is the *Instructions to Merikare*. The text which has come down to us is in the fragments of three papyri (Leningrad, Moscow and Carlsberg) dating from the Eighteenth Dynasty. Unfortunately the one which is most complete (that of Leningrad) has also been altered the most. This work was attributed to one of the several kings of the Ninth and Tenth Dynasties, all of whom bore the same name Kheti. In fact, it is impossible to identify its author; at all events, it does not seem to have been written by one of the Kheti kings, but during the reign of King Merikare, about 2100 (Lichtheim 1975, 97).

The work in question appears in the form of teaching lavished by an old king on his son and successor. As in the *Instructions* of the Old Empire it also exalts the crown and the dynastic princes, but in more personal terms, and putting more heart into it (Yoyotte 1960, 147). In comparison with the *Maxims of Ptahhotep*, we find a more subtle moral approach, which goes much deeper (Lichtheim 1975, 97). The father explains to his son how he must exercise power in order to be both a puissant and a virtuous king (Pirenne 1938b, 5).

After advice on repressing revolts, the security of the population and the protection of the frontiers of the country, special importance seems to be attached to behaviour based on goodness, wisdom and equity which evokes love and recognition (*DOTT*, 157; Simpson 1972, 182). In the section which contains advice on how to treat the nobles and other people (Lichtheim 1975, 98), it is said: 'Do justice and you will endure on earth. Quiet the weeper; do not oppress the widow; do not supplant a man in the property of his father; and impugn no officials in their posts. Be on guard against punishing wrongfully' (Daumas 1965, 131; Simpson 1972, 183). The author of the *Instructions* speaks out in favour of the great and the rich when it comes to choosing magistrates, since in their judgments they offer more guarantees of objectivity than the poor (Simpson 1972, 183). But when it is a matter of work in the strict sense no distinction is to be made in favour of the well-born man as opposed to the man of the people; the choice must be made according to the capacity of each (ibid., 184).

Towards the end of the *Instructions to Merikare* there is also a discussion of survival, the problem which so preoccupied the Egyptians, but here the moral aspect of the problem becomes much more important than before (*DOTT*, 157). Whereas in earlier times it was thought that immortality could be bought, above all with gigantic tombs and perpetual offerings, now the accent is put on moral values rather than on material goods. The memory lasts, thanks not to the memorial of stone but to the love that is borne, thanks to the good reputation that a person leaves behind. This development and spiritualization plainly appears in a passage where it is said clearly, as the Israelite prophets will come to say with particular force, that God prefers the virtues, the character presented by an honest man, to material offerings, to the 'ox of the sinner' (Wilson 1956, 120; Simpson 1972, 191).

The *Teaching of Amenemhet* I seems to have been produced during the reign of and on the initiative of Senusert I (1970-1936; cf. Lichtheim 1975, 135), but under the name of his predecessor Amenemhet I. Like the *Instructions to Merikare*, it is a royal testament which describes the experiences of the old king in order to instruct his son and successor so that he has a happy reign (Posener 1956, 63). But while Merikare is advised to surround himself with competent people, King Amenemhet recommends his son to mistrust his subjects, who are all potential traitors. However, immediately after this warning, steeped in scepticism, we find declarations in favour of justice and good-will: 'I gave to the poor, I raised the orphan. I gave audience to him who was nothing as to him who was something' (Daumas 1965, 401; Simpson 1972, 136).

But it is in the *Story of the Man from the Oasis* that we can see best the awareness of the need for social equality and the demand to realize Maat here on earth for the benefit of the neighbour rather than towards the gods (Wilson 1961, 114). This work, known under various names (*The Peasant's Lament, The Protests of the Eloquent Peasant, The Complaining Fellah*, cf. Lefebvre 1949, 41), is more than 430 lines long and with *Horus and Seth* is the longest of all the Egyptian literary texts (Lefebvre, 45). The four papyri which contain the copies of this story come from the Middle Empire (Lichtheim 1975, 169), but the original is earlier and relates to events which took place towards the end of the third millennium (Erman 1927, 116), under the last king of the Tenth Heracleopolitan Dynasty (Lefebvre 1949, X). Formerly studied predominantly, if not solely, from a literary and aesthetic point of view, for some time it has been reassessed as a valuable document of social history (Lanczkowski 1960, 51). It is cited among the works which inspired biblical thought (Cazelles, 1963, 33). Parallels have been drawn between the *Story of the Man from the Oasis* and the great Israelite prophets with Amos at their head (Lanczkowski 1960, 51).

This story is a testimony to human solidarity, a plea in favour of the poor and the oppressed. It tells of the misfortunes of a poor peasant, Khun-Anup of the salt oasis (Lefebvre 1949, 47), who, transporting goods in order to exchange them for food, is robbed of them by a man enjoying strong support at court. However, the peasant did not allow himself to be discouraged by all the difficulties he encountered and persisted in seeking justice. Charmed by his eloquence, the chief steward at the palace, Rensi, to whom the peasant complained, allowed him to plead his cause over nine sessions. The Oasian demanded Maat as a right from the one whose duty it was to dispense Maat (Wilson 1956, 120). The story ends with a very severe judgment: the aggressor is not only to repay what he has stolen, and all his own goods, but he himself is given to the peasant as his slave (Lefebvre 1949, 69).

This judgment is approved by the narrator, since in the story all the sympathies are with the man from the oasis. The moral of it is that the humblest can always claim his due and that true Maat calls for the effective application of justice. This very long story shows that 'Maat-justice was not a formal survival of the old order', but the positive quest for a new value. However, what is significant for the development of ideas on justice in Egypt is that the story, which enjoyed a certain popularity in the Middle Empire, subsequently went right out of fashion (Wilson 1956, 120-2).

Moreover, in connection with what I have just said, it should be recalled that the revolutionary movement was of relatively short duration. The nobles got the upper hand (Spiegel 1950, 7), and the return to the old state of things also showed itself on the spiritual level.

Alongside this attitude favourable to a change towards equality as expressed by the man from the oasis, there is the attitude which is hostile to it, even under the Middle Empire, and which recurs, as we have already seen, in the *Admonitions of Ipuwer*.

The manuscript of this work which we now have probably dates from the time of the Nineteenth Dynasty, but it is a copy of a much earlier work, the original composition of which may be dated at the beginning of the Twelfth Dynasty (perhaps at the beginning of the Second Millennium), when the recollections of the calamities of the revolution and the civil wars were still very much alive in the memory of the nation (Simpson 1972, 210). Nevertheless, we should add, in passing, that some would date the origins of the *Admonitions* to the beginning of the First Intermediate Period (Van Seters 1964, 13-23) and others to the Second Intermediate Period (Posener 1956, 28).

Ipuwer is one of those whose heart is with the nobility, with the people who vituperate the revolutionaries. He is an enemy of chaos, which he contrasts with the happy life of ancient times (Posener 1956, 28). According to him, revolution brings misery and hatred rather than justice and love of the neighbour (Spiegel 1950, 52). A supporter of the patriarchal ideal characteristic of the aristocracy of the Old

Empire, he passionately argues for the return of the old order (ibid., 36-8).

An extremely critical attitude towards the effects of the revolution also appears in the *Dialogue of the Despairing Man with his Soul* (Posener 1956, 43). This work seems to have appeared at the same time as the *Admonitions* (Spiegel 1950, 48), again in the Twelfth Dynasty (Lichtheim 1975, 163), and denounces the cupidity which has invaded people's hearts, the pride which has taken the place of gentleness. In these conditions the good man is humbled and the wicked man gains the upper hand; the just disappear; the man in whom one has put trust proves a criminal and the man with whom one lived as a brother becomes an enemy (ibid., 166f.).

The general anarchy which upset the relations between the different social classes, which ruined the nobility and favoured the rapid enrichment of ordinary people, is described in the *Prophecy of Neferti* (Posener 1956, 125). The work is preserved in one manuscript which dates from the eighteenth century, but according to Lichtheim it was written two decades after the *Teaching of Amenemhet* I (Lichtheim 1975, 172), and therefore in the twentieth century BC.

The prophet Neferti, summoned to the pharaoh's court,[8] depicts the revolution which overthrew Egypt, the misfortunes which fell on the country (Posener 1956, 125) in terms which suggest not only Ipuwer (Daumas 1965, 405), but also the diatribes of the great Israelite prophets (Amos, Isaiah, Jeremiah, Ezekiel; cf. Schulman 1971, 485). The country is ruined, hatred and violence reign everywhere, and people are only preoccupied with their own affairs and no longer think of their neighbours (Posener 1956, 42f.).

(iii) The New Empire

During the New Empire, the third main period in the history of Egypt, the growth of the country into a world power under the Eighteenth Dynasty much reinforced, if not engendered, the concept of a universal god, the sun; as he watched over all the earth and as he was the lord of all countries, in this way he could take on a more universal significance in the foreign colonies of Egypt which the old anthropo-morphic or zoomorphic gods lacked. Already under Amenophis III, the ancient name of the sun, Aten or the 'disc', was currently used, but it was when, towards 1375, Amenophis IV succeeded his father that the cult of this deity rapidly spread (Aldred 1968, 66), threatening to eliminate religious conceptions which had been respected for centuries.

The manifest zeal of the young pharaoh for the new faith was far from being approved and shared by the rich and powerful clergy of Amon, who became a serious threat to the authority and stability of the throne (*DOTT*, 143). So Amenophis IV and his supporters set out to combat Amon, the old god of Thebes (Breasted 1912, 318), who moreover also represented a certain universalist conception (Wilson 1956, 211). This did not prevent Amenophis from having his name proscribed, closing the temples, confiscating their goods and their personnel for the benefit of the royal house (Yoyotte 1960, 196). In the sixth year of his reign he changed his name from Amenophis ('Amon is satisfied [with this person]') to Akhenaten ('He who is serviceable to Aten', Wilson 1956, 215). Moreover, he left Thebes, the 'city of Amon', and installed his capital almost three hundred miles further north, in the province of Hermopolis, where he had a new city built named Akhet-Aten, 'the resting place of Aten' (Aldred 1968, 67), now called El-Amarna (Yoyotte 1960, 196). Thus Amon, an invisible and omnipotent entity, whose sanctuary could be approached only by a few elect, was replaced by Aten, the gleaming solar disc that nothing could mask (Wilson 1956, 217), and whose life-giving action of heat became the symbol of the new rationalist conception of the universe (Spiegel 1950, 61).

The central idea of the new faith was represented by Maat (*DOTT*, 144). The revolutionary propaganda was centred on Maat. Aten was called 'he who is satisfied with Maat', who accepts Maat, as the most sublime of offerings. Akhenaten officially called himself 'he who lives by Maat' (Wilson 1956, 218). However, the Maat which characterized the proselytism of the Amarna revolution did not signify rectitude or justice but truth, which was to be understood as 'the adoration of the forces of nature and not the artificial and distant activity of the old gods' (ibid., 214). It was a matter of subjective truth, that of the senses, and not of objective truth along the traditional lines of the term (*DOTT*, 144).

The king always added to his name the expression 'living from truth', and his behaviour proved that this was not pure theory but the acceptance of the facts of everyday life in a way which sought to be simple and not conventional. His family life was not hidden from the public eye (Breasted 1912, 377). He took pleasure in making public appearances, surrounded by his kin (Aldred 1968, 136), having himself depicted in the most prosaic attitudes and in dress which had nothing of protocol about it (Wilson 1956, 217).

J.Spiegel, to whom I have already referred, stresses some of the ideological affinities which he believes to have existed between Akhenaten and the protagonist of the revolutionary movement at the end of the Old Empire. Maat and man are at the centre of the preoccupations of both these figures. But between the one whom Spiegel calls the Regent and Akhenaten there is the same difference as there is between the original and the copy. What corresponds in the former to a natural spontaneous need takes on a forced and subjective character in the latter: what he undertakes is a revolution from above. The ideal of the 'Regent', a benevolent God who created the world for love of humanity, is replaced in Akhenaten by an aesthetic conception: he praises the world as a work of art created by God without truly taking seriously the ethical duty of the love of the neighbour which is at the centre of the idea that the 'Regent' has of life (Spiegel 1950, 78).

In the reign of Akhenaten, many people of humble origins seem to have had the chance of attaining important positions (Pflüger 1946, 268). At that time the senior administrative personnel seem to have consisted more of new men than of kin of the old aristocracy, but the administrative pattern had not changed (Yoyotte 1960, 199). There was nothing revolutionary in the social politics of Akhenaten (Aldred 1968, 260). We do not have the impression that the measures which he adopted originally came from the rise to power of a broad popular front. The ruins of Amarna show us a city full of villas and palaces in which the royal protégés enjoyed luxury and pleasures which were contrary to the spirit of equality. At Amarna people played at revolution, as they played at loving nature (Spiegel 1950, 78). Besides, only a short while after the death of Akhenaten very little of his work was left; neither the masses nor the great were touched by the grace of Aten (Yoyotte 1960, 199).[9]

Our knowledge of the teachings of Akhenaten comes above all from the great hymn to Aten (Barucq and Daumas 1980, 482) which is inscribed on the ruins of some tombs at El Amarna. In its sequences, its content and its forms of expression, it is often compared to Psalm 104 (Aldred 1968, 187-9). As a result of the parallel of structure and form existing between these two works, it has been claimed that there is necessarily a relationship of affinity between them and that the Hebrew psalmists must have known the hymn to the sun (Breasted 1933, 367; Wilson 1956, 227f.). However, it seems that these resemblances are the result more of generic similitudes between the Egyptian hymns and the biblical psalms than of direct dependence (Lichtheim 1975, 100). According to P.Auffret (1979, 171), the possible influence of the hymn to Aten on the general literary structure of Ps. 104 leaves room for Canaanite influence, which is largely predominant at the level of structures of detail, representations, imagery and modes of expression in the Psalm. J.H.Breasted (1933, 369) and the Egyptologists of his generation saw the hymn to Aten as a source of Hebrew monotheism, and via that of modern religion (Wilson 1961, 213). But this theory seems to have been finally rejected since it has been noted that the religion of Akhenaten was more a form of monoidolatry than of monotheism (Schulman 1971, 484): a kind of self-adoration in the form of egocentric megalomania (which sees the deity only as the giant shadow of the pharaoh, cf. Aldred 1968, 264), a personal cult to which the mass had no access. We should also note – and this is important – that we find no ethical preoccupations in the hymns to Aten, no rigorous stress on the moral norm which is so typical of Hebrew monotheism. The benefits of Aten were eminently material. The faithful were invited to show gratitude for his gifts, but no text encouraged them to express their gratitude by an exemplary inner life and behaviour. The universalism of Aten could implicitly have led to the recognition of equality between all men, but that does not appear in any text (Wilson 1956, 214).

Already under Amenophis III the stability and permanence of Egyptian power began no longer to be completely certain, but the process of decomposition intensified above all under Akhenaten (Wilson 1956, 218). Exalted by his religious ideas and absorbed in his great building projects at El-Amarna, he neglected affairs of state (Aldred 1968, 686), and realized only too late how critical the situation in the country had become. Syria, the most distant area which was most closely attached to the crown, was captured by the Hittite king, and its loss rapidly brought with it that of Phoenicia and Palestine. We have less information on the African empire, but its foundations, too, seem to have been shaken. These losses very probably produced disorganization in the economy, leading to unemployment and distress, which in turn created a certain state of disorder (Wilson 1956, 231).

The effects of the Amarna revolution (Aldred 1975, 53), the ruin and the neglect of the Eighteenth Dynasty, were to be combatted by the famous general Horemheb, already all-powerful under Tutankhamen and then under Ay whom he succeeded, apparently between 1350 and

1340 (Breasted 1948, 58). This last pharaoh of the Eighteenth Dynasty (some, e.g. Philips 1977, 121, would regard him rather as the first pharaoh of the Nineteenth Dynasty), in fifteen to twenty years of his pre-royal career (Hari 1964, 433) and in twenty-five to thirty years (Harris 1968, 95; Beckerath 1978, 49) of a well filled reign, produced a real Egyptian renaissance (Hari 1964, 433). Among the different measures which he took in order to put the country in order (Aldred 1968, 86), what seems particularly significant and important is the edict which it has proved useful to call the Decree of Horemheb (van der Walle 1947, 230).

The text of this decree is on a stele of black granite discovered in 1882 at Karnak by Maspéro (Bouriant 1885, 50). The original dimensions must have been about 2.80 metres broad by 3 metres high. It is the largest epigraphic stele in classical Egypt (Hari 1964, 305).

Horemheb sought above all to reorganize the administrative apparatus (Wilson 1956, 237), create tribunals throughout the country (Hari 1964, 316), and nominate judges (Roeder 1961, 91). But the decree was also aimed at warning against particular crimes; it was directed against the administrators and agents of the public service who were corrupt and guilty not only of appropriating goods but also of using force towards ordinary citizens (Wilson 1956, 238f.).

It is said in the prologue that 'Maat has come to join' Horemheb and that the latter 'devised a plan in his heart to protect the country', to 'combat evil and destroy the lie' (Hari 1964, 311f.). Then in the first part of the decree account is taken of a whole series of injustices and measures ordained by the king to deal with them: measures taken to prevent people from seizing transport vessels which made deliveries in the form of taxes; to come to the aid of the owners of ships from which cargoes destined for the king had been stolen; against those who appropriated deliveries in the form of taxes for the harem and for the divine offerings; to repress the requisition of the Kt plants (probably oleoginous) (Helck 1955, 119); to prevent people from extorting animal skins from the peasants; against extortion and corruption in the administration of revenues; against those who wrongfully took cereals and vegetables; to prevent people from unjustly exploiting the work of slaves (Van der Walle 1947, 231-4).

The decree proposed extremely heavy penalties for the guilty (false judges, looting soldiers, treacherous officials); they were to have their noses cut off and be sent into exile to the fortress of Sile (Hari 1964, 433), where there was an iron discipline (Wilson 1956, 238). In the case of soldiers who wrongfully took animal skins from the peasants and did not give them back, the law was applied to the guilty party 'in the form of one hundred blows of the staff and five wounds, and the skins which he had appropriated illegally were confiscated' (Hari 1964, 314).

According to Hari (433), these draconian measures were not dictated by imperious economic or political motives, or in order to regain respect for royal authority, which for so long had been flouted: we are to see in the decree a manifest desire to come to the aid of the poor and the humble, who could be imposed on and made to do forced labour.

Henri Cazelles, who follows J.H.Breasted (1906-7, 26) in translating the Egyptian term *nmḥ* as 'poor',[10] sees a parallel in attitudes towards the poor between the decree of Horemheb and the Covenant Code, but he recalls that the former is 'above all concerned to ensure the payment of tax and the good functioning of his administration'; these considerations 'are completely outside the perspectives' of the latter (Cazelles 1946, 165).

In one sense, as in the case of the Mesopotamian codes, it is not easy to get an exact idea of the motives behind the Decree of Horemheb. The commentaries, too, are far from being unanimous on this point; for example, alongside the view of Hari which I have just cited and which seems close to that of J.H.Breasted (according to whom it is a question of sane and philanthropic reforms and humane government), others are far less complimentary.

According to Pflüger (1946, 268) it would be a mistake to believe that Horemheb was moved by humanitarian motives. He was driven to ameliorate the lot of the workers by a need to make his reign popular, and therefore stable, and by the Amarna revolution, which was a warning. However, although he was motivated by a spirit of restoration, what he undertook was not simply a step backwards but the incorporation of revolutionary elements in a traditional mould.

It is in Roeder's version, revised by Professor Helck (Roeder 1961, 95) that we find after §23, which deals with the prohibition against confiscating bread from the homes of individuals, §24, the very title of which stipulates that the poor must be protected by the officials (ibid., 105). However, according to this author the moral that Horemheb proposes to his subjects is essentially practical: it is first and foremost a matter of relief from taxes (93).

The commentary by J.A.Wilson follows the same line, but it is even more severe. In his view, despite the concern of which 'the poor man' was the object, the measures taken in his favour were alien to all ideas of social justice: the legislator was above all concerned to protect the sources of national revenue. Thus the decree prohibits officials from requisitioning the boat which the contributor used to transport his taxes; soldiers from seizing skins destined for the tax collectors and seizing certain dye plants that had to be paid to the tax authorities. The tax collectors are also forbidden to falsify in their favour the measure used in the requisition of grain. The property of the humble folk, Wilson concludes, was only protected to the degree that the state took account of it (Wilson 1961, 228).

Alongside works associated with great names (Akhenaten, Horemheb), there are those which come from less well known figures or even others which are anonymous. They also deserve our attention because they help us to see better what characterizes the New Empire and distinguishes it from the First Intermediate Period and the beginning of the Middle Empire. This difference seems to consist in a certain eclipse of the idea of social justice which, with the return to stability and prosperity (Wilson 1956, 238f.), yields pride of place to preoccupations with personal success and a happy life; but in comparison with the old order it is now a matter of a more sophisticated 'utilitarianism', attenuated by a degree of personal piety, an inner spirituality, and feelings of humility and modesty (*ANET*, 420; Lichtheim 1976, II, 244).

We begin with two writings belonging to wisdom literature, two *Instructions*: the *Wisdom of Ani* and the *Wisdom of Amenemope*. In the former, which was almost certainly written under the Eighteenth Dynasty (Volten 1937-1938, 62), Ani, scribe of the palace of queen Nefertiri (wife of king Ahmes), recommends to his son Knenshotep that he should be generous to whoever is in his house, do good, extend his hand to his neighbour, not punish another's slave when he fails (Suys 1935, XVI).

As we can see, this teaching is not lacking in nobility and generosity; however, it seems to tend above all to give the young scribe the means of succeeding in life with the exact amount of virtue necessary and sufficient to this end (ibid., XIII). Composed in the heart of the middle class, the *Wisdom of Ani* seems to translate in its entirety a down-to-earth wisdom which corresponds to the idea that one has of Egyptian society: very gentle in outward form, with a refined and superficial politeness, compassionate towards the unfortunate but Epicurean and steeped in egotism (XII).

The Wisdom of Amenemope, which is later than the *Wisdom of Ani* (Posener 1973, 251; Peterson 1967, 121), is composed of a prologue and thirty chapters containing thirty precepts which the supervisor of wheat and the cadastre addresses to his son so that he too may one day become a just and honest official (Erman 1936, 222).

The *Wisdom of Ani* is perhaps more varied and more evocative; by contrast the *Wisdom of Amenemope* seems more profound and more moral (Daumas 1965, 412). Its prologue can perhaps be compared to that of the *Wisdom of Ani* (Suys 1935, XII), but then we find more elements relating to our subject than in the other work. It is generally thought that this work was composed about the Twentieth (Grumach 1972, 3,9) or the Twenty-First Dynasty (Peterson 1967, 121: towards the eleventh century), when the Israelite tribes were becoming a nation and where a large part of the knowledge that they had of Egypt which appears in the Bible came from the relationships that these two peoples maintained at specifically this time (Lichtheim 1976, II, 147). The tangible proof of these contacts is furnished by the striking and indubitable parallels between the *Wisdom of Amenemope* and the Proverbs of the Old Testament (Williams 1962, 106; Cazelles 1963, 33), above all in the section composed of chapters 22.17-24.22 which contains, in about thirty verses, the essentials of the Egyptian work in the form of a précis (Michaeli 1961, 120; Montet 1959, 8). Here I shall juxtapose the passages which seem particularly interesting:

The Wisdom of Amenemope	Proverbs
Incline your ears, hear what is said. Apply your mind to interpret them. To put them in your heart is beneficial...(I.5)	Incline your ear, and hear the words of the wise, and apply your mind to my knowledge; for it will be pleasant if you keep them within you (Prov.22.17f.)
Guard yourself against robbing the wretched and against being puissant over the man of broken arm (III, 1f.)	Do not rob the poor, because he is poor, or crush the wicked at the gate (of the city)... (22.22)
Do not remove the landmark at the boundaries of the arable land, nor disturb the position of the measuring cord (VI.1f.)	Do not remove the ancient landmark which your fathers have set (22.28)
Do not covet not a cubit of land, nor throw down the boundaries of a widow (VI, 1f.)	Do not remove an ancient landmark or enter the fields of the fatherless (23.10)

Do not labour to seek for increase, your needs are safe for you. If riches are brought to you by robbery, they will not spend the night with you (VII, 5-9)	Riches will disappear from your house. If you fix your gaze on it, it is already no more (23.4)
Do not tamper with the scales nor falsify the weights (XVII, 17f.)	A false balance is an abomination to the Lord, but a just weight is his delight (Prov.11.1)

(cf.Michaeli 1961, 120-2).

One has to be impressed by the nobility of these precepts, but it must not be forgotten that from the beginning of the prologue it is said that the aim of the instructions is to attain well being and prosperity here on earth (Lichtheim 1976, II, 148) and that one of the main themes of this writing is represented by the contrast and opposition between the immoderate and impetuous man and the peaceful, silent man (Simpson 1972, 241), who is above all in search of tranquillity (*DOTT*, 173).

Just as the Old Empire had the pyramid texts and the Middle Empire those of the sarcophagi, the New Empire had its *Book of the Dead* (Peet 1924, II, 202). What the first Egyptologists called the Bible of the ancient Egyptians, the oldest illustrated book in the world, is a collection in one more or less coherent whole of a number of texts of unequal length, each with its own title and illustration, its vignette. Written almost always on papyrus and bearing the name and titles of the dead person, this text went with him in the tomb like a book of prayers (Barguet 1967, 8) and was aimed at providing an assurance of eternal happiness (*ANET*, 34).

The *Book of the Dead* draws its content from a large number of texts going back to the First Intermediate Period and the Middle Empire, thus ranging from about 2200 to 1700. It would seem already to have formed an entity in the Eighteenth Dynasty (about 1500, cf. Barguet 1967, 9), but it subsequently underwent important changes, above all at the time of the Twenty-First Dynasty (Maystre 1937, 7) and the Twenty-Sixth Dynasty (about 650). While some papyri were stocked in bookshops where the purchaser might possible go, others were written to order, and the person who wanted them could choose from the mass of 'formulae' those which seemed most appropriate to him for opening the gates of paradise and safeguarding his soul and his body (Barguet 1967, 12).

Chapter 125 of the *Book of the Dead*, the most important, the best known and the most interesting, comments on a drawing representing the soul of the dead man who is watching his heart being weighed in scales before Osiris. The weight is Maat, at the same time truth, justice, equilibrium and equity. The vignette contains a declaration of innocence, a list of faults which the dead person says he has not committed (Daumas 1965, 265). Since the list is very long, I shall quote only part of it, representing the faults which seem to me to be most characteristic.

I have not committed evil against men
I have not mistreated cattle
I have not comitted sins in the place of truth
I have not done violence to the poor man
I have not defamed a slave to his superior
I have not cheated over land
I have not added to the weight of the balance (*ANET*, 343; Barguet 1967, 159).

To begin with these declarations of innocence were seen by scholars as the expression of an exalted ethic. Then a crude magical intent was detected in them. According to some scholars the whole of ch.125 is nothing but a magic formula which allows the dead person to avoid the consequences of judgment. In fact, though this cannot really be demonstrated with the help of the documents, the truth seems to lie between the two extremes (Daumas 1965, 265; Peet 1924, II, 202). The text of the *Book of the Dead* which goes with the mummy was only supplementary support for the magic of the rites, even if it was incomplete (Barguet 1967, 12). The interested party did not even need to know the text by heart; it was enough for a scroll of papyrus on which the words were written to be found beside him in his tomb (Peet 1924, II, 202).

This kind of personal apologia made by the dead individual therefore has little value for us if we want to appreciate the individual himself, but it shows what opinion expected of an official or a landowner, and how he had to conduct himself to merit a good funeral and a happy life in the next world. For the rest, if someone wanted to make his way and succeed in life, he had to observe the precepts of *savoir-faire* and behave with tact and delicacy in relations with his superiors and his equals (Meyer 1912-1926, 221).

This sketch is clearly far from being exhaustive; however, it does allow us to obtain a certain overall view which is perhaps not too far from reality.

Very soon we find in ancient Egypt the traces of a legal organization, notions of right and a sense of equity. However, in this society, which was so strongly hierarchical, where the pyramid is not only an architectural form but also the symbol of a certain social structure, what relates to social justice seems to proceed in accord with the laws of dichotomy, to favour distinct and superimposed social strata. There was the solution permeated with a desire for equality, a community spirit, which was represented by the popular uprising at the end of the Old Empire. Idealized by some and vigorously criticized by others, it seems to have had a very limited effect in both time and space. It achieved specific results only in the cities, where there were already certain precedents. Elsewhere, where this uprising signified an almost total break with all the institutions of the past, it was doomed to failure. What gained the upper hand was the tendency at the opposite extreme which, following a development in the form of a spiral, took the line of a certain geographical determinism in keeping with the configuration of the country.

The rich valley of the Nile protected by the desert (Frankfort 1948, 4), with few ways into it (Dykmans 1936-1937, I, 215), presented advantages but also dangers: the risk of isolation[11] and of the permanence of a world without change. Moreover, the fertile inundations which guaranteed a minimum of prosperity (Frankfort 1948, 4; Bonneau 1964, 64) would engender a conception of the eternal return favouring a static attitude (Wilson 1956, 313f.) which in the domain of social morality becomes a preference for tranquillity, the preservation of the existing state of things, and the maintenance of the benefits and privileges acquired. In these conditions Maat corresponded more to the concept of order (sometimes in the broadest sense of the word) than to that of justice.

PART TWO

Social Justice and Biblical Sociology: A Historical Survey

3

Justice in the Old Testament as seen by Old Testament Scholars

Our subject, treated above all from the perspective of biblical exegesis, has already been the concern of a whole series of works which began to increase in number from the middle of the nineteenth century onwards. Apart from the important place which is reserved for it in various aids to research (dictionaries, encyclopaedias and biblical lexica),[1] numerous studies have been devoted to it in the form of books or articles. These last are often cited in various bibliographies, but in a somewhat incomplete way. The list which I have drawn up and incorporated in the general bibliography at the end of this book is not exhaustive either; nevertheless it seems to include the main works on justice in the Old Testament written over more than a century in the modern languages of our cultural sphere; with some exceptions, the very titles speak for themselves.

Some of these studies confirm what we have already seen in the previous chapters, namely that thanks to the discoveries of the last two centuries it is possible to demonstrate from the texts the existence of a general aspiration towards justice extending over the various regions of the ancient Near East (Cazelles nd, 1). The quest for justice which appears in Israel has analogies to that which appeared among its neighbours. The Hebrew notion of justice can be compared with Maat (Brunner 1958, 426-8; Crenshaw 1970, 383), the deity, daughter of the sun god, Re, symbol of good order, of the true state of nature and society as it has been fixed by the creative act (Chalon 1973, 5). We find distant antecendents for the biblical word-pair *mishpat/ tsedaqa*, which is not an abstract formula but a notion profoundly bound up with the specific life of the people of Israel (ibid., 2), in Babylon and among the Western Semites. In the first case it takes the form of the pair *kittu/mêsharu*. The first term comes from the root *kânu*, a verb the primary sense of which evokes the idea of solidity and stability (8); but depending on the instance *kittu* is translated by terms as varied as truth, justice, correct procedure, loyalty, faithfulness, correction, normal state (*Assyrian Dictionary* 8, 468-72; Cazelles 1973, 61). *Mêsharu* comes from the root *eshêru*, a verb which first of all evokes good order, but which also embraces a whole series of meanings relating to the good growth of the harvest, the prosperity of animals and men, peace and the security of the kingdom (Chalon 1973, 9). In the case of these two verbs we thus have categories far removed from strict justice to lead us towards objectives of a much more pragmatic character (Cazelles 1973, 61).

In the Western Semitic context, in its Phoenician phase (ibid., 60), which corresponds to the immediate sphere of the Bible (Cazelles 1951, 185), the word-pair *kittu/mêsharu* becomes *sdq/m(y)shr*; the change of terminology does not seem to involve an important ideological modification (Cazelles 1973, 63).

We find the first attestation of this last word-pair in the fourteenth century BC in the *Legend of Keret*, which is one of the major works of Ugaritic literature (ibid., 62). *Tsdq* corresponds there above all to 'an idea of plenitude and abundance, the happy life where everything is in place and nothing is missing'; 'it represents above all an idea of concord, of social well-being' (Cazelles 1951, 185). Only in the Bible and above all, it seems, thanks to the prophetic movement (Chalon 1973, 27), did *tsdq* come to be associated with fidelity to the law and morality. The biblical authors also profoundly modified the idea of social justice when they substituted *mishpat* for *m(y)shr* (Cazelles nd, 9). Whereas the latter term was associated with the king assuring ease and a good life for his people (Cazelles 1973, 63), *mishpat* introduces the idea of a government subject to a norm; thanks to its revelation people know the will of their God (Cazelles, 9). Composed in part in a Canaanite milieu, the Bible came to draw on it, but also corrected the term it took over (Cazelles 1973, 73).

Mishpat, the first term of the biblical word-pair, is the Hebrew word used most often for law (Van den Ploeg 1943, 144), but it can also mean simply justice (Berkovits 1969, 189). It derives from the root *shapat*, which is usually tramslated by the verb judge. However, this 'judge' must not be understood in the modern sense of the term, namely, as pronouncing a judgment, a 'sentence'. The primitive idea of *shapat* was broader: it comprised all the actions which accompanied or immediately followed the primitive process that took place when two opposed parties presented themselves before the competent authority, each to claim its rights (Van der Ploeg 1943, 146).

Given that in primitive societies the law corresponded above all to customary right, *mishpat* often signifies custom or law, and it is only by a later development that it comes to designate the corpus of laws, and therefore simply legislation. At all events, *mishpat* is both more complex and more vague than our notions of law and judgment (ibid., 153). This term evolved above all among the prophets, where it shifted from its legal sense to an ethical and religious significance (Hertzberg 1922, 274). However, even in the derivative sense (fate, religion), *mishpat* represented something obligatory and necessary (Van der Ploeg 1943, 155), a set of religious rules in conformity with the divine will (Van der Ploeg 1950, 250).

Tsedeq or *tsedaqa*, from the root *tsdq*, is a term of unparalleled importance, above all in this book, and it has been the object of a large number of works. Of the roughly eighty studies which deal specifically with justice in the Old Testament and which make up our list, there are twenty-two which, as their titles explicitly indicate, relate more specially to the root *tsdq* and its derivatives,[2] five on *mishpat*[3] and two on both terms together (Chalon 1973; Cox 1977). *Tsedeq*, usually translated justice, signifies much more than equity in judgment (Cazelles 1978, 65), and the noun is very difficult to render in our modern categories (Cazelles 1973, 64). Some biblical scholars (Jepsen 1965, 80; Procksch 1950, 569; Scullion 1971, 336) draw a distinction between *tsedeq* and its feminine form *tsedaqa*: in the first instance the principle, just order, is said to be stressed; in the other, just behaviour. *Tsedeq* seems earlier, but *tsedaqa* comes to gain a certain preponderance in the biblical vocabulary (*tsedeq* 118 times to *tsedaqa* 158, cf. Cazelles 1978, 69). However, these distinctions are not very important; all commentators are agreed in admitting that *tsedeq/tsedaqa* represents by far the most important ethical concept relating to the social and legal life of the people of God (Procksch 1950, 568).

In analogy to *mishpat*, but to an even greater degree, the meaning atributed to the derivatives of the root *tsdq* varied and in time underwent changes which are of special interest to us.

In conformity with tendencies which appear after a time in Old Testament research (Orlinsky 1971, 1-18), the term *tsedeq/tsedaqa*, instead of continuing to be treated as a concept of an essentially religious (as a synonym for grace;[4] faithfulness to the covenant, Fahlgren 1932, 79; salvation, Dacquino 1969, 105; Kuyper 1977, 233-52) or legal kind (conforming to a norm, Kautzsch 1881, 59; Nötscher 1915, 4; or implying a punitive step, Monnier 1878, 23) comes more and more to be approached as a social phenomenon concerning relations between two parties (Cremer 1897, 58). People began to see that in ancient Israel behaviour was not judged in accordance with an abstract and absolute norm but was a function of concrete, human relations (for example, the covenant not only with God but among men).[5] The Christian theologians, for two millennia bent over the sacred texts without sufficient contact with Jewish thinkers, began to note that the concept *tsedeq/tsedaqa* (Bianchi 1973, 306) is a concept of 'real relation between two parties and not the relationship of an object under consideration to an idea' (von Rad 1965, 371).

H.H.Schmid (1968, 185) has brought out the broader aspect, the community sense implied by the root *tsdq*, and shows how it is used in a series of relatively distinct cases, notably in six different spheres: the law, wisdom, nature/fertility, war/victory over the enemy, the cult/sacrifice and royalty. An analogous demonstration has been made in another recent successful doctoral thesis, the author of which (who comments that he received Schmid's work too late to use it adequately) resorts to multiple meanings of the nouns *tsedeq/tsedaqa* and the adjective *tsaddiq*, which appear 481 times in Kittel's Hebrew text of the Old Testament, and which he compares with the Greek terminology of the Septuagint (Ziesler 1972, 39).

Thus thanks to all these works we can see the extreme diversity of meaning that the idea of justice takes on in the Old Testament. According to André Neher, it 'signifies at the same time veneration, respect, legality, love and charity. It symbolizes sacred virtue and secular honesty. It denotes equity and good law no less than strict law and severity. It embraces clemency and rigour. It represents above all sincerity, integrity, poverty and innocence' (Neher 1955, 10).

This characterization is probably too diffuse to satisfy a rigorous mind, but it rightly shows the difficulties encountered by scholarly research in giving a more concise definition; at the same time it gives an idea of semantic richness from the pluralist side, open and *ipso facto* already social, which is so typical of Old Testament justice.

However, despite the very important contribution of all these works, the type of investigation predominant in most of them does not correspond entirely to my preoccupation. They are concerned above all with the philological aspect, the theological or philosophical sense of the terms relating to divine justice[6] and the effects of providence and supernatural help assuring good order and peace, and relatively little with the human virtues of equity and respect for the law, detached from their social setting.

We must also remember that the majority of authors of these works approach the problem of justice, as elsewhere almost everything else connected with the Old Testament, as a preliminary phase which is of secondary importance in comparison with what we are taught by the message of the New Testament (Schultz 1862, 568).

In others of the studies that we have considered there is another important category of works which is often closely related: those where the problem of justice is touched on above all from the legal point of view. Their number increases significantly from the moment when, thanks to archaeological excavations and the discovery of different Mesopotamian codes, people began to believe less in the supernatural origins of the Pentateuch and the role played by Moses in connection with it (Jepsen 1927, 100; Powis Smith 1931; Gerstenberger 1965).These works, which are partly cited, *inter alia*, in certain specialist works (Cazelles 1957, 498-530; Falk 1966-68), are a valuable contribution to our knowledge of Israelite law as a whole and are also of considerable interest for our subject, all the more as the comparative approach seems to be gaining increased weight. I shall make use of them above all in the last part of this work.

The Old Testament is the principal source of information and we must draw on it in the first place. But as we are interested in the problem of social justice above all from a historical and sociological point of view, it seems wise to begin with a survey of what has been done in this sphere by a series of scholars who touch on the problem with which our survey is concerned. Moreover, it would be interesting first of all to cast a brief glance at the rationalist study of the Bible (Popkin 1969-72, 339-55) which, by a slow route, among other things leads to the sociological approach.

4

The Rationalist Study of the Bible and Justice in the Old Testament from a Sociological Perspective

(i) The rationalist study of the Bible

One of the most important figures of Jewish history after Moses, who brought about the synthesis of the scientific spirit with the spirit of rabbinic Judaism (Vajda 1947, 129), was Maimonides (1135-1204: cf. Maier 1972, 284ff.). Compelled to leave the land of his birth and having led a complicated existence in the various parts of the Mediterranean basin, he had the occasion to study and observe the many aspects under which justice or rather injustice appeared; he reserved an important place for it in his work.

The last two chapters of the *Guide to the Perplexed* are largely devoted to an explanation of the meaning of the words *hesed*, *tsedaqa* and *mishpat* (Maimonides 1928, 391ff.). After expounding the meaning attributed to them by the 'doctors', Maimonides refers to Jeremiah (9.23) and recalls that according to the prophet 'the most noble of ends' is not limited to the knowledge of God but is aimed at the knowledge and comprehension of his attributes: it is necessary to know his ways, and take as a model his actions which are *hesed* (lovingkindness), *mishpat* (judgment) and *tsedeq* (righteousness). Maimonides then adds that he considers it an essential idea, as the pivot of religion, to know that these divine attributes must be applied 'on earth'. Contrary to what 'those miscreants argue who believe that the divine providence stops at the sphere of the moon, and that the earth, with all that is in it, is neglected by God', the earth is also in some respects the object of providence. In declaring that the Eternal takes pleasure in exercising good will, justice and virtue, Jeremiah means to say, according to Maimonides, that man, 'having acquired this knowledge', by imitating the actions of God will be 'always determined to seek lovingkindness, judgment and righteousness' (ibid., 397).

However, although he is considered to be the apostle of rational religion, in conformity with the characteristics of his moral thinking at a certain stage of his development, Maimonides touches on the problem in question from a perspective in which the precept seems to get the better of the fact, the rule the better of observation. As we know, a normative attitude predominated for a very long time in the various spheres of human thought. Nevertheless, it diminished in the course of the major stages undergone by our civilization (the Renaissance, the Reformation, the Enlightenment). This change was usually slow and often difficult to perceive, but it also went ahead in leaps and bounds and then was represented by particularly striking positions.

In a perspective a bit like that of Maimonides, the problem of justice is also touched on by Spinoza, who had read the *Guide to the Perplexed*. The *Tractatus theologico-politicus* (1670) deals with the covenant which the Jews made with God and its moral consequences. Having come out of Egypt, being freed from intolerable oppression, having 'rediscovered their natural law', the Jews decided to transfer all their law not to a mortal authority but solely to God. Only God, writes Spinoza, was from then on their political head, and only the state thus constitued had the right to bear the name of the kingdom of God. In this organization 'the dogmas of the Jewish religion were not doctrines but declared rights and commandments; piety was accounted justice, impiety was wickedness and injustice' (Spinoza 1862, 294).

According to Spinoza, the difficulties presented by the interpretation of the Bible do not in any way affect the foundations of the faith (*EJ* 15, 283), which consists in believing in 'a supreme being who delights in justice and mercy and whom all who would be saved are bound to obey' (Spinoza, 1862, 255).

According to Spinoza, faith gives each person the total freedom to philosophize. It only condemns as heretics and schismatics those who profess 'beliefs capable of spreading hatred, quarrels and anger', but it considers to be believers 'men persuade to and practise justice and charity' (ibid., 258).

Another interesting thing is that Spinoza had been in contact with Isaac La Peyrère, that he knew *Prae-Adamitae*,[1] and that he gave a powerful impetus to biblical criticism. He declares that the method applied to the interpretation of the Bible does not differ in any way from the method one follows in the study of nature (ibid. 1862, 144). According to him, the Bible and its world can be treated not so much as revelation or providential history but as a primitive phase of human evolution. Using the psychology and sociology of the time (above all the analysis made by Hobbes), Spinoza interprets religion in terms of human fear and superstition. Contrary to La Peyrère, for whom the whole of the Christian world can be described in secular and natural terms, but for whom the Jewish world still remains providential, Spinoza resorts to a metaphysics according to which the Jewish-Christian world is an integral part of all the human universe which must be studied like anything else, being approached in terms of the new science of man (Popkin 1969-72, 346f.).

Richard Simon, who was considered at that time to be the greatest biblical scholar, if not in the world, at least in the Christian world, was strongly influenced by La Peyrère (Yardeni 1970, 191) and also by Spinoza (Auvray 1967, 201-4). In his *L'Histoire critique du Vieux Testament* (1678), the first serious attempt at the history of the Bible conceived of in a scientific way, he seeks to demonstrate how difficult it is to give an account of what God said or what he wanted to say; consequently he tries to find the best way of giving a faithful account of past events and evaluating them for his time (Popkin 1969-72, 347-50). He thinks that Rashi and the Jewish commentators, thanks to their better knowledge of the original language, were often more precise and nearer to the truth than Christian tradition, based on the Vulgate (Parkes 1961, 164; Steinmann 1960, 129f.).

In Great Britain, as a result of its political situation, thanks to the affinity between Anglo-Saxon Puritanism and Judaism (Dow 1891, 77; Larès 1974: the Puritans were obsessed with their desire to assimilate themselves to the ancient elect people, Lutaud 1973), attitudes to the Jews provoked and stimulated research. John Weemse, alias Wemyss, of Lothoquar in Scotland (a pupil of Jean Buxtorf Sr), published in 1620 *The Christian Synagogue* with numerous quotations from the Talmud, the authors of which seemed to him to be as trustworthy and competent as the church fathers (Parkes 1961, 155). John Selden, a lawyer and author of a brief *Treatise on the Jews in England* (1617), whose important works on the Jews appeared from 1631 (*De Successionibus*, cf.*EJ* 14, 1971, 1120), seeks to prove that the idea and application of justice formulated and demanded by rabbinism is the continuation of what we find in the Pentateuch (Parkes 1961, 163). Brian Walton, Bishop of Chester, who headed research into rabbinic literature both in church and lay circles, published the *London Polyglot Bible* in 1657, the wealth of information and accuracy in which are exceptional (Loewe 1961, 140). Twenty-nine years after the readmission of the Jews, around 1685, the important work of John Spencer, *De Legibus Hebraeorum Ritualibus*, which is considered to be the starting point for comparative religion, appeared in Cambridge (Parkes 1961, 163).

Basing himself on the indications already given by Spinoza, La Peyrère and Richard Simon, and unwittingly taking up an idea already put forward by his German precursor H.B.Witter (*Jura Israelitarum in Palestinam...*, 1711), but previously applied only to two chapters in Genesis, Jean Astruc (*Conjonctures*, 1753) sought to demonstrate that Genesis was composed by Moses from memoranda borrowed from different authors. Although Astruc did not have 'the broad historical perspective of a Spinoza' or the learning of a Richard Simon, 'his discovery, precise and with solid support, took biblical criticism further forward than the ingenious but fragile hypotheses of his illustrious predecessors on the same subject' (Lods 1924, 57). He laid the foundation for a literary criticism which was given expression in the so-called Reuss-Graf-Kuenen-Wellhausen theory according to which the Pentateuch was the result of the fusion of four documents: the Yahwist, the Elohist, the Deuteronomist and the Priestly Code (Steinmann 1954, 9).

The laicization and the desacralization of morality which increased over the period between the sixteenth and the eighteenth century became even greater in the next century. People then began to study the world of the Bible, freeing themselves from the grips of conventional sanctity, and this way of looking at things was no longer inevitably considered an insult to religion. Moreover this attitude was accompanied by efforts aiming to add to, if not to substitute for, biblical criticism in the abstract (whether theological and philosophical, or literary and linguistic) that which is situated in time and has a historical character (Hahn 1966, 3).

What had already been achieved by D.G.Niebuhr, father of modern history, for Rome (*Römische Geschichte*, 1811-1832, thanks to his penetrating criticism of the sources) was undertaken by others for the biblical world: by Joseph Salvador and Renan in France; W.M.L.De Wette, W.Vatke, H.Ewald (the successor of J.G.Eichhorn) in Germany (Kraus 1969, 174-208); H.H.Millman and A.Penrhyn Stanley in Great Britain; and A.Kuenen in the Netherlands. As to the Jewish historians, mention must be made above all of Leopold Zunz, Abraham Geiger, Isaac Markus Jost and Heinrich Graetz, the founders of the modern science of Judaism (*Wissenschaft des Judentums*, cf. Maier 1972, 548; Rotenstreich 1972, 21).

However, the majority of these historians considered above all the chronological sequence of events; they were interested more in the individual exploits, the great religious leaders, and less in what was typical, what related to the group, what formed the social foundations of the Old Testament. This gap was in part filled by John Fenton (who in *Early Hebrew Life: A Study in Sociology*, 1880, dedicated to his master H.Ewald, set out, in contrast to the historical and literary school, to examine the Old Testament from the point of view of content and not of form), by the Scottish anthropologist William Robertson Smith (cf. Black and Chrystal 1912, 181, considered as the precursor of J.G.Frazer and one of the main initiators, if not the main initiator, of the sociological method applied to the study of the Old Testament), and by a group of exegetes, above all from Germany and Scandinavia, who attached a particular importance to what was called the *Sitz im Leben* (cf. Jacob 1969, 297; the first of them, Hermann Gunkel, 1906, 1798f., 1862-6, stressed that literature in Israel was an integral part of the life of the people and that for grasping the essentials the typical is more important than the authors and their individuality). Some representatives of this group, for example G. von Rad (1966, 243-66) and his pupil K.Koch (1976, 266), show a very lively interest in the problem of justice (the former more in connection with a later period than the one that we are studying), but others, like J.Fenton and W.Robertson Smith, do not seem to be too preoccupied with it. However, there is a line of historians and sociologists who, even if they deal with Old Testament justice in a marginal or fragmentary fashion, make a particularly valuable contribution.

(ii) Justice in the Old Testament and the sociological approach

We begin with Louis Wallis, economist, sociologist and theologian (Troeltsch 1913, 454), whose work is almost entirely unknown outside the United States and whose books are usually inaccessible, even in the great European libraries other than the British Library.

He has been quite severely criticized, and has been accused among other things of having taken up the ideas of Max Weber without even having cited him (Hahn 1966, 173). However, as will become evident, his first striking works on Judaism appeared before similar studies from the German sociologist.

According to Wallis, the purely historical interpretation of the Bible is inadequate and must be completed with the help of sociology. The excessive separation between the different scientific disciplines prevents scholars from appreciating discoveries at their true value. They do not profit mutually from the respective results of their researches. If history, according to Wallis, is only a biography of human society, sociology seeks to describe the structure of this society and its functioning; its task is to connect the various facts and the various currents in order to examine them and present them as a whole (Wallis 1922, XXIII).

The importance attached by Wallis to the sociological method leads him to interesting views of a general kind about the very basis of the phenomena he studies.

In 'The Capitalization of Social Development' (published in the *American Journal of Sociology* of May 1902 and in part in *An Examination of Society*, which appeared in 1903), he discusses the relationship between the Semitic religions and the Christian church by retracing some aspects of social development from prehistory to the present day. What strikes him particularly is the transition from the living human species, through small scattered groups, nomads, towards the much larger sedentary groups. These communities in process of formation, in order to satisfy their many and growing needs, are in quest of material means, of capital, the importance of which will become increasingly important. Being unable to procure these means with the methods used at a primitive stage, they will have to resort to methods which will bring about a cleavage, a division of society into two opposing classes (Wallis 1902, 766).

Similar ideas to those which I have just described, above all in method, appear in a later study the very title of which indicates its main idea: *Egoism. A Study in the Social Premises of Religion* (1905). Like many others before him, Wallis considers egoism to be the principal motive for human activity. What is new is the idea that according to him the Bible puts us in the most direct contact (V) with this exceptional 'force' which animates the social mechanism (3). If the Bible has gained an incomparable pre-eminence, it is precisely thanks to the fact that it contains the best historical description of egoism (p.1).

As this motive has an eminently social character and is at the heart of the secular experiences of the people of Israel which arose out of the biblical conceptions (V), the Bible can only be understood correctly if it is approached from a sociological perspective (14).

Wallis stresses that in primitive religion the gods formed an integral part of society, and that no distinction was made, as happened later, between the human and the divine aspects of phenomena. In this connection he cites Robertson Smith (according to whom the social corpus was not composed solely of men but also of gods). He also comments that religion in the Bible is the product of conceptions common to all the ancient world: what relates to the history of Israel at its beginnings must be studied in connection with all the ideas native to this area of the world (16).

However, it is in 'Sociological Study of the Bible', a work published for the first time in the *American Journal of Sociology* (Sept.1908-Nov.1911), that Wallis discusses something that is of particular interest to us. He refers to Kuenen and Marti (117), to Budde, Kittel and Winckler (93f.), who raised the problem of the opposition between the characteristics of the life of the nomads on the one hand and sedentary people on the other. However, what was touched on more in passing by these historians becomes more important in Wallis's work. According to him, the dominant element in the history of the Old Testament is represented by the long struggle between these two groups, one of which has already achieved a certain level of material culture while the other is still nomadic but much more dynamic (88).

The first group was represented by the Amorites who, although long settled in the land, had neither political organization nor a religion with a national character. This society was formed by a series of cities, a group of independent states each of which worshipped its own god called Baal. The way in which these gods were represented corresponded to the economic and social conception specific to a sedentary and already somewhat static society: they were considered as the masters, the divine owners of the people, just as the main representatives of the upper classes were also called baals and were the human owners of this same people (XXVI).

The ordinary person was treated with little respect in this régime, and while the majority were subject to a certain form of slavery, a small minority of privileged people used the government machinery and religion to strengthen their hold still further (XXVII). These tendencies were violently resisted by the Israelites, who were attached to nomadism (a way of life based on the common exploitation of the earth; Wallis 1942, 31), where there was no place for individual property. And as the normal life of a migratory clan depended on the way in which each of its members was treated, the ideal of brotherhood came to play a very important role (Wallis 1922, 89). In conclusion Yahweh, the national God of Israel, is at the same time the symbol of the struggle against Baal and against injustice (ibid., XXVI). We find similar ideas in his last book, in which among other things he says, as I have mentioned, that the history of the Hebrews is a series of reacions against economic injustice (Wallis 1953).

As Wallis is also interested in the spread of the Bible down the ages and outside Israel, he studies the Reformation. Here he notes an analogy between the social conditions which predominated in Europe at the end of the Middle Ages and those which prevailed among the ancient Hebrews. The clash which occurred between Protestantism and Catholicism was, in his view, of exactly the same kind as the struggle between the supporters of Yahweh and those of Baal among the Hebrews. Just as the former, the supporters of Yahweh, rebelled against the despotic reign of the upper classes, against the extension of Amorite law and its hold on the primitive clans installed on the heights (Wallis 1922, 270), so the Reformation, that mixture of lay and religious elements, was from a sociological point of view a rebellion of the middle classes against the nobility, a protest against the special privileges of the Catholic church (ibid., 265).

In addition to the works which we have considered, Louis Wallis wrote *God and Social Process* (1935) and *The Bible and Modern Belief* (1949); here, and above all in the former, he paid a good deal of attention to social justice in the biblical period.

A very important stage in the sociology of religions generally and the study of the social problems of the biblical period is represented by certain writings of Max Weber. His main work on the question, *Ancient Judaism* (the German original was published in 1917-1919 in *Archiv für Sozialwissenschaft und Sozialpolitik* and in book form in 1921), begins with a declaration that we have a better understanding of the essence of Judaism considered from a historical and sociological perspective when we compare it with the system of castes which prevails in India. Although the Jews lived in a world without castes, they are considered by Max Weber to be a people of pariahs; i.e. living on the edge of society, separated from it for ritual, formal or practical reasons (Weber 1967, 3). To explain the phenomenon, Weber begins with a characteristic drawn from geography: the contrasts presented by the configuration of the countryside. The fertile plains on the one hand and mountainous and desert regions on the other produce great economic and social differences (10f.): at one extreme the patrician sphere of the cities, at the other the Bedouin nomads, and between the two the peasants living in the mountain country and semi-nomadic shepherds (54).

Like Wallis, Max Weber knew the works of Rudolf Kittel and Hugo Winckler, and was keenly interested in the relationships which were established between those who still lived at the stage of tribal organization and the representatives of urban society. He recalls that in the Canaanite period the Israelites belonged to the former category and that they united in order to defend themselves better and combat those in the second group. This struggle was aimed at 1. control of the great routes used by the caravans and a hold on the advantages that they represented; 2. a freedom from taxes and forced labour; 3. conquest of the cities in order either to destroy them or take them over from their ancient inhabitants.

This struggle, which Max Weber compares to what happened in Graeco-Roman antiquity or in a more recent period (for example in Switzerland, where the peasants tried to seize the Gotthard route) would correspond above all to a conflict between the inhabitants of the mountains and those of the plains. This form of opposition provoked by nature, the result of geographical configuration, came to an end in the period of the monarchy, but a new division took its place: that in which the patricians in the cities, this time Israelites, found themselves faced by a class that was more diversified than before, made up of proletarian Israelites (peasants in debt or those who had already lost their land, salaried workers, and so on) and a certain category of strangers (54-6).

According to Max Weber, the *berit* and levitism were the particularly characteristic features of ancient Israel (Raphael 1970, 309). As the centre of Jewish religion (Séguy, 77), the *berit* played a determinative role in the formation of the Israelite confederation. This covenant is in no way comparable to covenants made by individuals or groups taking God as a witness to the contract; it was a covenant made with God himself who thus became Israel's partner, who watched over the observance of the clauses of the pact (Weber 1967, 78). However, levitism went through periods of eclipse when the *berit* was questioned, or formidable enemies threatened the country, or injustice was rife. At that time exceptional men, the pre-exilic prophets, from Amos to Jeremiah and Ezekiel, appeared who denounced the misdeeds of Israel and declared that its punishment was deserved (Raphaël 1970, 309). Weber stresses that the prophets belonged to extremely varied social strata, and that it is wrong to claim that the majority of them came from indigenous proletarian spheres. However, despite the variety of their origins and their attitudes, their demands for social morality were identical. Weber explains this by the fact that their position was not determined by considerations of a political or social kind in terms of either domestic or foreign policy, but emerged from the *berit* and was dictated by purely religious motives. The prophets unceasingly demanded obedience to the commandments of love and social justice which favoured ordinary people, and they vigorously attacked the rich and the great. However, none of them championed a 'democratic ideal'; according to them the people needed to be guided, and what mattered most were the qualities of a guide. None of them claimed that it was right for the masses, oppressed by the great, to revolt. Any idea of this kind would have seemed to them to be the height of sacrilege. With the exception of Ezekiel, who during the exile conceived of the theological foundations of an ideal state for future times, according to Weber none of them developed a social and political programme (Weber 1967, 277). If they violently denounced slavery for debts, the seizure of clothing and the violation of regulations aimed at protecting ordinary people, it was because such acts constituted a break in the covenant made with Yahweh. The nomadic ideal that they commended with vigour, from the eighth century BC onwards, was in fact a defence, a reaction against the political and social achievements of the time in the name of the covenant made in the desert (Raphaël 1970, 314).

However, we should not forget that while the prophets were not political, their demands for the *berit* related as much to the social, political and economic sphere as to the religious (Séguy 1972, 84). According to Weber, the prophets were never disturbed about the 'meaning' of the world or of life (Weber 1967, 313). Their horizon was strictly limited to this world. Weber writes that even if Israelite prophecy was associated with a levitical preoccupation with the salvation of souls, it was only interested in the collective destiny of the people (308). With the failures and misfortunes of the present they contrasted the hope for a future when the people and its rulers would again become faithful to the covenant. Israel would then be governed in justice by a king of the line of David. The promise of the prophets relates to an earthly political future and not to one in the beyond (Séguy 1972, 87).

The writings of Max Weber on Judaism, like other parts of his work, are incomplete. And even *Ancient Judaism*, published in the form of a book, lacks a conclusion; it contains a number of errors and the arrangement leaves something to be desired; the result is that it is not easy to read and nor can its main ideas be easily disentangled (Guttmann 1925, 197).

Alongside these reservations about its form, some objections have been made to its content:

1. Like his theory of the economic consequences of Protestant Puritanism, Max Weber's view of the relationships between economics

and religion and Judaism is not entirely acceptable. The fact that the peasants and the semi-nomads, two groups whose interests were distinct, were united in fighting the nobility, would seem to indicate that economics was dependent on religion. He also gives an analogous interpretation of the role played by the prophets: their criticisms and attacks on the injustice and the misdeeds of the great were dictated only by ethical and religious motives and not by political and economic factors (Hahn 1966, 164). Now this interpretation does not seem to correspond to the facts, and even if it were partly correct, it would not be a basis for general conclusions applicable to the whole of society (Schiper 1959, 259).

Max Weber does not escape the frequent temptation of seeking to reconstruct in an artificial way something that is dead. In treating the Jews as a people of pariahs, he transposes into the distant past what was valid above all in a later period.[2]

He could not free himself further from this prejudice, this wrong-headed idea of a putative double morality of Judaism which would act in favour of fellow religionists and to the detriment of others (Guttmann 1925, 222).

The work of Max Weber as a whole, and on Judaism in particular, is more voluminous and more important than that of Wallis, but perhaps it is also more impregnated with preconceived ideas and fixed positions – and that is very dangerous, especially in a subject like ours. At all events it has to be recognized that nevertheless Max Weber made a great attempt at objectivity and that his conclusions are much less partial than those of Marx (1971) or his contemporary W. Sombart.[3]

In German-speaking countries a whole series of studies appeared, some of which antedate those of Max Weber and others succeed it;[4] however, as partly transpired from what happened next, they are not as important as *Ancient Judaism*.

Adolphe Lods[5], professor at the faculty of Protestant theology in Paris, the main successor to Renan at the beginning of the twentieth century,[6] was keenly interested, like Wallis and Weber, in the opposition between the traditional forms of existence and those that the Israelites found in the land of Canaan (Lods 1932, 376f.). Whereas among the nomads, pastures and springs belonged in an indivisible way to the whole community, when the Israelites became farmers and settled down, the more skilful, as a result of the growing security, were able to consolidate their gains and increase their lands. These economic changes were accompanied by social changes: the principle of equality among the members of the clan disappeared and the differences began to be more marked. Among the nomads, all ate the same simple food, wore the same crude clothing, lived in the same basic accommodation – the tent; riches were represented by the privilege of offering wider hospitality but did not ensure either influence or power. With the division of society into increasingly more differentiated categories, the great adopted a way of life which became more and more different from the primitive simplicity, and to satisfy needs which had suddenly arisen, they began to employ 'those weapons which their very wealth made available, with increasing harshness'. They profited from their situation as judges and nobility to strip those who found themselves deprived of natural defenders – in the first place the widows and orphans. They took advantage of the difficult situations in which the ordinary peasants found themselve to make loans to them: they called for ruinous pledges and finally took over the land of insolvent debtors, selling them with their children as slaves (ibid., 398).

Antonin Causse, who tried to apply the theories of the French sociological school (above all those of Lucien Lévy Bruhl)[7] to the study of the Old Testament and who knew the work of Max Weber (Causse 1937, 9), profited from the counsels of his teacher A. Lods, and also became interested in the social and moral crisis which Israel underwent as a result of the need to adapt to Canaanite civilization and to urban life (ibid., 37). The first two parts of his main work, *Du groupe ethnique à la communauté religieuse*, are devoted to this phenomenon. Causse recalls that to begin with Israel repudiated city civilization, but from the beginning of the monarchy it progressively adopted Canaanite customs and was under the influence of Canaanite culture. The village clans lost their independence and their importance diminished. The centre of gravity of Israelite society shifted towards the city where there were no longer the equilibrium and the stability of the old groups: the accumulation of riches in the hands of the privileged and the luxury which ensued created tension and engendered conflict (39-42). The primitive institutions did not disappear, but their very foundations were threatened.

These new conditions increased social mobility; hence there was a weakening of the bonds of affinity which allowed the individual to free himself from the obligations and the restrictions which the family group imposed on him. The old solidarity markedly weakened (47f.), the law of mutual aid and family protection was no longer observed in the same way (51); in legislation the individualist system began to gain the upper hand (50).

Causse ends this part of his analysis by declaring that there was a grave crisis, an attack on the very notion of the covenant, the weakening of the *berit*, 'this mystical relationship, more powerful than any physical bonds that can exist between human beings' (53).

Among the reactions that this crisis provoked, the most striking appeared in the form of the attitude adopted by the prophets. And as their criticisms, almost always with extreme severity and often with violence, seem to be the first written evidence of this state of affairs, it is natural that they should have become the focal point of the works in which the authors touch on the problem of justice. However, as we shall see, the way in which specialists on this question describe and interpret the phenomenon is not always the same.

Lods is nearer to Weber than Causse is: his interpretation of the role of the prophets is more idealist than that of his pupil. In his view the prophets, in reacting against Canaanite civilization, did not seek only to return to the past and defend the nomadic ideal (Lods 1937, 65); they were not simply social reformers: they aspired to a moral reform (ibid., 66), a new religious conception; they called for justice, absolute justice (Lods 1931, 314), which would be above the interests of the nation (Lods 1932, 423; Hahn 1966, 167-9).

Causse adopts a more sociological attitude. As is already partly indicated by the title of his first work, his thesis presented to the Protestant Theological Faculty of Montauban to obtain the degree of bachelor in theology, *Le Socialisme des prophètes* (1900), he presents them as collectivists, 'social revolutionaries who in the name of Jehovah the God of justice come to announce the destruction of a world based on egoism and iniquity' (93). He also draws attention to the fact that the Hebrew prophets 'never appeal to sanctions from beyond the grave', that they are hungry for 'earthly justice', justice which must be realized here on earth (82). In time Causse's views underwent some change; this already appears in his doctorate thesis presented to the Faculty of Protestant Theology at Geneva (Causse 1913), and the works which followed (Causse 1919, 1922; Lods 1922; Causse 1924), above all in *Du groupe ethnique...*, where he seeks to demonstrate that the attacks of the prophets on the disruptive influence of Canaanite civilization were the expression of the conservative attitude of Israelite peasants who desired to keep their primitive culture and their patriarchal organization (Causse 1937, 75).

Given that Causse took account of historical evolution, his interpretation came very close to that of Lods. Despite their conservative tendencies, the efforts of the prophets ended in a 'profound transformation of the primitive mentality and primitive social conceptions'. While wanting 'to restore the old solidarity of family and tribe', they proclaimed 'the monolatric character of Yahwism' (96f.). They drew on the very depths of popular religion, but they no longer conceived of solidarity between God and the group as a mystical and magic bond; they based it on an ethical foundation, on justice. 'Yahweh is the just God; Israel, the people of Yahweh, must perform justice' (100f.) By moralizing and rationalizing the cult, the prophets thus opened up, again according to Causse, the way towards an individualist conception of religion (106), and this appearance of the personal element signified that in relations between God and the faithful, the institutions of colleetive life had only a secondary importance (110).

On the whole, according to Causse, the work of the eighth- and seventh-century prophets mark a vigorous effort to rationalize religious tradition and social institutions. 'With them there comes about the transition from primitive collectivism to moral individualization.' They can perhaps be compared with the Greek philosophers of the Socratic period, but with the difference that among the latter the reforming principle is a theoretical reason, 'while among the prophets of Israel it is a matter of practical reason and not speculation' (112).

The works of Louis Wallis and Max Weber, and those of the French sociological school (of Lévy-Bruhl in particular) are known by J.Van der Ploeg, and we owe to him a valuable overall view of studies of the economic and social aspects of Israel before the monarchy (Van der Ploeg 1940). In 1943 there appeared his article entitled 'Shapat and mishpat' in which, like others, he recalls tha the notion of *mishpat* docs not correspond exactly to any of our own ideas (ibid., 152). In 1948 his *Les Pauvres d'Israël* was published; here he surveys what had already been said on the question and draws attention to the important fact that in the Old Testament 'the rich man as such is not considered the natural enemy of the poor', since 'the normal opposition was not between the rich and the poor, but between the poor and the wicked'. The prophets and the poor considered riches a great blessing that they did not want to abolish; it was poverty that they treated as an evil (Van der Ploeg 1950, 268).

F.Dijkema, a pupil of W.Brandt (who in 1899 in his Amsterdam university course examined the religion of Israel from a social and economic perspective), spoke out firmly in favour of the sociological approach, with reference to Van der Ploeg (Dijkema 1943, 18). This 'modernist' no longer shared the views of the followers of Wellhausen about the attitude of the prophets towards the cult; that is evident in his first study (1905) and in his other works, above all those published between the two wars (de Vries 1968, 121). The article which relates most closely to our subject, 'Le Fond des prophéties d'Amos', dates from 1943. As the title already indicates to some degree, here Dijkema seeks to describe the historical context, the economic and social structure which explain the attitude of Amos: his campaign against social justice which takes the form of attacks on 'the powerful landowners who claim the power of jurisdiction, the merchants who exploited the rural population, the perpetual wars bringing profit to some but harming others' (Dijkema 1943, 33).

Like the authors I have just cited, Dijkema pays detailed attention to the social and moral effects of the new forms of economic and political life: it is a matter of 'the agricultural society... weakened by growing capitalism', the degeneration represented by the replacement of Saul the peasant king and David the soldier king with Solomon the merchant-diplomat king (20).

In the wake of Solomon's policy and the contacts he established with the outside world, 'elements which did not exist beforehand began to dominate social life: a permanent modernized army, an organized class of officials, international trade, the new division of the kingdom, the financial régime'. But there was also a crisis, an impoverishment of the rural population (22).

The king, the permanent army and the great landowners profited the most from war, while the rural population reaped 'the bitter fruits of forced labour, taxes and devastation'. The contacts between the king and the people disappeared and the fate of the country was no longer in his hands; he became 'increasingly excluded from any involvement in the government' (24).

The peasants, formerly poor but nevertheless independent, became the prey of money-lenders and merchants who exploited them. A gulf opened up between the sumptuous life which appeared in the city and that which prevailed in the country (27).

What went hand in hand with this state of affairs and made Amos in particular so angry was the dishonesty and corruptibility of the judges. The representatives of the old families and tribes were pushed aside by the new bureaucracy, nominated directly by the king and the court, without account being taken of their ability or honesty. One of the most basic foundations of society is the impartiality of the judges. Now the complaints constantly repeated by Amos and the other prophets show us that this basis had been undermined. The judges are not subject to the laws and the powerful are free to do what they will (25).

In the eyes of Amos Israel is nothing but corruption, a negation of God. Punishment will come: the day of the Lord will not bring light but darkness (32f.). However, Dijkema stresses that Amos does not only announce disaster; he is not just the prophet of misfortune. The justice of God is fidelity to a word that has been given and therefore the evil will certainly be punished while the pious and the oppressed will be protected and recompensed (34).

In his doctoral thesis (*Le Développement du sens social en Israël avant l'ère chrétienne*), defended and published (1955) in Holland but written in French, C.Van Leeuwen refers among others to Robertson Smith, Max Weber and Van der Ploeg, but above all and very often to Causse. As he declares in the introduction, he wants to take account of the 'social structure' adopted by the faith to which the Bible issues a summons: he tries to identify 'the sociological factors' of the struggle that the legislators, prophets and psalmists wage for the benefit of social justice. In his view, the principle of justice that he is going to study 'far surpasses the role of historical conditions', and by social justice he does not mean an 'equal justice' for all but a 'special justice for the poor and weak' (11). In basing himself on the main works devoted to the problem of slavery which have appeared over past decades, Van Leeuwen tries to give an overall view of the phenomenon in question: he also examines it in relation to what happened in other countries in the ancient Near East. However, he deals above all with the most frequent case of slavery in the Old Testament: that which follows from the economic distress which forced free men to sell their children or to sell themselves (58).

This opposition between the two modes of existence, the two types of civilization specific to ancient Israel, is also taken into consideration by J.Pedersen, the leader of the famous Scandinavian Old Testament school (Ringgren 1971, 419). Like Causse, he cites in this connection passages of Jeremiah which deal with the contrast between ancient Jerusalem, the seat of justice, and the new state of things in which some amass riches and live in luxury while letting the poor die of hunger (Pedersen 1926, 375). However, as an anthropologist more than a historian, generally speaking Pedersen approaches the problems which interest us in a rather different way from the authors we have cited previously.

In two long chapters of his famous work *Israel. Its Life and Culture* (Danish 1920), entitled 'Righteousness and Truth' and 'The

Maintenance of Justice', he stresses that for the Israelites justice represents the essential problem of existence (374). He argues that while for Arabs the main cultural and moral value is honour, what counts above all for the majority of Israelites is justice. It resides at the very centre of the human being, in the deepest corners of his soul. Job, whose psychology is, according to Pedersen, typically Israelite, accepts the loss of all to which he was most attached, but what he will never be separated from is justice (367).

However, for the Israelites justice represented not only a personal value but an essential element of social health. The soul can only exist if it finds itself in a close organic relationship with other souls. The just man is 'a totality' with those with whom he has made a covenant (341). This does not transform society into an entirely uniform mass. The collective soul, like the individual soul, represents an organism formed in a very determined way in which each occupies the space to which he is predestined; it corresponds to the status attained by the soul in accordance with its possibilities of giving and receiving. Justice consists in maintaining one's status and that of others in conformity with the place one occupies within the covenant. Justice and truth are the expression of the realism characteristic of old Israelite culture which gives each what is due to him and as much as he can receive (343).

The changes which come about in the lives of the Israelite tribes after their settlement in the land of Canaan are examined by J.Lindblom in *Prophecy in Ancient Israel* (1962, entirely rewritten in comparison with the original Swedish text *Profetismen i Israel*, 1934). The author devotes an important part of this work to an analysis of the critical attitude that the prophets adopt towards the new state of things. Like Causse, he believes that the prophets have a nostalgia for primitive existence and also stresses that this is not a desire to return to nomadism but to agricultural life (V). The bias of the prophets towards the past has nothing to do with a reactionary conservatism or a dreamy romanticism. Their moral ideal is not a personal invention; it draws its strength from the experiences of life, in the tradition, and it is above all the fruit of teaching given in the sanctuaries.

Lindblom speaks of the social spirit of the prophets: their indignation in the face of injustice, their pleas for the oppressed, their sense of solidarity. At root, however, in his view theirs is a theonomic ethic inseparable from religion, in which humanitarian ideals, in the classical or modern sense of the word, is almost non-existent (344). According to Lindblom, the prophets are neither social reformers nor thinkers or philosophers. They are essentially *homines religiosi*. What is distinctive about them is a special gift which allows them to sense the divine, to receive revelations (1).

This way of envisaging the role of the prophets is represented by the fact that the main part of Lindblom's work is not dedicated to the social aspect of phenomena, but to the problem of the cult (351).

The contrast between the desert and cultivated land, between nomadism and sedentary life, is stressed in the work of Samuel Nyström, a pupil of Lindblom (1946, 220). In *Beduinentum und Jahwismus* (which, as the sub-title indicates, is a religious and historico-sociological study of the Old Testament), he describes the main phases of the process of sedentarization and then studies at length the attitude of the prophets and of Deuteronomy towards the life of the desert. It is Amos, Micah and Hosea who in his view prove to be most influenced by nomadic culture. This bias emerges from a social and moral perspective in their hostile attitude towards the accumulation of riches (126), luxury (132), urban life (134), and a criticism of the break-up of the old community life (137), a plea for the widow, the wise man and the stranger (139).

It is interesting to stress in connection with the first point in these charges that according to Nyström (who in this connection takes up an idea of Abram Menes that we shall be considering later), the prophets react not only against the effects of the economic system but also against the system itself, not only against the consequences but also against the principle of private property that results in these wrongs (131).

However, in this work, which is a doctoral thesis presented to the Theology Faculty at the University of Lund, the main role is attributed to religion. According to Nyström, we can only understand what this struggle between the desert and the cultivated land represents for Israel if we take account of Yahwism, since it is thanks to Yahwism that the nomadic ideal is humanized, and thanks to it that the old ideal of solidarity, which risked disappearing with sedentarization, could be preserved.

5

Justice in the Old Testament and the Kindred Approach of Historical Materialism

(i) The supporters of historical materialism

For almost all the authors with whom we have been occupied in the last part, the problem of justice has been raised in connection with certain confrontations between phenomena which are not always closely bound together at the heart of the same social system. Justice is considered in the context of the opposition between nomads and semi-nomads on the one hand and sedentary people on the other; the background is a confrontation between two worlds, two different phases of civilization.[1]

The writers to whom we shall now turn approach the problem of justice above all in the context of internal conflicts at the very heart of Israelite society at the point where the old ethical conception which was still predominant at the time of the arrival in the land of Canaan began to be undermined by the new forms of social and economic life (Kapelrud 1966, 197).

The majority of historians and sociologists belonging to the first group tend to make a connection between social justice and traditional values: those of the second, as we shall see, on the whole are biassed towards historical materialism and take account of the class struggle. This tendency is already evident in Robertson Smith and even in a sense in Max Weber, but it appears with even greater force among others from the 1930s on.

The first representative of this group, M. Lurje, takes account above all of the economic and social situation of the country. According to him the source of evil must not be attributed either to the cult of Baal or to the influence of the Phoenicians, but to living conditions, which were particularly critical at the time of the appearance of the great prophets.

The social differences and the class struggle caused great losses and considerable expense. The very heavy burden of taxes which the people had to bear was increased by the cost of the building of cities and palaces undertaken by its monarchs, as for example by king Ahab. The frequent droughts heightened the distress further.

This difficult material situation was made even harder to bear by a whole series of crimes of a moral kind: deception, corruption, the perversion of justice, usury, cupidity and at the same time, for some people, a sumptuous life well above the average.

It was this state of affairs that the prophets attacked. They are supporters of Yahweh, since Yahweh is the god of justice; the struggle for the power of Yahweh is a struggle for the rule of justice; the struggle on behalf of Yahweh is consequently the expression of a social movement (Lurje 1927, 57).

However, Lurje proves to be hard on the prophets: perhaps with the exception of Amos, in his view they were neither true democrats nor defenders of the poor. They thought that power in the hands of the proletariat would be the greatest of ills. They did not want a change of régime, they were supporters of the monarchy and the rule of the aristocracy. They did not formulate a programme which would put an end to the dispossession of the poor peasants for the benefit of the rich; according to them it would be enough for the great simply to change the way they behaved and not to oppress the weak so much.

However, although the prophets were not real social reformers, one can never stress enough, according to Lurje, the influence that they exercised on the social movement. They were the first publicly to stigmatize the misdeeds of exploiters in the severest of terms. They addressed the masses at the entrance to the temples and at the gates of the cities, and one can regard these meetings as the first political assemblies of the opposition party to be held in Israel and Judah. What Amos and Hosea said to Samaria was known some days later in Jerusalem, and the same sort of thing happened the other way round with the declarations of Micah and Isaiah. Little by little, the prophets began to write their speeches themselves or have them written by others, and this is what Lurje considers to be the beginnings of the political press in Jerusalem (59f.).

Hardly a year after Lurje's work appeared, and in the same collection (Beihefte zur Zeitschrift für die alttestamentliche Wissenschaft), the study by Abram Menes, *Die vorexilischen Gesetze Israels*, was published. Menes was a pupil of Hugo Gressmann, an admirer of Eduard Meyer, and also critical of the way in which Max Weber conceived of the economic and social structures of ancient Israel.

Perhaps even more strongly than Lurje, he stressed the importance of study of what is inherent in society itself. The criticisms of the prophets, their negative attitude to reality, cannot be explained by an attachment to old customs, to nomadic life. Their reaction is not provoked by an opposition between two different phases of cultural evolution, but by the opposition between the two principal social classes in the same society and at the same period (Menes 1928, 14).

Having recalled that according to Israelite tradition Moses was the source of all the laws, Menes stresses that the solution to this problem cannot be found either with the help of literary criticism or through the method of the history-of-religions school; it must take account of social and economic factors. What matters is not who produced the text or when that was done but the specific conditions at the time of the origin of the laws and the circumstances which produced them, the person who really inspired them. Like other contemporaries (Powis Smith 1931, 21), Menes does not believe in the role that Moses could have played in this respect and he goes on to try to demonstrate that it was the same with the role of the priests: before the exile they did not have a great deal to say in matters connected with the cult; so one could not expect that they would have participated actively in the elaboration of the laws.

The same is true of the Levites who, like the priests, did not represent a sufficiently homogeneous body. No longer being an organ of state, they were able to study the law, and transcribe or edit texts, but they were not their real creators. So proceeding by elimination one would be led to attribute the role of legislator to the king, who is often mentioned in this connection in the historical books. However, according to Menes even the kings did not do a great deal here. On the other hand, the traditions of the Pentateuch and the content of the historical books refer us in an appropriate way to another institution: to popular assemblies which were generally unknown in the Near East. Their roles emerge all the more clearly in the history of ancient Israel (Menes 1928, 21).

According to Menes, a distinction must be made between the smaller assemblies, those of the community and the tribe, on the one hand, and those which represented the whole country on the other. The former were held for matters of lesser importance and the others, for example, for the enthronement of Saul or for legislative reform; they were rarer and were summoned at the time of festivals.

Specifically in Israel, according to Menes, prophecy could grow only through the popular assemblies. These were democratic institutions which allowed the prophets to address the people and fulfil their roles as orators.

Another characteristic phenomenon, the covenant, is similarly explained by the popular assembly (22). As the Old Testament puts it, at the time when the covenant was made, the king had 'with him all the men of Judah and all the inhabitants of Jerusalem, and the priests and the prophets, all the people, both small and great' (II Kings 23.2). It is wrong to date the origin of the Book of the Covenant to the time of Moses; it is much better explained from what happened in the time of Elijah (23). As its content indicates, it represents a need for reform (25); it is the expression of the aspirations of the poor (43). The opening phrase, 'You shall not make gods of silver or gold beside me', is interpreted by some scholars as a prohibition against worshipping strange gods. Now according to Menes, in fact these are not images of gods but images of God; so this is not a matter of strange gods but of the image of Yahweh, and the prohibition originally related only to costly statues. This regulation was part of the struggle against luxury, which was similarly expressed in the precept calling for the building of altars of earth. This attitude which, according to Menes, bears the stamp of levitical origin, cannot be interpreted as a sign of attachment to nomadic customs, but is a reaction to the forms proper to a more advanced stage of civilization (25).

To have a better understanding of the Book of the Covenant it is also important to see what is said about the sabbath (36). Contrary to the widespread opinion according to which the sabbath primarily met cultic needs, according to Menes these themes were secondary to the needs of everyday life (38).

The essence of the sabbath is constituted by the ideal of the equality of all creatures. On that day all the differences are abolished between master and slave, wage-earner and master, man and domestic animal (39).[2] 'Six days you shall labour, and do all your work; but the seventh is a sabbath to the Lord your God; in it you shall not do any work, you, or your son, or your daughter, or your manservant, or your maidservant, or your ox, or your ass, or any of your cattle, or the sojourner who is within your gates, that your manservant and your maidservant may rest as well as you' (Deut.5.13f.).

This spirit of equity also appears in the regulations for the institution of the sabbatical year. Note, however, that Menes does not agree with the current interpretation according to which here the earth is to be left to lie fallow: 'Six years you shall sow your land and gather in its yield; but the seventh you shall let it rest and lie fallow...' (Ex.23.11).

In his view it is not a matter of abandoning the earth; this is a social measure to benefit the settlers and farmers who in this seventh year can keep all the produce of their land and do not owe anything to their lord (38).

A certain aspect of the sabbatical year particularly favours slaves: it is said, 'When you buy a Hebrew slave, he shall serve six years, and in the seventh he shall go free, for nothing' (Ex.21.2).

What I have just said in connection with the Covenant Code also applies to Deuteronomy. According to Menes, the centralization of the cult envisaged by some as the main objective of this code was dictated above all by humanitarian reasons: the slave was to be protected so that wherever he took refuge he would find the same prohibition against being handed over to the master from whom he had escaped. If we compare Deut. 22.4 and 23.16-17 it is clear that 23.16 assures the slave that he can take refuge where he thinks fit (55f.).

Nor does Menes agree with the general opinion that Deuteronomy was discovered or written by Hilkiah shortly before or in the time of king Josiah (64f.). Deuteronomy is not the result of an accidental discovery, the product of the efforts of an isolated thinker (66), or the result of measures adopted by a reforming king (67). It is the consequence of a whole series of circumstances and socio-political factors introduced with the assent of the popular party which was in favour of the reform and which found itself in power throughout the reign of Josiah (70).

In a chapter devoted to an analysis of the laws of Deuteronomy, Menes stresses that a reform of the rights of the debtor and the slave was the essential feature of the codes of the time; it corresponded to the aspirations of the indebted peasants and reflected the needs of the urban proletariat (78f.). What is striking in Deuteronomy is its concern for widows, orphans and the *gerim* (which can easily be explained if we take account of the decline into which the northern kingdom was entering and the ruinous wars being waged by Judah, the consequence of which was a catastrophc increase of the ranks of the proletariat, 85f.).

The popular assembly was the supreme organ of state in Israel, and the promulgation of laws was its main objective. However, the laws were at the same time said to have divine origins. The reconciliation of these two points of view is realized by the prophet: he is the intermediary between Yahweh and the people; he transmits the will of the one to the other. Menes stresses a very important aspect of this phenomena: according to him, as long as prophecy remained alive, the verdicts of Yahweh could not be considered immutable and Yahweh could introduce modifications. Moreover, it was not the hereditary and institutionalized clergy but free prophecy which was charged with revealing the divine will; in this way the risks of the bureaucratization of this function were avoided (90).

Law in antiquity was intended above all to protect property, and to a large degree the human being was also considered to be an object subject to the law of property. The debtor guaranteed his debt not only with his possessions but with his person. Similarly, the slave was considered not as a person but as a thing dependent on the will of his master. The Pentateuch as a whole represents a decisive change in this respect, progress which can serve as a model for the contemporary period. This comment applies especially to Deuteronomy, which is an important advance on the Covenant Code (117). While the greater part of the latter is aimed at safeguarding property, the law of possessions does not occupy the same place in Deuteronomy. This difference reflects a fundamental change in social structure. The Covenant Code met the needs of a predominantly peasant society which was above all afraid of theft, and damage caused to the harvest and cattle; Deuteronomy represented the attitude of the urban proletariat which did not have the same quantity of material goods and attached more importance to the protection of the human person (124).

(ii) Non-conformists close to some aspects of historical materialism

Ten years after Menes' study, in 1938, Louis Finkelstein's book, *The Pharisees*, was published. From the beginning of his work Finkelstein stresses that any part of the history of Israel must be studied in connection with the totality of which it is a part if it is to be understood and properly interpreted (1). As a result, despite its title, the work also takes account of the period which interests us and compares Pharisaism with prophecy. Moreover, in order to bring out the similarities better, it takes a great leap forward and establishes a parallel between the two currents in question and British Puritanism: these three movements are the consequence of the same type of social conflict. What happened in the urban Palestinian centre of Jerusalem in the eighth and third centuries BC respectively – the opposition of the workers and traders to the nobility, the clergy and the great landowners – corresponds to seventeenth-century London: the English metropolis in process of growing. Just as prophecy represented a factor which was to contribute to the engendering of Pharisaism, so this last, thanks to the English translation which made the Bible accessible to the people, served as a stimulus to Puritanism (XVIf.).

Stemming from the extreme polarization which characterizes the economic and political life of ancient Israel, the numerous social conflicts of which it was the theatre were usually reduced to a simple dichotomy between patricians and plebeians. Now the oppositions, the divergent interests, in fact proved much more complicated and diversified; they produced three or four and even more opposing parties. In the prophetic period the division was less complex than in the Pharisaic period, but in both cases it corresponded more or less to the same scheme. Prophecy and rabbinism were the result of these contradictory tendencies (3-6).

At the time his work was published, Finkelstein, a rabbi and representative of conservative Judaism, was teaching theology in a Jewish theological seminary in the United States. So he cannot be regarded as a partisan of historical materialism in the same way as Lurje or Menes. When he speaks of such and such a group he takes account not only of their economic needs but also of their spiritual aspirations. Similarly, when he discusses political divisions he refers to religious beliefs specific to patricians, plebeians or peasants (344f.).

However, in conformity to his sub-title (*The Sociological Background...*), he is interested in the sociological foundations of phenomena. In Chapter 15 ('The Prophetic Ideals of Equality') he analyses the sense of justice in the prophets not only in respect of their professional status and their environment, but above all of the economic and social structure and the conflicts which ensue (292). His main thesis is that prophecy expressed the aspirations of an oppressed and disinherited protesting minority (II, 462).

Finkelstein recalls that it is the work of the craftsman or merchant, where success is due to personal ingenuity, that develops a sense of independence, much more difficult to acquire the case of the peasant who is as attached to the soil as the beasts of the field which he uses. It is the city-dweller who has more possibilities of taking account of his own value and becoming aware of the discriminations against him. So it was not in the country but in the urban centre at Jerusalem that people began to be aware of the state of oppression, and it was there that the need for freedom which led to revolt began to germinate (302). This state of things, this difference between the unawareness of the countryman and the more awakened spirit of the city-dweller (306) confronted with injustice, is represented in the behaviour and attitudes of the first great writing prophets (294).

As long, for example, as Hosea lived in the country in the fertile north (295), where a degree of social peace reigned (301), and as long as he did not settle in a city (probably Samaria, 298), his indignation manifested itself above all against the cult of Baal, against duplicity, against arrogance – which in the eyes of a provincial were the main social vices (296). On the other hand, Amos, who left Tekoa, a region with rocky soil (which could not satisfy the most elementary human needs, 294), to settle in Jerusalem where the social conflicts were particularly virulent (304), denounces with extreme violence (294) those who 'sell the righteous for silver and the needy for a pair of shoes – they that trample the head of the poor into the dust of the earth, and turn aside the way of the afflicted' (Amos 2.6f.), who 'lie down on garments taken in pledge' (Amos 2.8), who 'store up violence and robbery in their strongholds' (Amos 3.10).

This difference in attitudes, attributed to the same reasons, also appears in two other prophets contemporary to Jeremiah, Nahum and Habakkuk. The former sees things with the eyes of a countryman (306) who, like Hosea, does not seem too amazed at the arrogance of the great going side by side with the exploitation of the weak (308). On the other hand Habakkuk, a city dweller, just as Nahum was a countryman (309), proves very aware of social misdeeds (317). Habakkuk compares the struggle against the weak nations and the powerful empires with the conflicts between the oppressed plebeians and the patricians: the external enemy, the invader, appears in his work in the form of the lord, the rapacious neighbour, the evil man who 'swallows up the man more righteous than he' (Hab. 1.13). He establishes a parallel between the increasing power of Chaldaea (which is soon to invade Judah) and the oppresive exploitation which takes place at the heart of the national community (311).

These differences between the various prophets also appear among some of them when we compare the successive stages of the life of one or other of them.

The first four chapters of the book of Jeremiah (those which correspond to the time of his youth spent in his birthplace of Anathoth) are devoted above all to the fight against idolatry. On the other hand, from ch.5, when he runs through the streets of Jerusalem and preaches in the capital, the prophet shows himself aware that the country is invaded by a much graver sin than before: there are evildoers who

lurk like fowlers lying in wait.
They set a trap;
they catch men.
Like a basket full of birds,
their houses are full of treachery;
therefore they have become great and rich,
they have grown fat and sleek.
They know no bounds in deeds of wickedness;
they judge not with justice
the cause of the fatherless, to make it prosper,
and they do not defend the rights of the needy (Jer.5.26-28).

Like Jeremiah, Micah also spent his youth in the country and he
only went to Jerusalem when he was grown up. The beginnings of his
prophecy, the first chapter (of the seven chapters in the book, only
the first three can be attributed to him with certainty), also relate
exclusively to the sins of the house of Israel represented by idolatry, and
only chs. 2 and 3 are devoted to social justice (305), the denunciation of
wickedness, the misdeeds of those who 'covet fields and seize them';
who 'oppress a man and his inheritance' (Micah 2.1-2).

When Ezekiel lived in a little Palestinian hamlet (314), his early
prophecies displayed a certain country crudeness (316), a spirit still
insufficiently aroused and unaware of social conflicts. His criticisms
were limited to denouncing idolatry, and did not relate to the problems
of human relationships and the tensions arising from them. However,
from a certain point he became the 'watchman of the house of Israel',
and began to play the vital role of the one who puts everyone on guard
against evil actions. Several factors acted in this direction: first,
probably the age (325); but the decisive role must be attributed to a
change of setting.

Deported to Babylonia, Ezekiel, like the other exiles of 597, found
himself in a complete vacuum. He could not take advantage of the
property he had left behind him, and his ecclesiastical prerogatives no
longer counted in a country where there were no Jewish temples. In
order to earn a living, he learned to engrave on brick in the fashion of
Babylonians and he was trained in the various building techniques.
Thus he was a member of the group of plebeians, the old artisans and
merchants of Jerusalem. He gradually adopted their points of view,
not only about the present situation (for example, the problems of
relations between Judah and Babylon) but also about questions relating
to the idea of God, the doctrine of individual responsibility and that

of social justice (329). In these conditions the oppression of the weak by the strong became for him a sign of the denial of God which was as strong as idolatry. The great iniquity of Jerusalem consisted not in its failure to submit to God but in its evil actions of which this plebeian prophet spoke so often (330). The major sin of Sodom was not its lack of hospitality but its arrogance and the fact that it perverted justice (331).

Going beyond all that had been taught by the prophets before him, Ezekiel declared all men to be equal. He introduced the term 'son of man' – which signifies that even the vehicle of the divine message is considered to be part of the multitude, that he is put on an equal footing with the others. In his eschatological vision, the territories attributed to the twelve tribes have to be strictly equal. Not only must the tribes must be treated in an absolutely equal way, but also the individuals who make them up (332). And so it is that Ezekiel ends up with the conception of the classless society (341).

As I said at the beginning, I shall limit this study to the pre-exilic period, but as has just emerged in connection with Ezekiel, the deportation presents aspects which are very interesting from our point of view, and since Finkelstein devotes some important pages to it, I shall extend somewhat the period covered by this book in that respect.

The prophets struggled for a long time against a false and narrow conception of God, but their own view was only accepted by a minority (II, 444). The deportation was needed for there to be a change. Then, for the first time in history, an important community dissociated the cult of its God from its ancestral territory; then too there arose the idea of a god not attached to a particular point of the universe, and the principle emerged that all countries and all human beings are equal in the sight of God (II, 443).

Another factor in the sense of equality and brotherhood was the overall structure of the exilic community. Almost all the peasants had remained in their homeland; those who were deported were the patricians, the landed nobility, the religious officials and the urban plebeians. Each group adapted in its own way (II,451) and the latter group gained the upper hand. That happened not only because there were more of them and the other classes had left everything behind, while the artisans and the merchants brought their professional skills with them, but also because the latter were better prepared from an ideological point of view (II, 457). For generations their spiritual leaders taught them that the community in which they lived was condemned to destruction and that they had to be ready for deportation and purification. In this community, reduced by Nebuchadnezzar to a plebeian economy, the patricians and the nobility were the losers and could not turn away from what they had rejected before. In this classless society they also had to accept an ideology in conformity with the lesson of the prophets (458).

This acceptance of prophetic doctrine necessarily entailed the decline of the prophetic movement as an institution. From the moment when prophecy ceased to be the voice of an oppressed minority and corresponded to the aspirations of the majority, there was no further need of criticisms and protests; there was need rather for positive and specific instruction. The prophet gave place to the scribe, the master, the teacher. Rather than be told what it was necessary not to do in order not to die, people had to be told what had to be done to live. So it was in Babylon that there began the transformation of the prophetic religion into a system of norms and prescriptions known as legalism.

This change is generally thought to be a regression, as though the constructive work of the legislator were on a lower plane than the criticism of the prophet. In reality, there was neither progress nor setback. The scribe was the disciple, the continuation of the prophet. The only loss was that poetry gave way to prose (462).

Despite what I have said on the subject of the choice of authors belonging to this second group of historians and sociologists and their attitude to phenomena which are not an inherent part of the society that we are examining, I shall take account here of a study by Michel Astour in which a very important place is reserved for the cult of Baal and the influence of the Phoenicians. However, my decision would seem justified by the way in which these problems are treated and by the fact that on this occasion an additional light is shed on the attitude of the prophets, who would appear moved not only by a feeling of solidarity with the oppressed and an attachment to a traditional mode of life but also by a certain concern of interests, the well-being, of other members, if not the whole of the community.

Astour recalls that according to legend, the main object of the hate of the ninth-century prophets was Queen Jezebel, daughter of the king of Tyre and Sidon and spouse of King Ahab. Among the numerous crimes of which she was accused the main one was that of favouring the cult of Baal. The centre of this cult was in Samaria, in the temple built on the occasion of the marriage of Jezebel with Ahab (Astour 1959, 36). This union, the consequence of the treaty with Tyre, entailed the arrival of a large number of Phoenician merchants whose custom was to group themselves in cultic associations and to found sanctuaries dedicated to their gods. And as the temples in antiquity were not just places of worship but also treasuries, banks which played an important role in the economic life of the country, according to Astour it follows that it was not the hatred of Baal which provoked the destruction of his temple at Jehu's *coup d'état* and the overthrow of the dynasty of Omri, but on the contrary the existence of the temple which excited the hatred of the god to whom it was dedicated. As a foreign excrescence, the temple of Baal in Samaria was an advance post of Phoenicia in Israel (ibid., 37).

This hostile attitude towards the Phoenician merchants is also evident among the prophets of the eighth century and in the course of the following centuries. Amos reproaches Tyre for having forgotten the brotherly alliance and having sold captives *en masse* to Edom (Amos 1.9). Hosea accuses Canaan (Phoenicia) of having false balances in its hands and loving to deceive (Hos.12.8). As this influence of the Phoenicians did not change much between Solomon (who gave the king of Tyre grain and olive oil in exchange for wood imported from Lebanon) and the sixth century, we find attacks of the same kind in Ezekiel, who desires the destruction of Tyre since by the extension of its commerce this great maritime city has been filled with violence, and by the iniquities of its trade it has profaned the sanctuaries (Ezek.28.16-18; Astour 1959, 54).

As is already indicated in these few quotations, the prophets reproach the Phoenician merchants not only for cheating and exploiting, but for introducing elements which disrupt the traditional and patriarchal mode of life of the Hebrew people. These accusations correspond to the sentiments of the masses of the people, for whom the luxury shown by the Phoenicians was a blatant example of social injustice and corruption.

However, those who seem to have adopted the most hostile attitude towards this Phoenician influence were the non-Phoenician merchnats. There were not many of them, but even at this time there were indigenous Israelite merchants represented by these nomadic tribes of the semi-desert region of the Palestinian south, grouped in the region of the southern area of the great route linking Tyre with Elam. Chief among these was the sect of the Rechabites, which seems to have been a branch of the Sinaitic population of Kenites who inherited from them the reputation of being allies and friends of Israel; they were known for not having abandoned their nomadic customs on contact with the agricultural civilization of Palestine: not cultivating the soil, not building houses and not drinking wine.

Now it seems certain that the prophets, or at least some of them, were influenced by the Rechabites; and if we take account of the hostility that both of them show towards the temple of Baal, and the natural rivalry between the Rechabites and the Phoenicians, it seems possible, according to Astour, to conclude that the prophets shared with the Rechabites in the same coalition of discontented people who struggled against the Phoenician hold and sought to reserve for the benefit of nationals the exploitation of commercial routes, which represented the main source of the riches of the country (55-6).

It seems to me worth while ending this survey of the second group of authors with G.E.Mendenhall. He represents an original point of view, non-conformist in relationship to the main commentators on the Old Testament. He cannot be considered a supporter of historical materialism since, as he himself declares, he attributes a vital, if not decisive, importance to the role played by ethics (Mendenhall 1973, xv), religion (ibid., 214) and ideology (Mendenhall 1969, 435). But like Lurje and Menes he is above all, if not exclusively, interested in what happens within Israel, in what forms part of the social structure itself. His account of the way in which the twelve Israelite tribes settled in Palestine and in northern Transjordan differs from the usually accepted view (Weippert 1969, 433) and provoked lively reaction (de Vaux 1969, 272-6; Smith 1969, 19-35); however, according to some this event has rarely been described in so convincing and expressive a way (Halladay 1973, 474). I am not qualified to participate in the discussion, nor do I intend to, but as with other authors, I shall only be taking up those parts of Mendenhall's work which have a bearing on our subject.

As he announces at the beginning of the article which seems to be the essential part of his work, Mendenhall seeks to substitue a very different model from the 'ideal' model put forward by a whole series of Old Testament specialists. He is opposed to the 'archaeological' conception commended by W.F.Albright and taken up by his disciples, notably G.E.Wright and J.Bright, according to whom Canaanite cities will have been destroyed at the end of the thirteenth century and reoccupied by a population with inferior material culture represented by the Israelites – proof of an invasion *en masse*, a systematic military conquest. Nor does he agree with the 'solution from history' proposed by A.Alt and developed by M.Noth, according to which the settlement will have taken place by a peaceful infiltration of the less populated regions in which the tribes successively settled bit by bit (Mendenhall 1962, 67).

In fact there was no real conquest of Palestine. From the perspective of secular history concerned with sociological phenomena, the event in question will have consisted of a simple peasant revolt. In order to understand what happened, according to Mendenhall, we need to remember that at the Amarna period the first Israelites, whom the Bible also calls Hebrews or Apiru, were under the domination of Canaanite cities against whom they rose to free themselves (ibid., 75).

This movement of discontent had been polarized by the arrival of a group of escaped slaves from Egypt who, being unable to count on the aid of any other community, united in the same faith in a new god, Yahweh, with whom they made a covenant and to whom they transferred all the powers and attributes of their lords. Their arrival west of the Jordan gave the revolt a warlike character. Although the Canaanite kings united to defend themselves, they were exterminated or driven out and their cities were destroyed (73). Victorious, the Israelites, having succeeded in liberating themselves, did not want to reconstitute the same type of autocratic, tyrannical society under whose yoke they had been subjected (77).

The submission of individuals and groups to a divine master in the form of a covenant, and the spirit of solidarity reigning at the heart of this newly created community, meant that its members could and really did break all ties of religious, economic and political dependence on Canaanite society, to which they opposed Yahwism (75). This rejection of a markedly stratified society inevitably went hand in hand with a special stress on the principle of absolute equality in the application of the law and an exceptional concern for the slave.

Another striking feature of Israelite religion in its earliest stage appeared in the form of a profound desire to keep the peace: this was the opposite of late Bronze Age Canaan in which, as the Amarna letters illustrate so well, the continual struggles of the cities against one another did great harm to the peasants. According to Mendenhall, the behaviour of ambitious rulers, planning to ruin and dispossess the peasants by preventing them from cultivating their land, apppears clearly in the letters of Rib-Addi (77).

As to the covenant between Yahweh and Israel, Mendenhall stresses that was a covenant with each family, if not with each individual, and since protection was the first objective of this type of contract, the result was that all were protected and all were equal before God; each one profited from the same law, no matter what his social and economic status. That, according to Mendenhall, was the source and the very foundation of justice; the decisive factor on which was to depend the vital place that it had in Israelite law (Mendenhall 1954, 39).

It was the attraction of this egalitarian conception which, according to Mendenhall, played an essential role in the extension of Israel. Like David Koigen (1934, 13, cited by Neher 1950, 43, who saw the exodus as neither a national nor a political episode but essentially as a social revolution, the mass freeing of slaves), he does not see Israel as an ethnic group which became a religious community; rather, the contrary happened. The relatively rapid transformation of a small group into an important unit dominating almost all the heights of Palestine and a large part of Transjordan could not happen as the result of a simple demographic thrust. The group expanded quickly thanks to the adherence to it of a majority of the inhabitants of the region, in whose eyes the concept developed by the Israelite community presented more advantages than the system on which they depended under Canaanite domination (Mendenhall 1961, 43).

PART THREE

Nomadism, Prophecy and the Social Laws

6

Nomadism and Social Justice

As I indicated at the beginning, almost all the authors with whom we have been occupied in the preceding parts deal with justice in a somewhat marginal and fragmentary way. The historical survey which I have just made therefore leaves us unsatisfied. To satisfy our curiosity better and to try to find at least a partial explanation of this almost unparalleled intensity with which the thirst for justice shows itself in Israel, our most promising course would seem to be to resort to sociology based on the dynamic concept of the global phenomenon (Gottwald 1979, 70f.), taking into consideration every aspect of the phenomenon in question in the form of a whole in which all is related, all interpenetrates. It is necessary specifically to take up all the essential themes of the biblical story which deal with the problem of justice: the memory of slavery in Egypt (Nahmani 1964, 76), nomadism and prophecy, and study them, taking account of the historical setting and the social structure of the country at the time with which we are concerned. However, work of this kind requires very considerable knowledge of the Old Testament and multi-disciplinary research which goes far beyond my ability. So I shall just touch on nomadism, prophecy and the social laws of the Pentateuch. It seems to me that it is in the context of these phenomena that we have most chance of bringing out the problem of justice in its dynamic form.

As we have already seen (for example with Weber, Lods and Causse), biblical history usually reserves a very important place for nomadism, but, as we know, its importance must not be exaggerated. Moreover, it is to be remembered that most scholars nowadays say that the ancient Hebrews were no more than semi-nomads.[1] However, we must not go to the other extreme, and above all in this connection it would probably be wrong to deny or minimize excessively the role of this factor (Mendenhall 1973, 174; de Geus 1976, 211), which also plays a role among other ethnic groups (Gottwald 1979; Rogerson 1978, 98f.).

Neither the Israelites nor their ancestors were ever great Bedouins; they never seem to have led the life of the open desert (de Vaux 1961, 4; Mark 1936, 13). We first meet the patriarchs as small cattle-breeders (Goitein 1955, 25). It is as a semi-nomad that Abraham lived before his departure for Canaan and Jacob lived during his stay with Laban (de Vaux 1949, 15). It is no less true that the Isrelites or their ancestors lived for some time in the desert (de Vaux 1961, 4). It is striking and almost unique that despite quite a long period of sedentary life in Egypt to begin with, and even after finally settling on the soil of Canaan, the Hebrew people continued to have nomadic aspirations (Neher 1955, 154), to consider this form of life the best (Wright 1955, 5).

Some modern writers also idealize nomadism (Caquot 1977, 341). According to Renan (1887-97, I, 13), 'The life of the tent is that which leaves most room for reflection and passion. In this form of austere and grandiose life was created one of the spirits of humanity, one of the forms under which genius... comes to express itself and to live.. They were truly the fathers of the faith, those chiefs of nomadic clans who went over the desert, serious, honourable, full of horror for pagan pollution, believing in justice.'

A whole part of the legislation preserved in the Pentateuch, which we already touched on in an earlier part of this study, can only be understood against the background of a nomadic stage of civilization (Dhorme 1937, 58). According to some scholars who take up the ideas of M.Weber and Pedersen (Gerstenberger 1965, 115-17; Fohrer 1965, 72), the apodictic formulation of biblical laws finds its source, its *Sitz im Leben*, in a quasi-nomadic mode of life (Prévost 1976, 358; von Waldow 1970, 185).

The Hebrew patriarchs seem to be pastoral figures living in tents, who take their flocks and herds to watering places, who stop at privileged places to find rest and relaxation (Dhorme 1937, 63). In fact this way of life was not as ideal as some would have us believe. In it war was an endemic state and people had to struggle to keep alive (Causse 1926, 9). However, it was the difficulties rather than the ease, or rather the alternation, the mixture of the two which called for 'a distinct pattern of society and a code of behaviour all of its own' (de Vaux, 1961, 4), moving in the direction of a spirit of solidarity and equity which was more developed than elsewhere. The uncertainty and dangers of the migratory life of the desert favoured equality and created an atmosphere of freedom (Silver 1928, 1). 'In the desert,' recalls de Vaux (1961, 4), 'the unit of society must be compact enough to remain mobile but strong enough to ensure its own safety: this unit is the tribe'. All the members of the tribe regarded themselves as descendants of a common ancestor (who here was a man and not a sacred being as in Egypt); all were equal in law since the same blood, real or supposed, ran in their veins (Moret 1941, 277). In the desert there is no wall for protection, hence the vital importance of leadership, the need for discipline (Weingreen 1967). But the mobility of the nomadic life 'prevents the definitive fixation of power with a given group' (Neher 1955, 1). There are no hierarchical relationships (Moret 1941, 1). When difficulties arise, when war threatens the security of the nomadic group, an individual with particular wisdom or great courage establishes himself as chief, but he only remains *primus inter pares*, and once the danger is past, he returns to his habitual place (Gordis 1971, 22). In these conditions, political power can hardly become important and prestigious enough to come before ethics, moral values, above all given the belief of the Hebrews, according to whom all men, created by God in his image, benefit from the same rights and must assume the same responsibilities (Kübel 1870, 21). The recollection of this state of things, this egalitarian structure, explains one of the main foundations of the Old Testament laws according to which, contrary to what we find elsewhere (for example in the Code of Hammurabi), compensation and penalties do not vary with membership of a particular social class: the principle of an eye for an eye and a tooth for a tooth is applied to everyone (Ex.21.23-25; Deut.19.21; Lev.24.19) except for the slave – though he is not treated as a simple object but benefits from numerous favours (Kübel 1870, 71; Balscheit and Eichrodt 1944, 10-14).

In the desert, an individual who parts company with his group must be able to count absolutely on the welcome of the groups he meets or which he joins; anyone may need this help and everyone must give it (de Vaux 1961, 4). The dangers presented by the world around do not encourage accumulation and individual possession (Finkelstein 1946, I, 359; Hecataeus of Abdera in Reinach 1895, 19). Wealth in material goods has a relatively secondary role in these conditions; generosity, hospitality take on a particular importance (Nyström 1946, 14). In the desert, where there are neither police nor justice over the tribes, the group is united in crime and punishment (de Vaux 1961, 4). All this creates a feeling of solidarity, an obligation which in an imperious way requires the whole group to ensure the protection of all its feeble and oppressed members (ibid., 11; Jacobson 1942, 114-35).

Something else that also works in the same direction and is a prefiguration of one of the most characteristic features in Jewish history is the fact that these semi-nomads, living on the periphery of groups and societies which are numerically more important, more stable and more structured, are aware of being in the minority, of being different. They feel a sense of insecurity, if not fear, which impels them to cling together and to help one another with a fervour rarely encountered elsewhere. This appears above all in difficult periods, at moments of crisis when the very existence of the group is at stake: at the time of the exodus and during the exile when, faced with misfortunes on an apocalyptic scale, their bonds of solidarity are reinforced and the social barriers are lowered to eliminate all that could bring separation (inequality, injustice).

What I have just said in connection with nomadism and human migration leads me to say something about some aspects of the circulation of goods. In fact these two phenomena are quite closely interlinked, both generally and in connection with our subject.[2]

According to Kautsky (1910, 191), the first people to devote themselves to commerce will probably have been nomadic shepherds; the extremely limited resources of the countries in which they lived would encourage them to get goods produced in more favoured regions; they profited from this occasion to acquire more than they needed themselves to sell it on to others.

According to C.H.Gordon (1958, 28-31; 1962, 35), the Hebrew patriarchs will have traded and Abraham will have been a rich merchant (*tamkarum*). This theory does not seem to have gained general acceptance (de Vaux 1965, 18). However, as it generally seems to be admitted that the first Hebrews were sheep breeders or caravaneers, we can infer that on passing through regions, they spent time in places where they had more opportunities and possibilities than others of laying down their 'spears', of 'substituting the treaty, the gift and commerce for war' (Mauss, 1923-24, 184).

Israel was on the very frontier of the East and West (Steinmann 1954, 22), at the crossing of the two main trade routes of antiquity (Rathjens 1962, 118): one linking Egypt with Syria and Mesopotamia, the other going from Phoenicia to Arabia (Kautsky 1910, 174). A continual wave of Egyptian and Assyrian soldiers, Babylonian priests, Phoenician merchants and Bedouin Arabs broke across this country (Baron 1952, I, 17). There were exceptional possibilites for 'opposing without massacring and giving oneself without sacrificing one for the other' (Mauss 1923-24, 185; 164), of applying the formula 'give as much as you take' (Woolley 1935, 124-9; Lehmann 1953, 15-20).

When it goes beyond the stage of gift or barter, the exchange of goods calls for the use of weights and measures used in such a way as to guarantee a minimum of fairness in transactions. The importance attached to them in the biblical period (Bertheau 1842, 114-20; Yadin 1961, 16) is indicated by the seriousness with which the phenomenon is treated in the different parts of the Old Testament (Diringer 1942, 82). It is said in Leviticus, 'You shall do no wrong in judgment, in measures of length or weight or quantity; you shall have just balances, just weights, a just ephah and a just hin' (19.35f.). And in Deuteronomy: 'You shall not have in your bag two kinds of weights, a large and a small. You shall not have in your house two kinds of measure, a large and a small. A full and just weight you shall have; that your days may be prolonged in the land which the Lord your God gives you. For all who do such things, who act dishonestly, are an abomination to the Lord your God' (Deut 25.13f.).

When we remember that the balance, an essentially functional instrument, becomes the symbol for justice in the broadest sense of the word, we may ask whether the practices of commercial life did not serve among other things as prototypes of a totality of moral precepts. In the course of their stay in centres of economic and cultural life will not the patriarchs and then the prophets have found what could serve as a stimulus which, while reinforcing their thirst for justice, allowed them to express themselves in a more vivid way and with more precision (Gray 1962, 174; Clévenot 1985, 31)?

7

Prophecy and Social Justice

The biblical prophets who occupy such an important place in the history of humanity and who are considered by Asher Ginsberg (= Ahad Ha-am, cf. Haran 1972, 151; Rotenstreich 1972, 84), Buber (Glatzer 1963, 354) and many others as the most significant figures in Jewish history, deserve special attention.

Prophecy is an almost universal phenomenon (Powis Smith 1918, 2; Rowley 1956) which was particularly widespread throughout the Near East; however, outside Israel, above all in the sphere with which we are concerned, it seems to have remained somewhat marginal and episodic. So-called prophetic literature appeared in Egypt (Herrmann 1963, 47-65) in periods of decadence and social trouble, but the genre of lamentation hardly prospered among this happy people. In Mesopotamia, in these regions 'of great river floods and the onset of invasions, where people sought above all to exorcise fear, despair and war, the main role of the oracles was to guard people against anxiety and uncertainty' (Ramlot 1972, 1206). The correspondence of the kings of Mari (about the eighteenth century BC) refers to prophets or prophetesses called 'respondents' or 'ecstatics' (Cazelles 1974, 11). In Canaan the stele of king Zakir of Hamath shows us that the kings consulted their gods through the prophets; there were also seers and ecstatics there. However, in the end we do not know very much about this west Semitic prophecy (Cazelles 1973, 338f.). As to Greece, as in Egypt there were wise men there, but in the city they looked for order, equilibrium (Neher 1966, 51), happiness (Despotopoulos 1969, 303) rather than justice, in which they were interested more for its consequences than for justice itself (Vlastos 1972, 95; 1947, 156-78; Kaiser 1969, 327).

On the other hand, above all in connection with the problem that we are studying, it was in Israel that prophecy occupied a central place; it made a deep mark on religion, political institutions and even social structures. Expressing the disquiet and discontent which, above all from a certain time on, seized a large part of the population, in the fulfilment of their mission the Hebrew prophets did not come up against the insurmountable barriers set up elsewhere by the powerful central powers against any criticism from below; their voices had more chance of getting through, of rising to the surface and making themselves heard even by the greatest. King David, who sent Uriah to his death in order to take possession of Uriah's wife Bathsheba, acted like so many others, but he bowed to the condemnation of Nathan and accepted punishment (Neher 1974, I, 316).

The Hebrew prophets who more particularly interest us here, and who have already been mentioned in the second part of this study, had predecessors: they were not created all of a sudden but were the offspring of a long tradition and the sons of their fathers (Porteous 1967, 53; Gunneweg 1959, 120; Anderson 1966, 83; Wilson 1978, 8). But if the first prophets proclaimed above all the omnipotence of God and made cultic demands, their successors specially stressed the fact that the real covenant with Yahweh had to find expression in action; worship of Yahweh which did not go along with fair behaviour was a blasphemy leading the faithful into error (Rivkin 1971, 10). From the eighth century on, faced with crisis, the new prophets, led by Amos (the first of the writing prophets, cf. Cohen 1965, 153), moved by an exalted ideal and profoundly shocked by the multiplication of abuses (Soares 1915, 215), spoke directly to the people, and did not so much attack individual crimes as condemn, if not the whole system (Koch 1971, 238f.), at least the officials and the privileged (Donner 1963, 245).

At one stage the role of the prophets seems to have been exaggerated. Wellhausen, Duhm and their numerous successors considered them the true founders of the religion of Israel (Clements 1973, 15), and the most noble realizations of Israelite law were attributed to them (ibid., 23). Thanks to more recent studies the problem is now put in a more sophisticated form. The prophets do not seem to have considered themselves the vehicles of a new conception of God or a new moral teaching (16). The foundations of the law, strongly impregnated with morality (the concept of the covenant), appeared before the prophets (23; Bach 1957, 24; Lewy 1957, 325). On the other hand, we should not forget that the relationships which were established between the prophets and law usually represented bonds of close interdependence; the prophets could refer to an already existing tradition of law, but they themselves exercised an influence on the recognition and the development of this law (Clements 1973, 24). At all events, they were not interested in the formal side of law but in the spirit in which it was steeped; they did not seek to reform the laws but above all to raise the moral level of humanity (Eberharter 1924).

There are countless works devoted to the Israelite prophets.[1] Above all in earlier times the prophets were most often regarded as the emanation of a supernatural force, the expression of the divine will (Welch 1912, 53; cf. Buber 1949; Rosenzweig 1921; Heschel 1962; Neher 1955, 4, etc.). However, as we saw in the second part of this book, after a certain time an increasing number of authors were also interested in the prophets as social reformers, spokesmen of the aspirations of the people (Robertson Smith 1881; Darmesteter 1892; Cohen 1924, I, 306; II, 398; Lods 1937; Kaufmann 1960, etc.). Moreover, as a whole these two points of view tended to draw together, the difference between them seeming to diminish. It is usually accepted that unlike the priests, the prophets were not 'established' (Baron 1952, I, 87), attached to particular periods and places, fixed in time and space (Schofield 1969, 112), that they were not cultic personnel (Bright 1981, 264). They inveighed against the abuse of ritual (Rowley 1967, 174), though as the Scandinavian school has demonstrated, they were not entirely hostile to the cult (Gunneweg 1959, 112; Rowley 1951, XVII; Eissfeldt in ibid., 120). They seem frequently to have delivered their messages in holy places and to have used ritual terminology (Bright 1981, 264). If they had been asked whether they considered themselves primarily to be religious reformers or social reformers, they would probably have protested violently against this distinction (Baron 1952, 88). They had a unitary conception of things (Cazelles 1951, 171); they sought a synthesis between politics and ethics (Rothenstreich 1972, 84); the social element in their message is simply an epiphenomenon of morality (Neher 1950, 251); according to them social crimes become religious sins. But given the time in which they were living and which produced them, given that they spoke at a time of political and economic crisis, it is on society that the attention of some of them seems chiefly to have been fixed (Lindblom 1962, 343; Caquot 1970, 436). The strictest criticisms of Amos relate to social injustice (Koch 1971, 242).

In this perspective of a stress on the social element, we should recall another dichotomistic distinction. For some scholars the prophets are primarily traditionalists or conservatives, for others innovators or even revolutionaries. However, on the whole here too people began by not going too much to extremes: the majority of contemporary exegetes adopt a moderate point of view.

According to W.C.Graham, the prophets seek to introduce more transformations than innovations and are far from acting as partisans of the class struggle (Graham 1934, 74). According to von Rad (1965, I, 66), they are rooted in tradition with their gaze fixed on the future, and for H.W.Wolff (1964, 220) they draw on the past but are reformers.

Kapelrud (1966, 194), Reventlow (1962, 116) and Fohrer (1967, 27) tend towards an interpretation which firmly puts the prophets among the conservatives. However, for Jacob (1963, 297) they were simultaneously revolutionaries with an eye on the past and conservatives animated by a passion for the future; similarly, according to Ramlot (1968, 188) the prophets do nothing without invoking tradition, and yet these are new times for their great message. Other scholars think that the prophets knew how to utilize the past for the needs of the present (Gordis 1971, 24). Amos, for example, cannot be considered the spokesman of a class, nor can he be described as either a revolutionary or a reactionary (Fendler 1973, 32-53).

As emerges already in part from what I have just said, it seems very difficult, if not impossible, to extract a uniform prophetic doctrine, and in addition it is also necessary to take account of the individuality of the great prophets, each of which had his own ideas and his own feelings (Caquot 1970, 436). However, they all seem to have had something in common: a realistic attitude. They had a horror of verbiage, of over-abstract eloquence. In contrast to the false prophets, they were interested in the concrete (Wolff 1978, 26) and were far from living shrouded in a veil of illusions (Buber 1964, II, 948). Preaching about the future was not the essential element in their proclamation; it is rather the fruit, the final result, of a deepened knowledge of the world around them, the present and the past (Herrmann 1967, 6).

Contrary to the views of some scholars (Troeltsch 1916, 1-28; Weinrich 1932; Albrektson 1972, 56), the prophets that we are studying seem a long way from being utopians (Elliger 1935, 15). Drawing on tradition, on the experiences of the past, involved in the experiences of the people, up to date with what was going on (Gottwald 1964, 358), they had a totality of knowledge and information which allowed them to achieve an amazing lucidity and objectivity in their judgments on all human affairs (Homerski 1972, 38), to see things as they really were (Kleinert 1905, 5; Soares 1915, 212). Their social demands bore a great similarity to the ancient laws; their frequent declarations in favour of the oppressed, the widow and the orphan, corresponded to the heavy losses experienced by Israel in the course of wars (above all with the Aramaeans and the Assyrians), as a result of which in many families there were only widows and orphans deprived of all protection (Balscheit and Eichrodt 1944, 38).

If we take Isaiah as an example, the two features that seem most striking about him are the practical character of his action and his realism. Without forfeiting any of his inspiration and poetry, he would seem to have been very positive, very close to actual fact (Brunet 1975, 226). At all events, the label of ecstatic does not seem to suit Isaiah: his ecstasy, if he had any, left no traces; his spells of exaltation were integrated into a very active existence and were expressed in texts which were fully in keeping with life (ibid., 229). The famous passage

> Woe to those who join house to house,
> who add field to field,
> until there is no more room,
> and you are made to dwell alone in the midst of the land (Isa. 5.8)

represents a condemnation which relates less to the literary tradition and more to the legal practice of the time (Dietrich 1976, 225).

The Hebrew prophets come from the most varied backgrounds, but even those who were not of plebeian origin seem to have developed in this direction (Weber 1967, 96). Isaiah, who had aristocratic origins, played a role which could be compared with that of a tribune of the people (Finkelstein 1946, I, 301).

These 'ministers of disquiet' (Ramlot 1972, 1207) sought the absolute, their attention always directed upwards, but at the same time they were very aware of all that was part of everyday life. They went up and down the length of the country; they visited any place where they thought that they could fulfil their mission (Baron 1952, I, 87); they mingled with the crowds and the masses both in places of worship and in the markets; they spoke directly to the people and it was only subsequently that their speeches and their sermons appeared in writing (Lindblom 1924, 8). Unlike the false prophets, they were not professionals. Their activity arose out of an inner need; it was personal, and not either honorific or that of an interested party. Amos has his *Sitz im Leben* in tribal wisdom (Jacob 1973, 421); the abuses of luxury make him really suffer. Before prophesying he carefully observed his surroundings (Robertson Smith 1881, 128).

The relatively rapid changes in the period when the prophets were active made them somewhat nostalgic for the past; indeed this nostalgia in some ways resembles that found in aspects of Romanticism in the

West.[2] But these changes at the same time compelled them to face a whole series of new needs. And on top of these inner upheavals, these economic and social transformations, there were dangers coming from outside – the almost continual threat of extermination by their numerically superior neighbours – the dramatic constant of almost all Jewish history.

The situation to which I have just alluded forced all those who had a sense of collective responsibility to be almost continually on the moral alert; they could not allow themselves, as happens in societies of a static kind, living at one remove from the great social and political upheavals, either to turn aside from or to be uninterested in the essentials of both material and moral life. And since, despite the rapid changes, Israelite society in the eighth and seventh centuries was not yet too hierarchical and socially differentiated, since the needy masses had not yet been entirely marginalized, and the 'priestly caste' and above all the prophets were not yet turned in on themselves, the prophets were involved in the common experience of the group, and In contrast to what happened in Greece and Rome did not risk lapsing into abstract speculations, purely theoretical considerations, which were restricted to the privileged, those above the pressures of everyday life (Neher 1948, 30-42).

At the time when the prophets were living, it was difficult for them to employ a language different from the one that they did use. However, their solemnity, their lyricism and their poetic expressions cannot be compared with the shadowy discourse of an oracle (Dubnow 1925, I, 228); their dominant feature is neither mysticism nor magic, but comprehensibility and rationality (Weber 1967, 314).

According to the prophets, by continual effort human beings must develop the divine spark of life of which they are the vehicles. But the spiritual values they acquire must not be restricted to their inner being; they must be applied to real life. The behaviour of human beings must correspond to their principles (Vellas 1964, 108). A distinctive feature of the Old Testament is that it lacks what is generally understood as theology. Thoughts on the nature of God are not considered in the abstract, but are immediately related to the world of action (Welch 1936, 69; Türck 1935, 28). Whereas elsewhere great importance is attached to divine grace and predestination, the prophets regarded men and women as free and moral beings from whom right behaviour could be required (Baeck 1918, 14). They stressed the obligation not only to believe but to act (Shaskolsky 1970, 26). According to them, justice is not an abstract value existing outside real life and society (Pedersen 1926, 352). For the prophets, injustice is the main reason for the wrath of God (Lods 1932, 466f.). Those who seem to be among the first, if not the first, in history to introduce the primacy of morality (Kaufmann 1937, 345) attach more importance to good morality and behaviour than to the cult. According to them, God does not ask for sacrifices and offerings but for love, truth, faith, equity (Gressmann 1924, 335). Theft which damages the an individual, people will say in time, is a greater crime than sacrilege (Baron 1952, II, 254).

Free from all priestly obligations (Clements 1973, 121), Amos revolts in what is probably an unprecedented way against a cult limited to purely external forms: in the name of God he cries:

> I hate, I despise your feasts,
> and I take no delight in your solemn assemblies.
> Even though you offer me your burnt offerings and cereal offerings,
> I will not accept them,
> and the peace offerings of your fatted beasts
> I will not look upon.
> Take away from me the noise of your songs;
> to the melody of your harps I will not listen.
> But let justice roll down like waters,
> and righteousness like an everflowing stream (Amos 5.21-24).

He was the witness and victim of many forms of injustice, so he was particularly preoccupied with the fate of those who have a difficult life (Koch 1971, 242) and is very harsh about all forms of exploitation.[3] He denounces those who oppress the poor and ill-treat the needy (Amos 4.1), those who 'sell the righteous for silver and the needy for a pair of shoes', who 'trample the head of the poor into the dust of the earth, and turn aside the way of the afflicted', who 'lay themselves down upon garments taken in pledge' and 'who drink the wine of those who have been fined' (Amos 2.6-8). With special vehemence he turns against speculators who, to the detriment of the needy, hoard wheat and then sell it more expensively, and in addition falsify the 'scales of deceit' (Amos 8.5).

Hosea also proclaims that Yahweh 'desires steadfast love and not sacrifice, the knowledge of God rather than burnt offerings' (Hos.6.6), and condemns those who 'remove the landmark' (Hos.5.10), who 'make idols' (Hos.8.4) of their silver and gold, who love fraud by which they amass wealth (12.8f.).

Similarly, according to Isaiah God has 'had enough of burnt offerings of rams and the fat of fed beasts'; for him incense is an abomination, his soul hates new moons and solemnities. He does not listen to those who multiply prayers and whose hands are full of blood; rather, he calls on people to abstain from doing evil and to learn to do good: to seek justice and 'correct oppression', to defend the widow and orphan (Isa.1.11-17), not to scorn the real owner of the vine, not to 'crush' the people and 'reduce the poor to nothing' (Isa.3.14f.).

According to Micah, what God requires of people is not holocausts, 'thousands of rams and tens of thousands of rivers of oil', but that they practise 'judgment', love piety and walk 'humbly' with their God (Micah 6.6-8). And as Micah, like Amos, is also keenly interested in the fate of the poor and oppressed (Koch 1971, 246), he condemns those who 'devise wickedness', who 'covet fields and seize them', who 'oppress a man and his house, a man and his inheritance' (Micah 2.1f.). As for the 'heads of Jacob' and the 'rulers of the house of Israel' who should 'know justice' but who 'hate the good and love the evil', who 'eat the flesh' of the people and 'flay their skin from off them', they will cry to Yahweh but he will not reply to them and will 'hide his face' from them (Micah 3.1-4).

According to Jeremiah, holocausts are not pleasing to God nor are sacrifices acceptable to him; he has no need of the 'frankincense which comes from Sheba and sweet cane from a distant land' (Jer.6.20). True piety and knowledge of God are represented by the practice of judgment and justice (Jer.22.15-16): it is necessary to snatch 'the spoil from the hand of the oppressor', not to molest or violate 'the host, the orphan, the widow' (Jer.22.3), not to build 'one's house by injustice', not to make one's neighbour serve for nothing (Jer.22.13) or to fix one's eyes and one's heart only on profit (Jer.22.17).

Zephaniah and Habakkuk who, like Jeremiah, are to be dated to the last third of the seventh century, the time of Josiah's reform, vigorously attack what is going on around them: justice is the main remedy that they commend. Zephaniah condemns the corruption which reigns in Jerusalem:

Woe to her that is rebellious and defiled,
the oppressing city (Zeph.3.1).

Her officials within her
are roaring lions;
her judges are evening wolves
that leave nothing until the morning (Zeph.3.3).

All these are doomed to destruction since in his heart Yahweh is just (Zeph.3.5), and it is only the 'humble of the land', those who execute the judgment of Yahweh, who seek justice and humility who will perhaps be sheltered 'on the day of the wrath of Yahweh' (Zeph.2.3).

From the beginning of his prophecy Habakkuk complains about the oppression of the weak by the strong, about the violation of law. He sees before him iniquity, plunder, strife and contention: a state of affairs where 'the law is slacked and justice never goes forth' (Hab.1.3f.). And as I have already remarked in connection with Finkelstein's work, even when Habakkuk turns against the conquerors, his condemnation partly takes the form of a social sermon:

Woe to him who heaps up what is not his own (Hab.2.6).
Woe to him who gets evil gain for his house (Hab.2.9).
Woe to him who builds a town with blood, and founds a city on
    iniquity (Hab.2.12).

The concern for salvation, the hope of a reward in the other world, may have a positive effect on our behaviour here on earth, but if too much attention is attached to the beyond, we run the risk of making ourselves insufficiently attentive, if not indifferent, to everyday reality. This second possibility seems relatively limited, if not completely eliminated, in Judaism taken as a whole and above all at the time we are considering. As is recalled so strikingly in the Talmud (where it is said that an hour of good works in this world is better than the whole of a future life, Schuhl 1878, 505), Judaism is primarily interested in the fate of humanity here on earth (Baron 1952, 9). The problem of the other world, belief in the resurrection of the dead, does not have a central place in the pre-exilic Old Testament (Lods 1906, 42). Immortality is considered to be a divine attribute (Bruppacher 1924, 47).

The idea of individual life after death is alien to the biblical thought of ancient Israel, which is concerned above all with the eternal duration of the group. The Israelite dies but Israel continues: the individuals pass on but the elect people continues to exist (Martin-Achard 1956, 25). Individualist eschatology only becomes important when with the loss of national independence the people feel threatened in every aspect of their existence (Huppenbauer 1962, 149). The fate of the individual then becomes a preoccupation, and the problem of resurrection one of the themes of Israelite belief from the exile on (Herrmann 1965, 306; Hammershaimb 1966, 112). But even from this time there is no duality between body and soul, no incompatibility, no break between life and existence after death (Baeck 1948, 184; Thomson 1970, 46-55). As it appeared in the Psalms and the wisdom literature, immortality was above all the continuation of existence here on earth and not a new life in the beyond (Vawter 1972, 165).

At all events, we find almost no indication of a preoccupation with the resurrection in the prophetic writings of the period in which we are interested (Causse 1908, 19; Bruppacher 1924, 47; Virgulin 1972, 49-60; Keller 1974, 28). Almost no place is reserved for the vision of the beyond (Baeck 1948, 39). The prophets seem to have been indifferent to the prospect of a future life (Wiener 1912, 69), though perhaps we should not deduce too much from this silence (Jacobs, 1964, 411). However, we should not forget that in contrast to the official representatives of the cult, the prophets usually led the same existence as those without privileges, as all those who could not expect too much, who looked for an improvement of their fate here on earth. And as their difficult life, often full of privation, did not have a monastic character (Neher 1955, 174), they did not turn their backs on reality. What the prophets called for, in contact with the great mass of people, was dictated by good sense; what they advised was not too far removed from the everyday and had no need of justification or of sanctions drawn from an imaginary world (May 1923, 28).

This realistic side, coupled with their state of insecurity, the virtual impossibility of finding a fixed position in space, of forming attachments (in the twofold sense of the word) to the material, necessarily led to a certain mobility, a capacity to adapt, an availability which is the *sine qua non* of every quest for social justice. Being in direct contact with the difficulties and privations under which the great majority suffered, the prophets could not lapse into immobility, into adopting the *status quo* as definitive and defending acquired privileges.

In accord with what I have already said about this capacity to draw on the past and at the same time to turn towards the future, the prophets seem to have been well aware of the role played by time (Jacob 1973, 293); they knew that nothing can stay in the same place and took account of the fact that in the universe, in the world which surrounds us, everything is subject to change and continual development (Cohen 1924, 325). Thus as long as they remained the representatives of a living prophecy, even the verdicts of Yahweh were not immutable for them (Menes 1928, 90). The judgments passed on God and nature cannot be definitive and unchangeable (Welch 1936,

70). There is no order established once and for all (Weber 1967, 132). There is not even an institution which deserves to be preserved for its own sake: each individual's value depends on his or her possibilities of adaptation to the changing conditions in which human needs must be satisfied (Graham 1934, 73).

According to the prophets, all the laws were provisional and conditional; they could not claim immutability, since such a demand would restrict God's freedom of action and that could not be tolerated (Rivkin 1971, 14). This approach was represented among other things by the application of the laws of the year of jubilee, based on the principle that God is the sole proprietor of the earth (Nahmani 1964, 21), the aim of which was to protect and at the same time to limit the rights of private property: the outgrowth of riches and the accumulation of land (Kübel 1870; North 1954, 217; Neufeld 1958, 53-124).

What I have just said would seem to match the finalist, teleological and dynamic approach of Jewish historical thought as distinct from the causal, static and critical conception which is predominant among the Greek historians (Boman 1960, 123ff.; Barr 1969; Sekine 1963, 66-82; Wildberger 1963, 83-117). The thought of the Hebrew prophets, which some scholars have compared with an arrow aimed at the future (Serres 1976), seems to fit well into the tradition of the specific nature of Jewish discourse which 'in its strictest tradition already splits into a twofold articulation...: a vehicle both of the strictest tradition attached to the specific sacred rigour of the law and at the same time of the most advanced narratives, giving unforeseeable impetus to the questioning practice of the Talmudic commentary and the most subversive insights in the history of Western thought' (Boyer 1975, 46).

Research into conceptions of time in the Old Testament is still far from entering a definitive phase (Petitjean 1976, 400), but it seems worth while drawing attention to this problem, and it is also interesting to recall in this connection that one of the essential traits of Judaism, as opposed to what Christianity was to commend, is that the expected world has not yet arrived (Condon 1970, 279). Besides, even the other world does not await man as a haven of security, where he could perhaps enjoy rest and refreshment, 'for there is no rest for the righteous, even in the world to come, where progress, journeying and effort still await them' (Neher 1966, 147).

The realism, the faculty of adaptation, the mobility, if not the dynamism, that we rediscover in the prophets and then throughout

Judaism risk being interpreted in terms which attribute a crudely utilitarian and opportunist side to the Jews (Sombart 1911, 423). In order to avoid this error, it must not be forgotten that Judaism is in principle non-dualist (Parkes 1969, 33), that the universe of true Judaism is that of unity (Buber 1920, 20).

The prophets, who were interested in every aspect of existence, tried to reconcile the physical with the spiritual, the concrete with the utmost idealism (Baron 1952, 20). Almost always leading a very hard life, full of privations, they did not support asceticism, and they did not seek to exterminate the human desire for material goods: they did not consider riches and the satisfaction of physical needs to be evil in themselves (Graham 1934, 64); they did not seek to abolish private property (Eberharter 1924, 60). Hosea was not hostile to the fertility cult (May 1932, 98). Jeremiah deplores not only the disappearance of spiritual values but losses of a material kind (Jer.3.24, cf. Graham 1934, 63). Conscious of the fact that the nation was already showing certain signs of exhaustion, of the attenuation of its dynamism (ibid., 56), the prophets proved enemies not only of everything that harmed moral values but also of whatever weakened the economy (63). But as the lack of balance, the economic and social crisis that the prophets denounce, is represented by far too unequal a distribution of goods (66), and because these benefits are used badly, the prophets attack cupidity (64) and the attribution of too great importance to material riches (60). Without wanting to put the brake on economic activity, they call for it to be subjected to a degree of control. According to Graham, on the lips of the prophets terms like goodness, honour, trust, fidelity, decency, justice represent their attempts to keep the profit motive, the pursuit of personal interests, within the framework of a certain moral discipline (63-5).

On the other hand, in conformity with one of the basic principles of Judaism which consists in not *a priori* favouring the poor in the face of the rich, as we have already seen, the prophets attack the wicked rich (Eberharter 1924, 62-5), but not all the rich without distinction. They are the defenders of the poor, the weak, the oppressed; they turn against the privileged, the kings. Not, however, as partisans of the class struggle so much as those with a concern for a life-style, a type of culture, in which violent confrontations will be lessened, if not eliminated (Graham 1934, 63-5; Kaiser 1969, 327).

Passionately concerned for justice, deeply affected by moral degradation and the disintegration of ancient values (Eberharter 1924, 17ff.: urban customs were increasingly gaining the upper hand over the country way of life, nomadic or semi-nomadic traditions), the prophets attained in their diatribes a degree of intensity and hardness comparable to the qualities attained by iron when subjected to sharp changes of temperature. What is attributed to revelation and divine inspiration seems above all to be the effect of this shock, this confrontation between a particularly intense history, an exceptionally dramatic human experience and a long-drawn-out current of ethical aspirations (Craghan 1972, 259; Dion 1975, 34), which had reached a very advanced stage. By stimulating people's minds this confrontation allowed the human conscience, thanks to the prophets, to rise to an exceptional level, to attain the threshold of transcending itself.

As almost always happens in the sphere of morality, in the case in which we are interested there was also a considerable difference between the norm and the existing state of things, between what was commended by the prophets and reality. The very tone in which they argued for justice was itself a sign of its extreme inadequacy (Crenshaw 1970, 380-95). And the fact that the prophets were not only so frequently ill-treated by the authorities but very often vigorously criticized by the population (Walter 1900, 263; Shaskolsky 1970, 28) seems to be additional proof of what I have just said.

However, we should not forget the numerous cases of moral ascendancy and specific influence that the prophets exercised over the behaviour of kings (Samuel over Saul, Nathan over David, Ahijah the Shilonite over Jeroboam, Elisha over Jehu and so on; cf. Rowley 1938, 174; Parkes 1971, 24).

We should also recall the interdependence between the law and the teaching of the prophets which according to some scholars had some effect on the social boldness of Deuteronomy (Brunet 1975, 235). Weinfeld (1972, 293), for example, does not agree with this last assertion, but as I have already said, it seems certain that the prophets exercised considerable influence on the different spheres of social and moral life, above all when we take account of their long-term effect. The prodigal teaching of the prophets often did not have any great direct effect on their contemporaries (Kohn 1956, 40; Finkelstein 1969, 3), but it acted as a powerful leaven, a long-term catalyst. The interventions of the prophets in domestic and foreign policy met with setbacks, but the disciples of these prophets collected their oracles 'and the great legal collections represented by the collections in the Pentateuch would seem increasingly to be an echo of the prophetic word' (Cazelles 1971, 512). It would seem to be largely thanks to the teaching of those who succeeded them (the rabbis) that the growing domination of economic power was limited in relationships between Jews, that an excessive social and legal disenfranchisement of the economically weak and of slaves was prevented. By adopting a scale of social criteria with priority given to education and teaching, Judaism offered everyone a certain minimum of opportunities to be judged at his or her true worth, and each person was given an inalienable dignity (Goldberg 1975, 153).

Whereas the history of other peoples is usually centred on the powerful, those who hold power (monarchs, great military leaders, the main dignitaries of the church: Ramlot 1972, 186), the Jews saw that the key figures in their destiny were the first and the main ones to protest against evil and defend justice (Bright 1981, 264f.).

Christianity can rightly boast of very many figures with a very high moral standing, but the thirst for justice does not occupy the same place in Christianity, and does not attain the same degree of intensity (Bamberger 1969, 319) as it does in the prophets. Perhaps with the exception of the church fathers, the quest for justice does not play the same role as a common denominator, a guideline, as it does with the Hebrew prophets (Agus 1957, 291).

In the course of the first half of the nineteenth century in the West, a period which has a certain resemblance to the time of the first great Hebrew prophets (Agus 1957, 291), there was a quite homogenous group of social reformers made up above all of so-called utopian socialists who, concerned for justice, reacted vigorously against the unbridled pursuit of profit, the growing power of money, the stress on social inequalities. But although in some respects the utopian socialists and even Marx are the spiritual heirs of the biblical prophets, they are above all intellectuals addressing their equals, representatives of the upper classes. By contrast the prophets – closer to the people, to everyday reality, enemies of theoretical analysis and complicated legal formulas – speak as much to the heart as the mind: their voices pass more easily over the barriers set up by space, time and human egotism.

8

The Social Laws of the Pentateuch

The aims pursued by the social legislation of the Torah are closely correlated with the ideal of the prophets (Clements 1976, 51f.). We need to examine this legislation as a complement to our investigation of prophecy in the previous chapter. The legal texts in question are not 'the product of speculative human brains' but are 'rooted in the life of Israel'; 'they are not abstract decrees but the expression of the religion and life of Israel in the face of the influences and threats of the surrounding peoples' (Cazelles 1966, 855). They reflect values of Israelite culture which are no less significant than those which we find in the prophets or in the psalms (Greenberg 1960, 27).

(i) Biblical law and cuneiform law

Thanks to research and archaeological discoveries undertaken above all from the beginning of this century we know 'that the people and state of Israel were formed within a world which had already evolved' (Cazelles 1977, 329), that therefore biblical law emerged in the context of a great legal corpus covering the various regions of the ancient Near East (Boecker 1976, 12) and that cuneiform law (Cardascia 1956; 1966; 1977, 63-70) played a very important role in the first stages of Israelite law (Paul 1970, 104; Schottroff 1977, 8).

Some statements by the prophets and some commandments in the Israelite codes, above all those which are not yet strictly juridical (Cazelles 1946, 79), show marked similarities with certain passages in the prologues and epilogues of the Mesopotamian codes or certain works of Egyptian literature which stress the need for justice. On both sides pity is taken on the fate of the poor, the victims of the oppression of the powerful. However, differences arise at the level of application.

Given the importance that the sacred gained within the chosen people and the significance that the Old Testament attaches to history (Graetz 1936, 20; Rivkin 1971, XVIII; Meyer 1974, 29), justice in ancient Israel more than elsewhere has a basically religious stamp (Paul 1970, 41; Jackson 1971, 207). Whereas in other countries of the Near East at that time justice was also seen as the emanation of the divine essence, in Israel it is considered to be the indivisible prerogative of a single God (Fensham 1962, 135; Van der Ploeg 1951, 296; Horst 1972, 201; Locher 1982, 132ff.); this exclusive power of Yahweh does not allow of other masters than him in this sphere either.

'The Israelite king,' wrote Cazelles (1978, 65), 'receives from his God the virtues of right and justice, *mishpat* and *tsedaqa* (Ps.72.1), just as the Pharaoh received Maat, justice or truth, from Re, the supreme God, the Babylonian king received *kittu* and *mêsharu* from Marduk and the Phoenician king had divinized right and justice (*mshr* and *tsdq*).' In an analogous way to the other sovereigns of the ancient Near East, the Israelite king had the duty of protecting the weak and the poor, the widows and the orphans (Van der Ploeg 1969, 514). But in Israel the king is not god (Gaudemet 1967, 106) as the Pharaoh is, nor his vicar, as the Babylonian prince is (Cardascia 1956, 68). The submission of the king to the will of Yahweh was constantly required (Caquot 1959, 31); as the instrument and servant of God he has to act in accord with the divine will (Gaudemet 1967, 106).

Given the semi-nomadic past of Israel and the 'relics of the practices of primitive Semitism' (Cazelles 1977, 199), together with its experience in Egypt and the covenant with Yahweh (Paul 1970, 27), the life of the king of Israel was for long an integral part of the life of the people (Cazelles 1973, 199). As in the ancient tribes, in many respects the king remained a chief among equals (*primus inter pares*) and was in no way above the law (Paul 1970, 33).

In Mesopotamia (except in the period of 'primitive democracy' in most distant times, when all the 'elders' enjoyed the prerogatives of government, de Fraine 1954, 59), and in Egypt (except during the transitory rise to power of the mass of the people at the time of the 'revolt'), the king was the supreme legislator and the intermediary between the gods and the people. In this respect the Israelite king played only an instrumental (ibid., 75) and functional role (391). He may have been the anointed and even the son, but there was tension and opposition in his relationship with Yahweh (Ellul 1967, 268). He had judicial power but no legislative power; he did not create the law (Garelli and Nikiprowetzky 1974, 295). He was not charged with making edicts or with supervising the observance of the law as was generally the case in the Mesopotamian laws and especially in the code of Hammurabi (Leemans 1950, 128). He was not the source of law like the Pharaoh (Tanner 1967, 249), and it seems possible to posit a clash between the law representing his will and the tribal bond which played a vital role among the Hebrews (Harari 1971, 52f.).

At the time of the monarchy, writes Van der Ploeg (1969, 463), the supreme judicial power in Israel was embodied in the king, who at the same time had administrative and executive powers. But the monarchy did not introduce a new judicial system into Israel or one which was inspired by models from neighbouring countries. Nor was it involved in the action of local legal bodies which were and remained the main judicial organ (Macholz 1972, 182). During the earliest stages of the monarchy (Saul, David, Solomon) the 'intercessors' (*pelilim*) of tribal society and the 'elders', who became local judges in the cities instead of tribal chiefs, were retained (Cazelles 1978, 64). Royal jurisdiction simply appeared as a new instrument to the degree that it related to cases or groups related to the monarchy. Beyond that the monarch took over the judicial role of the leader of the army in the period before the state, and probably also the duties of the 'judges' of the same period (Macholz 1972, 187).

From the death of Solomon onwards, the monarchy no longer brought unity. The prophets gave the words of God a meaning which made the people understand that faith and hope in the God of Israel called for more than a simple monarchical ideology (Cazelles 1973-4, 7; 1980, 9).

Thanks to the judicial reform of Jehoshaphat, achieved in the middle of the ninth century (II Chron. 19.5-11), royal jurisdiction in Judah underwent important modifications in its dispositions and organization at the end of the eighth century. This does not appear to have been a reform of the administration of justice, above all in terms of jurisdiction, but on the contrary to have been the creation of a homogeneous 'state' judicial system with a complicated structure. The Deuteronomic regulations relating to jurisdiction (Deut.16.18; 17.8-12) are based on this system but seek to reform it: the structure of the jurisdiction is maintained, but all royal influence is eliminated (Macholz 1972, 340). The nomination of judges and commissioners will no longer be made by the king but by the people or its representatives. Although the judicial system is maintained as a whole, this denial of the administrative authority of the king in fact amounts to a denial of his judicial competence (ibid., 335). The two 'laws of the king' (Isa.8.11-18; Deut.17.14-20) do not allude to a power of the king; on the contrary the first guards against his arbitrary acts and the second orders him to have a copy of the divine law and to conform strictly to it. Moreover, it is interesting to note that outside the text to which I have just referred the king is not mentioned anywhere in the Deuteronomic code.[1]

The second-person singular address which Yahweh uses to the faithful in the codes of the Pentateuch indicates that he is addressing the whole people, everyone (Noth 1943, 136; Wright 1950, 69; Galling 1951, 134). By the will of God the whole society becomes the repository of the law and is responsible for it and its application (Paul 1970, 38). Every individual who is part of the community is involved (Goldberg 1977, 152; Porter 1965, 365; Weinfeld 1973, 63). The laws dictated by God are not just communicated vertically (from God to the faithful) but are also propagated horizontally, in a democratic way, from man to man.

Another important difference between Israel and its neighbours consists in the fact that among the latter, as also later among the Greeks (Momigliano 1978, 23), justice was sought more for the economic and political advantages that it could present (Paul 1970, 41; Greenberg 1960. 19; Philips 1970; Jackson 1973, 16). For example the prologue to the code of Lipit-Ishtar is concerned with well-being (*ANET*, 159) and the prologue of the Code of Hammurabi with prosperity (164) as a corollary of justice. By contrast, in Israel, while the interested party is not completely excluded (e.g. Deut.6.18), much stress seems to be have been laid on the quest for justice for its own sake; as is expressly said in Deuteronomy, 'Justice, and only justice, you shall follow, that you may live' (16.20).

This importance attached to justice is represented by a great effort at impartiality. Already in Mesopotamia, for example, in the *Hymn to Shamash* the judge is encouraged to show himself to be impartial in his judgments. In Egypt, in the *Hymn to Amon-Re* there is a eulogy of the vizier devoted to the poor, whose judgment is impartial (Fensham 1962, 138). But the Israelite codes seem to be more explicit in this respect. We read in the Covenant Code: 'You shall not follow a multitude to do evil; nor shall you bear witness in a suit, turning aside after a multitude, so as to pervert justice; nor shall you be partial to a poor man in his suit' (Ex.23.2f.). An almost identical point of view appears in the Holiness Code: 'You shall do no injustice in judgment; you shall not be partial to the poor or defer to the great, but in righteousness shall you judge your neighbour' (Lev.19.15). In Deuteronomy God instructs the judges: 'You shall not be partial in judgment; you shall hear the small and the great alike' (Deut.1.17), and as for God himself, he is 'not only great, mighty and terrible' but 'impartial and incorruptible' (Deut.10.17).

It emerges from what I have just said, that the monotheistic principle as it is formulated in the Old Testament ('Hear, O Israel, the Lord our God is one Lord', Deut.6.4) implicitly signifies that the law of justice, like the laws of physics, must reign at the heart of all humanity, without any discrimination of nationality or social class and transcending all privileges (Wallis 1935, 259).

(ii) Goodwill towards the poor

In the ancient Near East, as probably almost everywhere else, people were not entirely indifferent to the poor and the disinherited. The Mesopotamian codes which we have already considered have passages which support the weak who are oppressed by the strong, above all in the prologues and epilogues. As we have seen, the princes and kings (Urukagina, Gudea, Lipit-Ishtar, Ur-Nammu and Hammurabi) declare that they have taken just measures to protect the poor, that they are preventing the powerful from ruining the weak, that they are seeing that the rich does not wrong the orphan nor the powerful man the widow. In Egypt, Amenemhet I says in his teaching that he has made gifts to the poor and brought up orphans (*ANET*, 418), and in the *Story of the Man from the Oasis* we are told of the great steward Rensi, 'father of the orphan, husband of the widow' (*ANET*, 408). As for Ugarit (de Langhe 1957, 65f.), the Ras Shamra documents have not so far revealed the existence of codes, but the mythological poems allude to the judicial activity of the rulers and the protection of the poor. In the *Legend of Danel and Aghat* (Column A.V, 6-8) the sage Daniel (or Danel) 'sat at the entrance of the gate beneath the trees which were by the threshing floor; he judged the cause of the widow, tried the case of the orphan' (Gibson and Driver 1978, 107; Vesco 1968, 252; Caquot 1974, 443). In the *Legend of Keret*, his son, Yaṣib, impelled by his inner demon to dethrone his father, king of Khubur, cries out (Caquot 1974, 100): 'Hear, I beseech you, O noble Keret. You do not judge the cause of the widow, you do not try the case of the importunate. You do not banish the extortioners of the poor, you do not feed the orphan' (VI.40-48, Gibson and Driver 1978, 102).

In Israel, before poverty began to be idealized, the first and principal current passing through the Old Testament regarded poverty as a scandalous state which should not exist among the chosen people (Gelin 1953, 13). From Amos to St James, and from Deuteronomy to

Jesus, the Bible regards poverty – and the sense of the word reaches far beyond a simple lack of money – as a state about which one cannot have a good conscience (ibid., 151). Mercy, charity and love for the poor emerged a long time before the Christian era (Van Leeuwen 1955, 12). The realism of traditional Israelite piety is represented among other things by the special importance attached in it to the protection of the poor (Maier 1972, 386). In a country which still retained the memory of the practices of semi-nomadism, it was thought that from an ideal point of view poverty should be unknown (Van Leeuwen 1955, 42), that its existence amounted to a negation of the happiness for which the Lord intended his people. In fact as long as the people were not too far removed from the traditional way of life the difference between the rich and the poor did not go too far. While there were rich men, there does not seem to have been a rural proletariat – each person owned his family land (Causse 1922, 51) – nor any division into organized classes, the Hebrews all being in principle the *rea*, the 'neighbours' of one another.

At all events, under the pressure of factors connected with the settlement, the division between rich and poor grew more marked and raised social problems which the stronger economic class tended to resolve to its advantage. The rich *baal* sought to enslave not only the stranger, the *ger* whom he hired, but also the Israelite who was forced into debt and had to provide pledges. Moreover, working on the land, while more remunerative for the rich, was much more demanding on subordinates than pastoral occupations (Cazelles 1946, 135).

In this period, which in some respects already heralds the 'time of misfortune' of which Amos speaks (5.13), the number of poor increased and the situation of those whom the Old Testament denotes by the terms *ani, anaw, ebyon, dal* (Van Leeuwen 1955, 14; Gelin, 1953, 19) became more and more difficult. Not only were they the main victims of material misery, but they had no legal identity; anyone could oppress them without running the risk of legal action (Fensham 1962, 139). In order to re-establish a certain social balance, to reduce injustices if not to eliminate them, some action was very soon taken in their favour.

From the 'earliest collection of legal sentences' (Cazelles 1966, 810), the Covenant Code, which in fact proves to be a compilation of laws, we find several imperatives (Cazelles 1946, 107) which seek to ensure a minimum of legal protection for the poor – 'You shall not pervert the justice due to your poor in his suit' (Ex.23.6) – or a minimum of material aid: 1. in the form of a loan for food, comparable to the

Roman *mutuum*, which did not bear interest (ibid., 134): 'If you lend money to any of my people with you who is poor, you shall not be to him as a creditor and you shall not exact interest from him' (Ex.22.25); 2. in the form of a periodical abandonment of the harvest: 'For six years you shall sow your land and gather in its yield; but the seventh year you shall let it rest and lie fallow, that the poor of your people may eat and what they leave the wild beasts may eat. You shall do likewise with your vineyard, and with your olive orchard' (Ex.23.10f.). This last commandment will surprise us less when we remember that the Covenant Code relates to the conditions in which the Hebrews lived during the period between the entry into Canaan and the foundation of the state (von Rad 1966, 14). Their customs were still steeped in the tradition of the life of the desert (Jepsen 1927, 97) and their occupations were still essentially pastoral (Cazelles 1958, 113; Steinmann 1954, 54; Van der Ploeg 1951, 31), with cattle-breeding as a vital priority (Cazelles 1957, 503) and the products of the soil supplementary to that (von Rad 1966, 14). The latter could be given away without the giver entirely losing his resources.

However, despite these first measures, the situation of the poor got worse and worse. The development of urban civilization, going hand in hand with the advent of the monarchy, only aggravated the problem (Neufeld 1960, 37). The increase in riches and prosperity from which in time the whole country benefited was enjoyed almost exclusively only by a privileged class. The inequality in fortunes multiplied injustices and upset social relationships (Causse 1922, 51). The great landowners profited from crises and wars to accumulate land and increase their domains. In this way they inaugurated the régime of *latifundia* (Bardtke 1971, 239f.). Established in the cities, they cut themselves off from the rural proletariat which they had created. It was in the city that trade guilds came into being, grouping together specialist workers at the expense of the traditional divisions. David, far from putting a brake on the development, relied on a foreign guard for support and superimposed on the old structures an administrative body of new men. The splendour of the palace, the weight of taxes and the different international involvements (trade, wars, alliances) created a climate which had not existed before (Gelin 1953, 15).

The Deuteronomic code, which came after the Covenant Code, was related to a society which had long since become sedentary and centralized, which knew of commerce (Cazelles 1957, 503), and in which the economic and social disparities were becoming increasingly shocking. But as it, too, drew on the more noble traditions (Lewy

1957, 324; Nicholson 1967, 122; Merendino 1969, 402) of the distant past (Speiser 1960, 39), whose spirit it renewed (Buis and Leclerq 1963, 5), its reaction against poverty was even stronger than that which appeared in the Covenant Code. The latter, a compilation which seems to go back to a period between Joshua and Samuel, represents in Israel 'a first effort to legalize moral and religious life', a 'first mixture of human formulae (*mishpatim*) and divine commandments (*debarim*)' (Cazelles 1946, 28). The Deuteronomic Code, which dates from the monarchy (von Rad 1966, 15) and seems to have been produced in the second half of the eighth century (Buis and Leclerq 1963, 16), was in all probability discovered in Jerusalem in 622, but contains texts which come from one of the sanctuaries of the North (Shechem or Bethel, von Rad 26). King Josiah was inspired by it for his reform (L'Hour 1963, 2). It marks an important step forward over what had previously been accomplished. It extends to all Israel the legislation which in the Covenant Code is limited to the city (von Rad 1966, 27). It represents the transition from a limited collection in which casuistic and statutary laws predominated, to a code of laws in which the human side becomes of capital importance and gains the upper hand (Weinfeld 1972, 283).

According to the majority of biblical scholars (Weinfeld 1962, 244) the moral and human side of Deuteronomy 'came to birth from the prophetic sphere' (Gelin 1953, 22). However, for others (e.g. Kaufmann, Weinfeld), it must be attributed above all to the wisdom literature.[2] In reality, Deuteronomy draws on all the ideas and currents (von Rad 1966, 25) which were spreading across the country and were prevalent in the local environment. Considered as one 'of the finest books of the Bible', it achieves a remarkably balanced synthesis of all the currents of thought which moved the people of the covenant (Buis 1969, 5; 1976, 192). It is primarily interested in human beings, and above all in those whose possibilities of defending themselves are limited (Weinfeld 1962, 243). It is distinguished by its lofty spirit and 'filled through and through with paraenesis aimed at paralysing poverty' (Gelin 1953, 22). It preaches that the notion of poverty must be unknown in Israel, which lives in a state of grace with Yahweh (Van Leeuwen 1955, 42). 'But there will be no poor among you (for the Lord will bless you in the land which the Lord your God gives you for an inheritance to possess), if only you will obey the voice of the Lord your God, being careful to do all this commandment which I command you this day' (Deut.15.4). In fact this ideal proved incapable of realization. The law takes account of that, but it does not want, does not accept that people should be resigned and give way to it (ibid., 42). Even if poverty is an inevitable evil, everything must be done to try, if not to overcome it, at least to reduce it as much as possible. Deuteronomy prescribes solidarity among brothers and generosity towards the poor: 'For the poor will never cease out of the land; therefore I command you, You shall open wide your hand to your brother, to the needy and to the poor, in the land' (Deut.15.11). That is very characteristic of Judaism, for the law prescribed by God is not beyond human possibilities, and does not go over into the abstract (Cazelles 1966, 818): 'For this commandment which I command you this day is not too hard for you, neither is it far off. It is not in heaven... Neither is it beyond the sea... But the word is very near you; it is in your mouth and in your heart, so that you can do it' (Deut.30.11-14). It is concerned with specifically allowing the needy to relieve their most essential needs: 'When you go into your neighbour's vineyard, you may eat your fill of grapes, as many as you wish, but you shall not put any in your vessel. When you go into your neighbour's standing grain, you may pluck the ears with your hand, but you shall not put a sickle to your neighbour's standing grain' (Deut. 23.24f.).

Evidence of goodwill towards the poor may be found in the Holiness Code which, as we shall eventually see, in many respects represents an even more developed form of the *mishpatim* than the Deuteronomic Code. If we are to explain this, we should recall that if the Holiness Code would seem to be an essay in codification of the same kind as Deuteronomy, Israel is above all considered to be a ritual community, centred on the temple where the holiness of Yahweh dwells (ibid., 827). The great social and political problems of Deuteronomy are not touched on (824), and the Holiness Code seems to have been produced against a background of the specific conditions in which, as we saw in connection with Finkelstein's book *The Pharisees*, ethical prophecy ceases to be the voice of an oppressed minority and becomes the possession of the majority. It is in this atmosphere that the vision of future Israel is worked out, as an ideal model steeped in a particularly lofty humanitarian spirit (Wallis 1935, 284).

According to some scholars the Holiness Code is earlier than Leviticus as a whole (Gamoran 1971, 132). Like Deuteronomy, it presupposes earlier collections and draws on primitive materials (Cazelles 1966, 825). The authors represent conservative sacerdotal tendencies and seek to rescue ancient traditions (ibid., 822). That is why their imposing edifice was for the most part formed of very ancient stones (Lods 1937, 263; Garelli and Nikiprowetsky 1974). Thus they took up the famous law about the corner of the field and the leaving of the gleanings: 'When you reap the harvest of your land, you shall not reap your field to its very border, neither shall you gather the gleanings after your harvest. And you shall not strip your vineyard bare, neither shall you gather the fallen grapes of your vineyard; you shall leave them for the poor and for the sojourner' (Lev.15.9f.). The first law goes back to a very old religious rite (Beer 1911, 152) which among other people consisted in reserving a part for the God of the harvests and fruits: Yahweh, the God of Israel, left this part for the poor among his people (Cazelles 1958, 90). Similarly, leaving the gleanings, which was primitively an offering to the spirit of the fields, is transformed by Israel into a social law.

In any comparison of the laws which I have just mentioned with those in the two previous codes with similar aims, one difference seems to be worth bringing out: in the Covenant Code and the Deuteronomic Code we have help for the poor in the form of access to food, while in the Holiness Code, in addition to the gift of what falls to the ground, the law about the corner of the field seems to offer a chance of sharing in the very act of production.

(iii) The protection of the widow and orphan

Alongside the poor *par excellence* we find the widows and orphans (i.e. those without a father), whose situation was far from being enviable. In addition to the sorrow with which widowhood could be accompanied, it almost inevitably meant poverty. By losing the legal protection of her husband, the widow sometimes found herself burdened with children or the debts left by her husband. This precarious situation made her easy prey for all kinds of exploitation. The orphan, whose fate was closely bound up with that of the widow, robbed of a father's support, had no protection against the vicissitudes of life. If the father had left debts, the son could be reduced to slavery by the creditor (Vesco 1968, 251).

The widow and the fatherless seem to have been the object of some concern among Israel's neighbours (Cazelles 1946, 78). According to the Code of Hammurabi and the Assyrian laws, the formal situation of the widow would seem to have been better than in Israel (Vesco 1968, 252). In Babylon she had a right to some of her husband's estate. The widow or the repudiated wife could even in some cases enjoy part of the estate equivalent to that received by a child (Code of Hammurabi §§137, 173, 180-2) and regain full control over her dowry (Van Leeuwen 1955, 27). The Assyrian laws seem to contain analogous dispositions (de Vaux 1961, 35). By contrast, the Israelite widow did not enjoy any right of succession and the estate fell entirely into the hands of the sons of the dead man, and if he had none, those of his daughters. If he did not have any children, the estate went to his brothers, his father's brothers or the nearest relative.

Given this situation, it is not surprising that the Old Testament has a quite special bias in favour of this category of the poor. Protected by the religious law, they find themselves commended to the charity of the people (ibid., 40). Nowhere outside Israel is so much stress and emphasis placed on the kinship between God and these poor and on the assurance of his forthright intervention on their behalf (Vesco 1968, 252). The Covenant Code forbids the ill-treatment of these defenceless creatures, of whom people are tempted to make victims, for they will be heard by Yahweh and avenged: 'You shall not afflict any widow or orphan. If you do afflict them, and they cry out to me, I will surely hear their cry, and my wrath will burn, and I will kill you with the sword, and your wives shall become widows and your children fatherless' (Ex.22.21-23). The word for ill-treat in the ancient texts, *te'annun* in the *piel*, denotes violence and physical cruelty which could go very far (ibid., 251).

The Deuteronomic Code, which corresponds to a more developed stage, touches on the problem from a perspective the repressive side of which gives place to more positive measures. The widow and the orphan, who are defenceless, have the right to the legal protection of the Lord and his people: 'You shall not pervert the injustice due to the sojourner or to the fatherless, or take the widow's garment in pledge' (Deut.24.17). 'Cursed be he who perverts the justice due to the sojourner, the fatherless, and the widow' (Deut.27.19). However, as well as these curses, an important place is given to the problem of material aid. At the time of the harvest and the wine harvest, and the gathering of olives, the stranger, the fatherless and the widow have the right to glean, and Deuteronomy recommends that sheaves and fruit should not be gathered too meticulously (Causse 1922, 75). 'When you reap your harvest in your field, and have forgotten a sheaf in the field, you shall not go back to get it; it shall be for the sojourner, the fatherless, and the widow. When you beat your olive trees, you shall not go over the boughs again, it shall be for the sojourner, the fatherless and the widow. When you gather the grapes of your vineyard, you shall not glean it afterwards; it shall be for the sojourner, the fatherless and the widow' (Deut.24.19-21).

Every third year, independently of the sabbatical year during which the tithes cannot be paid because there are no harvests, everyone is to put aside a tithe[3] by means of which he shall provide food not only for the levite and the sojourner, but also for the widow and the fatherless. 'At the end of every three years you shall bring forth all the tithe of your produce in the same year, and lay it up within your towns; and the levite, because he has no portion or inheritance with you, the sojourner, the fatherless, and the widow, who are within your towns, shall come and eat and be filled' (Deut.14.28f.). This offering is accompanied by an obligation to make a declaration at the sanctuary before the Lord, the aim of which is to ensure that nothing has been kept back of the prescribed tithe (Lesètre 1926, 1433). 'I have removed the sacred portion out of my house, and moreover I have given it to the levite, the sojourner, the fatherless, and the widow, according to all thy commandment which thou hast commanded me; I have not transgressed any of thy commandments' (Deut.26.13). This declaration can be explained by the fact that the tithes were raised and distributed in the villages outside the control of the priests.

The widow and the orphan also had the chance of joining in festivals, in religious ceremonies and family rejoicing (Causse 1922, 740). For example at the harvest festival (called the Feast of Weeks) or the Feast of Tabernacles (before the harvest or grape harvest), 'You shall rejoice before the Lord your God, with your son, your daughter, your manservant, your maidservant, the levite who is within your cities, the sojourner, the orphan and the widow who are in your midst' (Deut.16.10-13).

As well as having these various advantages, the widow benefits from a special protection over the pledge given on the occasion of a loan: 'You shall not take a widow's garment in pledge' (Deut.24.17).

(iv) Protection for the stranger

Before even the widow, the orphan and the poor generally, the Israelite codes mention the sojourner (the stranger, the guest). As we shall see, this choice does not seem to be a purely fortuitous one.

Alongside the free Israelites who made up the 'people of the land' and passing strangers, the *nokri*, who, for example as prisoners of war, only stayed temporarily, part of the population was made up of strangers with permanent residence, the *gerim*, singular *ger*. This typically Israelite category (Van Leeuwen 1955, 81) comprised the ancient inhabitants (who had not been assimilated through marriage or reduced to slavery) and immigrants and refugees. Their status has similarities to the Arab *djâr*, the 'neighbour', and the Spartan *paroikoi* (De Vaux 1961, 10). Dhorme compares them with the 'clients' in Rome, whom he calls 'guests'. For the Israelite, to be a *ger* was to have the status which the Israelites had in Egypt: to be in a foreign land, with a dependent status in which one was given all the unpleasant work (Cazelles 1946, 78).

The Code of Hammurabi draws no distinction between the people of the land and strangers. In Babylon, a cosmopolitan city and the centre of international trade, the foreigner (David 1950, 155; Falk 1964, 115) was most often a rich man, and it was all too likely that he would make the citizen his victim (Vesco 1968, 250). Those who brought their money and resources were welcome and had a share in all rights and duties: this city, which lived above all on commerce, was open to anyone who wanted to try his luck. But it was merciless on anyone who had no good fortune (Van Leeuwen 1955).

In Ugarit, the immigrants had the same rights and the same duties as the native population: they paid taxes as they did, performed military service and devoted themselves to commerce, manual work and intellectual pursuits (Astour 1959, 74). Things were different in Israel, where the privileges of the elect people involved a difference in status between the Israelite and the stranger (Vesco 1968, 251).

In everyday life there was no barrier between the *gerim* and the Israelites: as we shall see later, in connection with slaves, they sometimes made fortunes. From the religious point of view they were more or less subject to the same rules as citizens: they had to observe the sabbath; they could offer sacrifices; and they participated in religious festivals, etc. However, these resident foreigners, while being free and distinct from slaves, did not have all civic rights, and as land remained in Israelite hands, they were reduced to hiring out their services (Deut. 24.14), to earning their living, for the most part the hard way, as day workers. Generally poor, they were classed with the needy, the widows and the orphans, with all those who were 'economically weak', and commended to the goodwill of the Israelites (de Vaux 1961, 73f.). They had to be protected, not only by pity, goodness and charity, but also by a sense of humility which can be explained from the very history of the people of God (Vesco 1968), by the 'two basic experiences in the life of Israel: that of oppression and that of the brotherly solidarity experienced after the liberating intervention of Yahweh' (ibid., 242). Israel was not to be proud of its power and riches and to say 'by my own might I have done all this'.

Israel owed everything to Yahweh. It had to remember that it, too, was a *ger* and a slave in the land of Egypt (Causse 1937, 165).

So it is not surprising that the Covenant Code already shows great human concern for the *ger*: 'You shall not wrong a stranger or oppress him, for you were strangers in the land of Egypt' (Ex.22.21). The first verb used in this verse, *yanah* (exploit, molest, abuse), denotes the exploitation of a weak person by a strong one. The second verb, *lahas*, of which the strict sense is 'press' (press a door against someone pushing it), 'squeeze up' (squeeze up against a wall), in this context denotes the oppression of one people by another. We find them again in parallel with the verb 'make to stumble', and this evokes the situation in which Israel found itself in Egypt. At one time a stranger itself, Israel has no better way of keeping that memory alive than by not oppressing the stranger (Vesco 1968, 249).

This prescription, formulated in Ex.22.21, is taken up again in Ex.23.9: 'You shall not oppress a stranger; you know the heart of a stranger, for you were strangers in the land of Egypt.' In Egypt, Israel lived the life (literally the *nephesh* of a stranger). The use of the noun *nephesh*, primarily denoting breath, seems to allude to the physical rhythm of work and rest; the stranger must be allowed room to breathe (ibid., 250).

At the end of the monarchy there was an influx of refugees from the old northern kingdom. The number of *gerim* increased in Judah and the Deuteronomic code seems to have taken account of this state of affairs. As in the case of the widow and the orphan, it took more specific measures than the Covenant Code in favour of the stranger and adopted a much more humane attitude. Like the levite, the widow and the orphan, the stranger could benefit from the triennial tithe (Deut.24.29), glean in the fields, gather the olives left on the tree, and go over the vines (Deut.24.19-21). Moreover, not only does Deuteronomy, like the Covenant Code, stress that the Israelites should remember that they were slaves in the land of Egypt (Deut.24.18,22); for that reason they must love the stranger (Deut.10.19).

As to the Holiness Code, it also proved to be more generous than the other codes. The stranger must not only be left the corner of the field and be allowed to glean (Lev.19.9-10), but he must also be allowed to benefit from the sabbatical year: 'The sabbath of the land shall provide food for you, for yourself and your male and female slaves and for your hired servant and for the sojourner who lives with you...' (Lev.25.6). What seems particularly important is that the Holiness Code goes even further than the Deuteronomic code in feelings of love towards the stranger: 'When a stranger sojourns with you in your land, you shall not do him wrong. The stranger who sojourns with you shall be to you as the native among you, and you shall love him as yourself; for you were strangers in the land of Egypt' (Lev.19.33f.).

(v) Respect for the wage-earner

A new category of the economically weak can be added to those with whom we have already been concerned. As the economic situation got worse, alongside the foreign mercenaries, the *gerim*, there were also Israelite mercenaries. The amassing of land by the royal family and the powerful, the very heavy taxes on behalf of the central institutions, and above all the disasters at the end of the eighth century and the Assyrian enslavements made the situation very difficult for the smallholder who could no longer maintain his own property (Van Leeuwen 1955, 71). The impoverishment of numerous families and the loss of land compelled an increasing number of Israelites to fall back on paid work. Since at this stage people were above all hired for agricultural work, these wage-earners became above all shepherds, harvesters, vineyard workers, and so on. They were engaged either by the day, as 'day workers', or by the year.

According to the Code of Hammurabi, the workers received a shekel a month during the major periods of work and a little less for the rest of the year, but some contracts fixed much lower sums. The Old Testament does not give us any specific information about the wages of these workers, but it is certain that their situation was difficult and they had to be protected (de Vaux 1961, 76).

As emerges from what I have just said, the appearance of wage earners comes relatively late and it is not surprising that the Covenant Code does not speak of them. On the other hand the Deuteronomist calls for respect for the paid worker: 'You shall not oppress a hired servant who is poor and needy, whether he is one of your brethren or one of the sojourners who are in your land within your towns; you shall give him his hire on the day he earns it, before the sun goes down (for he is poor and sets his heart upon it); lest he cry to the Lord, and it be sin in you' (Deut.24.14-15). Leviticus takes the same line: 'You shall not oppress your neighbour or rob him. The wages of a hired servant shall not remain with you all night until the morning' (Lev.19.13). Moreover, the Holiness Code ordains that the wage earner shall have his share in the advantages of the sabbatical year

(Lev.25.6), and if a slave succeeds in freeing himself but has decided to stay as a paid worker in the service of his old owner, the latter shall not 'rule him with harshness' (Lev.25.53).

(vi) The status of slaves

Slavery, disseminated over various countries of the ancient Near East (Lauterbach 1936, 22), appears in forms which have marked similarities in their origins, their functions and their character (Mendelssohn 1949, 121). However, as this institution functioned in economic and social conditions which varied in time and space, 'cases are rarely identical and solutions are almost always different' (Cazelles 1946, 150).

A comparison between the Code of Hammurabi (§§117, 118) and the Covenant Code (Ex.21.2-11) shows that in both cases there is slavery for similar reasons, and in both cases freedom comes after a certain time (after three years with Hammurabi and after six with the Covenant Code). Moreover the texts are even strangely parallel in announcing this freedom, though the solutions are conceived in a very different spirit (ibid.). In the first case we have a class society (Klima 1953, 143) in which only a slave of patrician origin can be freed, while the other made no class distinction provided that it was a Hebrew who had to be protected against degradation (Van Leeuwen 1955, 59). Furthermore, thanks to Van Leeuwen's study, we have been able to note that the situation of slaves in Israel was generally much better than that in neighbouring countries: in contrast to the working conditions which prevailed in the great centralized exploitation which was predominant in Mesopotamia and in Egypt, in the small agricultural properties of the ancient Israelites, where the work was done by the proprietor, his family and a limited number of slaves, the latter were treated in a way as members of the family to which they belonged (ibid., 67). They became almost companions whose services were appreciated at their true worth (André 1892, 4).

We should remember that of all the peoples of the ancient Near East, Israel was the only one, after a certain period, which did not take slavery for granted (Maarsingh 1961, 154), the only one from a certain stage of its development to condemn, if not outright, at least in many respects, what all the other countries accepted without the least objection. Whereas nowhere in the very rich Sumero-Akkadian literature do we find any protest against slavery nor any expression of sympathy for the victims of this institution (Mendelssohn 1949, 123), even before Job attacks slavery outright (Fuchs 1935, 82), the Holiness Code, as we shall see in detail later, prohibits it in dealings between Israelites.

But when there was no trade in the country and no other source of revenue than agriculture, if he was not to die of hunger or to go begging, a man deprived of his patrimony clearly had to put himself at the service of those who were more fortunate than he (Kahn 1867, 9). The Covenant Code and the Deuteronomic Code, developed in other circumstances than the Holiness Code, took account of the realities of the time and accepted slavery even between Israelites. However, they introduced a series of restrictions, above all in Deuteronomy, which seek to make the institution as humane as possible.

In the Covenant Code, 'When you buy a Hebrew slave, he shall serve six years and in the seventh he shall go out free, for nothing' (Ex.21.2), and in the Deuteronomic code the Hebrew slave is freed after six years: 'If your brother, a Hebrew man, or a Hebrew woman, is sold to you, he shall serve you six years, and in the seventh year you shall let him go free from you' (Deut 15.12), but in the latter the tone is more human (the legislator introduces the term brother, Alt 1953-59, I, 292, and instead of purchase which, according to von Rad, would presuppose the case of a man who is not free, the man sells himself voluntarily). In that case the initiative would be taken by him and not by the master, as in the previous case.[4]

Deuteronomy also adopts a more liberal attitude towards women, whom it allows to sell themselves, something which does not happen in the Covenant Code. The changes that had taken place in the law of property which, in time, began to give the woman the right of inheritance, allow her to be in the same situation as the man possessing land (von Rad 1966, 14).

Deuteronomy also has a more humane attitude over the freeing of slaves. According to the Covenant Code, both male slaves and their wives can be freed but only if they were married before: 'If he comes in single, he shall go out single; if he comes married, then his wife shall go out with him. If his master gives him a wife and she bears him sons or daughters, the wife and her children shall be her master's and she shall go out alone' (Ex.21.3f.). And if an Israelite father, poor or in debt, sells his daughter (de Vaux 1961, 86) 'as a slave, she shall not go out as the male slaves do' (Ex.21.79). By contrast Deuteronomy, which takes up and amplifies the texts of Exodus, allows all slaves, both men and women, to benefit from the privileges of the *shemitta*:

in the seventh year there will be not only the remission of debts but the liberation of all slaves. There is no restriction in Deuteronomy, as there is in the Covenant Code, against the wife of the slave who marries in the house of her master and whom he keeps to increase his stock of slaves. According to the Deuteronomic approach, the master cannot have a hold on the private life of the slave or his wife; the slave is considered a citizen, a brother who sells only his services and not his person to his master. And as a citizen enjoying the same rights as his master, the slave leads a free family life, independent of any interference on the part of his master. Moreover, while the refusal of freedom by a slave is attributed in the Covenant Code above all to the fact that he does not want to leave his wife and children – 'I love my master, my wife, and my children, I will not go out free' (Ex.21.5) – in Deuteronomy this refusal is explained solely by his love for his master and the house where he is happy: 'If he says to you, "I will not go out from you" because he loves you and your household, since he fares well with you' (Deut.15.16). Note that this facility for choosing between staying and going is accorded both to the man and the woman and also that it is not by chance that the term 'master' is not used in the passage of Deuteronomy that I have just quoted. Given that the slave is thought to be the 'brother' of the proprietor, it would be inappropriate to apply the title 'master' to the latter (Weinfeld 1972, 282).

Those men and women who choose to stay, after a ceremony which seems to have its origin in nomadic life (piercing the ear), acquire the special legal status of a 'perpetual slave' and are received into the community of the family of their master. Deuteronomy shows a sign of goodwill and generosity to those who go which has no counterpart elsewhere. As it is not enough to give the slave his or her liberty but he or she also has to have something to live on and to be protection against distress, Deuteronomy prescribes: 'And when you let him go free from you, you shall not let him go empty-handed; you shall furnish him liberally out of your flock, out of your threshing floor, and out of your wine-press' (Deut.15.13f.).

This reinforcement of the humanitarian spirit can also be seen in connnection with runaway slaves. Among Israel's neighbours the extradition of runaway slaves was required, and anyone who discovered one received a reward (Maarsingh 1961, 154). The Code of Hammurabi pronounces the death penalty for 'aiding and abetting a fugitive slave, refusing to give him up or merely hiding him' (de Vaux 1961, 87). The Laws of Eshnunna also protect the owner against the flight of slaves: according to §51, a male or female slave of Eshnunna bearing fetters, a chain or the mark of a slave is not allowed to leave the gates of the city of Eshnunna without the permission of his master (Van Leeuwen 1953, 65). By contrast, Deuteronomy 'forbids anyone to hand over a slave who has escaped from his master and sought refuge; he is to be welcomed and well treated in the town he has chosen' (de Vaux 1961, 87). Israel has to be a vast refuge (Maarsingh 1961, 154). 'You shall not give up to his master a slave who has escaped from his master to you: he shall dwell with you, in your midst, in the place which he shall choose within one of your towns, where it pleases him best; you shall not oppress him' (Deut.23.15f.). Deuteronomy, like the Covenant Code (Ex.21.16), also proves extremely strict on anyone who kidnaps a brother Israelite to sell him as a slave (Fuchs 1955, 31). 'If a man is found stealing one of his brethren, the people of Israel, and if he treats him as a slave or sells him, then that thief shall die' (Deut.24.7). There is a similar ruling in the Code of Hammurabi (§14), but it only concerns the child of a patrician (*awilum*; Maarsingh 1961, 154).

The Holiness Code does not forbid a stranger living in the country to possess slaves: 'If a stranger or sojourner with you becomes rich, and your brother beside him becomes poor and sells himself to the stranger or sojourner with you, or to a member of the stranger's family...' (Lev.25.47). However, this right is qualified by two restrictions: 1. The right of redemption at any time ('then after he is sold he may be redeemed; one of his brothers may redeem him, or his uncle, or his cousin may redeem him, or a near kinsman belonging to his family may redeem him...'(Lev.25.48f.); 2. freeing of the slave in the year of jubilee ('If he is not redeemed by one of these means, then he shall be released in the year of jubilee', Lev.25.54).

As for the Israelites, they can have foreign slaves in perpetuity ('As for your male and female slaves whom you may have: you may buy male and female slaves from among the nations that are round about you... and they may be your property... to inherit as a possession for ever...', Lev.25.44-46). However, we should recall that even the Covenant Code prescribes the immediate liberation of male and female slaves if their master puts out an eye or breaks a tooth (Ex.21.26f.).

The principle of slavery is not questioned, but in its quest for an ideal the Holiness Code does not assume that the slaves of Israelites are themselves Israelites ('If your brother becomes poor beside you, and sells himself to you, you shall not make him serve as a slave, he shall be with you as a hired servant and a sojourner', Lev.25.39f.).

As in so many other cases, there was a considerable gap between the regulations and what was actually done. The biblical narratives demonstrate that there were many Israelite slaves and that they included not only malefactors sold to compensate their victims (Ex.22.2) and those who were sold through poverty (Lev.25.39) but also debtors reduced to slavery by their creditors (II Kings 4.1; Amos 2.6; 8.6; Prov.22.7, cf. Urbach 1964, 4; Sarna 1973, 147).

Jeremiah shows us that the law on the liberation of the Hebrew slave after six years of service was not respected. All 'the authorities and the people' who on the orders of king Zedekiah had committed themselves to free their slaves, 'obeyed and set them free. But afterwards they turned around and took back the male and female slaves they had set free, and brought them into subjection as slaves...' (Jer.34.8-11). According to the books of Ezra (2.64f.) and Nehemiah (7.67), of more than 42,360 people who returned from Babylonia there were 7,337 male and female slaves (Cohn 1971, 1657).

Another aspect of the question is indicated by the situation of foreign slaves whom the Israelites obtained by war and trading; these found themselves treated much less favourably than Israelite slaves (Kahn 1867, 138). Nevertheless they, like the others, were accorded the advantages of a weekly rest (Ex.20.10; 23.12; cf.Deut.5.14), and benefited from a safeguard for their life which had no equivalent in other legislation (Urbach 1964, 40). If a man strikes his male or female slave fatally 'he shall suffer vengeance...' (Ex.20-21). It is true that the penalty is expressed rather vaguely, but it seems to have been capital (Kahn 1867, 91).

It is clear that the protection of the slaves that the Torah seeks to assure is very inadequate, but on the whole the Jewish law was much in advance of other legislation in antiquity (ibid., 138). The conditions of slaves in Israel, writes Cardascia (1956, 90), would seem to have been the least unfavourable of all those that have been revealed to us by ancient law. There are many complex reasons for this state of affairs. One which certainly played by no means a negligible role was that the Israelite legislators tried to oppose the creation of overly distinct social classes, remembering that the Israelites had all been slaves in Egypt (Van Leeuwen 1955, 60). On the other hand the Bible and then 'tradition' steeped them in the idea that the Hebrews are above all servamts of God and that they have no right to alienate their freedom: the Hebrew who sells himself is just as much failing in his duty as the one who becomes his accomplice by buying him (Kahn 1867, 9). According to Kahn (10), 'it has to be acknowledged that, painful and degrading though slavery may have been, it had a certain attraction for feeble spirits, intolerant of the harsh toil of life and the heavy responsibility of freedom; it assured at least everyday food, lodging for the night, and clothing as covering; and what more do people need for whom struggle is a misfortune and liberty a burden? But this was something which the Jewish law did not tolerate: in making a concession to poverty it conceded nothing to idleness.'

(vii) The prohibition against lending for interest

Since indebtedness (Buis and Leclercq 1963, 167) in Israel was one of the reasons, if not the main reason, for the loss of family property and slavery, the prohibition against lending for interest has an important place in Israelite legislation in favour of the poor. This practice, accepted in dealings with foreigners, is categorically prohibited between Israelites, nor is any distinction made between a limited interest and an unlimited, usurious rate.[5]

Such an intransigent position contrasts vividly with the other countries of the ancient Near East (Gamoran 1971, 127), where what in Israel was regarded as an intolerable practice among brothers was not considered a fault (Vesco 1968, 248). In Mesopotamia usury was not a sin. Among the Assyrians, interest on money was fixed according to the law of supply and demand (Van Leeuwen 1955, 51). In the Mesopotamian legislation prior to the Laws of Eshnunna, there is no limit on the level of interest and no restriction on means of recompense from the defaulting debtor (Szlechter 1955, 18). However, in the course of the period which extends from the Laws of Eshnunna to the Code of Hammurabi the right of the creditor, hitherto arbitrary, began gradually to be subjected to some restrictions. These two legislations provide for a legal level of interest: 20% for lending money and 33.3% for lending grain (ibid., 21f.). The free lending of advances is not unknown in Babylonia (Vesco 1968, 248): article 48 of the Code of Hammurabi exempts the debtor from interest when for example a storm has flooded his house or when drought prevents germination (Van Leeuwen 1955, 51). However, in no case is lending at interest prohibited or even discouraged (Gamoran 1971, 127). While the Covenant Code does not provide any sanction against the insolvent debtor, in the Laws of Eshnunna and the Code of Hammurabi he can be imprisoned (Vesco 1968, 248); the creditor can seize the debtors and the members of his family and his slaves (Szlechter 1955, 21).

These divergences can be explained for the most part by the very important difference that there was at the time between the economic and social structures in Israel and those among its powerful neighbours. The laws relating to lending at interest which were promulgated in Mesopotamia concerned countries which were ruled by a very strong central power (Klingenberg 1977, 24), whose economies included not only agriculture but also commerce (Gamoran 1971, 128) and a very developed system of credit (Klingenberg 1977, 34). When Israel began to prohibit lending at interest, it was still at the stage of being a tribal community without class division and without a well-established state power. Its economy was based almost exclusively on stock-breeding and agricultural work. At the time of the judges and the beginnings of the monarchy, trade was still almost entirely in the hands of the Canaanites, the Philistines and the Phoenicians. It was only in the reign of Solomon that this situation began to change (ibid., 24).

E. Neufeld (1955, 370) tries to show that Israelite society, governed by the Covenant Code, already had some experience of trade and that it was at a level of civilization comparable to that of its neighbours. However, he is somewhat isolated in his views and the majority of scholars, if not all of them, think that at this period Israel was mainly a people involved in agriculture on a small scale in which money had to serve above all for buying consumer objects (Van Leeuwen 1955, 52) and in which commercial transactions had no part. In these conditions the demand for commercial loans was almost non-existent (Gamoran 1971, 128) and the loans mentioned in the Torah served more to relieve the essential needs of the poor and hungry (Klingenberg 1977, 24).

The prohibition against lending for interest appears for the first time in Israelite legislation in the Covenant Code (Ex.22.24) which, as we have already seen, seeks to make loans for food a *mutuum* (a free contract between friends) and not a *nexum* by which the borrower confers on the lender a power which can come into force if he does not redeem the loan by repaying it (Cazelles 1946, 192). The Israelite legislator wants to prevent the poor of Israel from becoming the prey of their creditors (Causse 1922, 73); he wants to break the fatal chain of indebtedness (pledges, interest, loans) which was often the main cause of impoverishment (Vesco 1968).

This first prohibition against lending for interest was formulated very precisely, and extended considerably in the Deuteronomic Code. What in the Covenant Code appeared more in the form of a general statement of principles, becomes a norm in the latter. While the former tells the creditor not to treat his debtor 'as a usurer' (Ex.22.24), the other for the first time uses the technical term *neshek* for interest and prohibits collecting it when lending money and food and 'anything that is lent for interest' (Deut.23.20).

The difference between the two codes seems to be attribuable to the fact that Deuteronomy is legislating for a later period. After a respite represented by the prosperous reigns of Jeroboam in Israel and Azariah (Uzziah) in Judah, during almost the whole of the first half of the eighth century (Neufeld 1955, 354), the situation in the country grew steadily worse (Baron 1952, 67), especially as a result of progressive cupidity, an increased development of *latifundia*, an increase in taxes and the growing burden of different levies (von Rad 1966, 106). The continued process of social differentiation went hand in hand with economic decline, and each national or international catastrophe had a harsh effect above all on those at the bottom of the social scale. The rich profited from it to enrich themselves still more (Baron 1952, 68). The poor peasants found it harder and harder to make ends meet and were forced to borrow on very disadvantageous conditions (von Rad 1966, 106). Hence the pressing need to protect the main victims of this state of things.

However, in spite of these changes, at the time with which Deuteronomy is concerned, Israel still remained almost exclusively a nation of peasants (ibid., 148). According to Klingenberg (1977, 34), on the whole the economic and social structure of the country did not differ much from that reflected in the Covenant Code. Moreover, although there is no explicit mention of the status of borrowers, it seems that it is to favour the same category of the poor that Deuteronomy promulgates the law against interest (Gamoran 1971, 130), like the Covenant Code and the Holiness Code (Lev.25.35-37).

As to sojourners, Deuteronomy does not make any prohibition against the levying of interest. 'To a foreigner you may lend upon interest, but to your brother you shall not lend upon interest...' (Deut.23.21). At this time, all the merchants in Israel were foreigners (von Rad 1966, 148), and it seems logical to suppose that the loans which were made to them by Jewish farmers bore interest, since they represented not only a service rendered but also 'the risks of capital and its unavailability to the lender' (Salomon 1932, 17).

It goes without saying that the laws against interest corresponded to the state of economic development of Israel (Meislin and Cohen 1964, 266). But since for Israel, above all at the beginning of its existence, the ties of blood and the feeling of brotherly unity were very powerful (von Rad 1966, 148), it is not surprising that lending without interest was based in biblical law above all on moral considerations (Szlechter 1955, 22). There was no distinction, as in Roman law, between *ius* and *fas*. The prohibition against lending for interest was formally based on the precept of love for the neighbour and the fear of God (Klingenberg 1977, 52). The children of Israel were not to be victims of their brothers, of their thirst for possessions. As the elect people, they had to apply the laws of solidarity (ibid., 25).

We may wonder how far the law in question was respected and applied. From the fact that Ezekiel, Psalms and Proverbs expressly condemn lending at interest we can infer that the prohibition was often violated. But since throughout the Old Testament there is not a single instance of a loan for interest, it might suggest that the precept was observed at least to a certain degree (Vesco 1968, 247).

The law on lending is followed very closely by that on the pledge. In the Covenant Code, immediately after the verse on lending there is a verse aimed at protecting the pledge which the debtor gives his creditor. It presupposes a poor man who leaves his garment as a sign of his commitment. Already at Nuzi, for example, the garment plays an important role in contracts: it is a substitute for the person. The Covenant Code perpetuates this tradition of the garment, but humanizes it by demanding that it should be given back almost immediately: 'If ever you take your neighbour's garment in pledge, you shall restore it to him before the sun goes down' (Ex.22.26).

Deuteronomy sees this problem in the same spirit and goes even further in a humanitarian direction. It does not allow the creditor to retire at night while keeping the pledge of his debtor, since the latter must lie down in his garment (Deut.24.12f.). And there is a new development: it imposes restrictions on the creditor as to the choice of his pledge (Weinfeld 1972, 289); it forbids the taking of objects which are basic necessities as pledges: the hand mill or one of the two millstones which were probably used to prepare the daily meal: 'No man shall take a mill or an upper millstone in pledge; for he would be taking a life in pledge' (Deut.24.6). Moreover Deuteronomy forbids a creditor to enter the home of the debtor to take a pledge: 'You shall stand outside, and the man to whom you make the loan shall bring the pledge out to you' (Deut.24.11).

As to sanctions, in case of failure, the Deuteronomic code shows a more developed awareness than the Covenant Code (Lewy 1957, 323). The latter warns that if the creditor behaves badly towards the poor man, the latter can be sure of being heard if he cries out to God. On the other hand, if the creditor behaves fairly and returns the pledge at the due time, then according to Deuteronomy the unfortunate person will bless him and he will be 'just' before God (Deut.24.13).

Deuteronomy, moreover, commends a special measure which we do not find elsewhere: the remission of debts. The increasingly precarious situation of the Israelite peasants at the time of the monarchy was further worsened by the advent of the commercial economy. This state of affairs prompts the legislator to take up the old agricultural law of leaving the harvest every seven years (which we find among the measures of the Covenant Code to help the poor) and to extend it to a new area. The expression used for abandoning the harvest every seven years (Ex.23.11, in Hebrew *shamat, shemitta*) is applied to the sphere of debts: 'At the end of every seven years you shall grant a release... every creditor shall release what he has lent to his neighbour: he shall not exact it of his neighbour, his brother, because the Lord's release has been proclaimed. Of a foreigner you may exact it; but whatever of yours is with your brother your hand shall release' (Deut.15.1-3).

The term for remission (your hand shall release) corresponds to the image of the hand which opens to let go what it holds. The exact bearing of this insitfution is not specified. Was it a moratorium remitting the payment of debts for a year, or rather a final annulment of all debts contracted over the previous six years? The warning in v.9, 'Take heed lest there be a base thought in your heart and you say, "The seventh year, the year of release is near" and your eye be hostile to your poor brother, and you give him nothing' (Deut.15.9f.), is better understood if it is a final remission, but it also indicates the difficulties in applying such a measure.

(viii) The sabbath

The different laws that we have examined in this chapter bring out well the hold which religion had on the economy. However, this phenomenon, which was the starting point for the research undertaken by Max Weber on the great religions of the universe, emerges again in a special way with the sabbath, the most characteristic (Lemaire 1973, 161), if not the most important, institution of Judaism (Harrelson 1977, 234; Eisenberg and Abecassis 1978, 169).

The majority of biblical scholars have been more inclined to study the origins and history of the sabbath, but recent studies are more concerned with the consequences of this institution for the life of the individual and society (Andreasen 1974, 469). Our preoccupation will be in this direction.

The etymology of the word sabbath (which is a transcription of the Hebrew *shabbat*) and the origins of the institution are very complex (Kraus 1966, 81ff.) and are still not well known (Hulst 1966, 152). Some scholars seek them in Babylonia and particularly in the Akkadian word *shapattu*, which denotes the day in the middle of the month, the day of the full moon, which was a day when the gods' heart was appeased and therefore a day of good omen (de Vaux 1961, 476). Others do not accept a direct borrowing from Babylon but, impressed by the similarity of the terms, think that the sabbath came to Israel through the Canaanites (ibid., 478). There is also a view that the sabbath has a Kenite origin. The Kenites were smiths who exploited the ancient mines of Sinai: for them the prohibition against kindling fire on the sabbath (Ex.35.3) marked the interruption of their ordinary work (376).

However, none of the theories I have just mentioned has provided adequate arguments (Caquot 1960, 3), and in a general way the sabbath can be explained by an almost universal custom which consists in observing rest days and festivals recurring at regular intervals (de Vaux 1961, 480; Andreasen 1971). At all events, whatever may have been the origin of the sabbath, the Israelites developed it and observed it rigorously (Van Leeuwen 1953, 68). It originally had a religious value, a special sense which made it a specifically Israelite institution (de Vaux 1961, 480; Hallo 1977, 1-18).

In Genesis the sabbath, which has not yet been given its name, is simply the seventh day (Cazelles 1946, 69), which evokes the completion of creation. We should note that when the seventh day, the sabbath, is mentioned, it is generally added that God rested on it. We rediscover this notion of rest in the Bible, but later (Eisenberg 1978, 169). To begin with, it is simply said that 'on the seventh day God finished his work which he had done, and he rested on the seventh day from all the work that he had done' (Gen.2.2). The primary meaning of the word sabbath is cessation (ibid., 174). God has to limit his work. He has shown his power not by giving himself free rein but by limiting his power. Here the Bible teaches us that all potential power needs a brake if it is to constitute authentic power (173).

Before the settlement, as emerges from Num.12.15, the rhythm of seven days was still connected with a cessation of activity, pauses on the people's journey (Cazelles 1977, 4). The earliest references to the sabbath that we find in the Old Testament (Andreasen 1974, 457) show us that to their great astonishment the Israelites found a double quantity of food on the sixth day, but as there was no manna on the seventh day, they ate on that day what they had put aside the day before (Ex.16.4-35). In this way they discovered the mystery of the seventh day, the mystery of the day of rest dedicated to the Lord (Lohfink 1976, 404).

In the old Covenant Code, marked by the process of settlement, the rest on the seventh day is not yet festive (Cazelles 1977, 4), but we find there the appearance of social considerations which do not yet exist in the verses to which I have just referred (Ex.16.4-35). That could be explained by the fact that after the settlement the relationships of equality from before the conquest faded out, and more and more Israelites lost their freedom. So that they had some right to free time, to rest, a special regulation was needed (Andreasen 461). The Covenant Code requires (Kraus 1966, 80) that after six days of work man shall rest so that his ox and ass can rest and the son of his female slave and the sojourner can get their breath back (Ex.23.12). In the ritual decalogue (Ex.34.11-26), which already bears the stamp of agricultural civilization (it contains a number of ritual prescriptions about the festivals of the harvest and the grape harvest, cf. Cazelles 1957, 503), no reason is given for the rest on the seventh day, but it is immediately followed by rest 'at ploughing time and at harvest' (Ex.24.21) and, given its context, one can see here the introduction to the festive rest of the following verses ('You shall celebrate a feast of weeks... and the feast of the harvest...', Ex.34.22: id., 1977, 4).

In the Decalogue, as in Ex.16.23, the sabbath is named, and the rest on the seventh day is festive: 'Remember the sabbath day, to keep it holy. Six days you shall labour, and do all your work; but the seventh day is a sabbath to the Lord your God; in it you shall not do any work, you, or your son, or your daughter, your manservant, or your maidservant, or your cattle, or the sojourner who is within your gates. For in six days the Lord made heaven and earth, the sea, and all that is in them, and rested the seventh day; therefore the Lord blessed the sabbath day and hallowed it' (Ex.20.8-10).

Here as elsewhere, Deuteronomy, which seeks to reinforce the moral aspect of the Hebrew laws (Weinfeld 1973, 243), takes an important step forward in a humanitarian direction in relationship to the other commandments. Whereas the first version of the Decalogue (Kessler 1977, 6) associates the sabbath with the creation of the world, the second, that of Deuteronomy, connects it with the exodus from Egypt: 'You shall remember that you were a servant in the land of Egypt, and the Lord your God brought you out thence with a mighty hand and an outstretched arm; therefore the Lord your God commanded you to keep the sabbath day' (Deut.5.15). This historical motivation of the sabbath seems meant to reaffirm the social implications of the festival (Andreasen 1974, 292). And perhaps even more important here in humanitarian terms is a formula that we do not find earlier, the addition (ibid., 285), 'that your manservant and your maidservant may rest as well as you' (Deut.5.14).

The passages I have just cited seem to justify the judgment of those who declare that 'the sabbath hallows the victory of the spiritual over the temporal' (Munk 1947, 129), that 'the liberation of all men from all hierarchy and all domination, even if only for one day a week, was one of the most revolutionary ideas in the Bible' (Eisenberg 1978, 188). We should note that this kind of equality, between master and servant, already appears in texts relating to the reign of Gudea, prince of Lagash, in the third millennium (Andreasen 1974, 461). However, there they seem to be limited to commandments which remain in the sphere of theory, without any great effect on real life.

As we have just seen, even animals may rest on the sabbath day, and here the Bible gives an extremely topical lesson since, despite the significant progress achieved, above all in recent times, in our attitude towards nature, the right of animals to rest, to humane treatment, has still to be introduced and established in a satisfactory way in much of the world.

The aspects of the sabbath which I have stressed are particularly important for us, but they do not give a complete idea of the spirit in which this time of rest is to be spent (Delahoutre 1977, 22). The sabbath, which has many meanings (Weil 1975, 13), is not solely aimed at freeing human beings from work and external oppression. It also seeks to free them from themselves (Andreasen 1973, 297) in their innermost being, and in this respect it can also play a vital role in the present-day world.

Modern man is moved by the unbridled pursuit of profit, a quest for material advantage and constant progress. To restrain this disastrous course, it is necessary to follow the divine example put before us by the Bible; in order not to succumb to temptations of unlimited growth, not to allow oneself to be entirely taken over by material things, human beings, like God, must know how to say 'Enough is enough' (Eisenberg 1978, 173), since the world may well be destroyed if such growth takes on excessive proportions (Safran 1977, 138). Judaism in principle favours technical progress, but 'to the degree that human beings make use of it for their development rather than being enslaved by it' (Friedmann 1975, 87). The sabbath is the day on which we learn the art of leaving technological civilization behind and 'attaining a degree of independence from it' (Heschel 1957, 129f.).

In the biblical perspective work is not an end in itself. The sabbath was not created with a view to the six days, but the six days of the week are focussed on the sabbath (ibid., 113). The sabbath rest must be creative leisure (Eisenberg 1978, 173), be caught up into a festival (Lohfink 1976, 407). The Jew who really respects the sabbath does not limit himself to simple rest. In its negative form ('freedom from'), freedom from work must be displaced by its positive side ('freedom by': cf. Negreti 1973, 289; Hansel 1975, 34). By ceasing to be the servant of 'external and internal pharaohs', the faithful give themselves to the service of God and consequently of humanity (Safran 1977, 138).

Rest for humanity is matched by rest for the earth (Munk 1947, 127). In the Bible there is a deliberate parallelism between these two phenomena (Cazelles 1946, 92). The verses about rest on the seventh day of the week (Ex.20.8-10; Ex.23.12; Deut.5.13-14) have analogies with the verse on the law that the slave must be freed after six years (Ex.21.2) and with the law about the remission of debts in the seventh year (Deut.15.1), but above all with the regulations relating to the sabbatical year (Ex.23.11; Lev.25.3). The sabbath is the seventh day of the week, just as the year from which the master does not profit is the seventh year, the sabbatical year. It is a matter of limiting the profit that man can make not only from men and animals, but also from the earth (ibid., 96).

As for Ex.23.11, which has already been discussed in connection with measures to favour the poor, some scholars (Baentsch, Beer, Causse, Jepsen) claim that here we have a rule for a fallow year. We find this term in the Revised Standard Version and many other modern translations of the Old Testament. However, when we remember the great social inconveniences which this measure posed, and when we study the vocabulary, it is evident that the land could not have been left fallow. It was cultivated, but once the harvest was reaped, it was not taken in; the corn was left spread on the ground to be there for those who needed it (92). Note that according to N.P.Lemche (1976, 43), it is improbable that this measure was applied in all Israel at the same time; it is more probable that each farmer adopted the measure at regular intervals in rotation.

While in the case that we have just considered we have a periodical abandonment of the harvest for the poor, the Holiness Code understood this old custom differently: as an expression of the intuition that the earth needs rest, to recoup its strength (Munk 1967, 127), the sabbatical year brought the earth itself into harmony with the great rhythm of work and rest which governs human life in the framework of the week. These periods of voluntary rest allow men to express to God their submission to him in trust and remind them that they are not machines for producing things. 'When you come into the land which I give you, the land shall keep a sabbath to the Lord. Six years you shall sow your field, and six years you shall prune your vineyard, and gather in its fruits; but in the seventh year there shall be a sabbath of solemn rest for the land, a sabbath to the Lord; you shall not sow your field or prune your vineyard. What grows of itself in your harvest you shall not reap, and the grapes of your undressed vine you shall not gather; it shall be a year of solemn rest for the land. The sabbath of the land shall provide food for you, for yourself and for your male and female slaves and for your hired servant and the sojourner who lives with you; for your cattle also and for the beasts that are in your hand all its yield shall be for food' (Lev.25.2-7).

The text that I have just quoted does not indicate clearly whether all the land must lie fallow in the seventh year (cereal crops and vines are only cited as an example) or whether only the harvest and grape harvest are prohibited and other cultivation is allowed. Nor can we see clearly whether the prohibition against harvesting and gathering in grapes is absolute or relates only to the way it is done: there is no harvest organized by the owner, but each person, including the owner, can use what has grown of its own accord (ibid., 247).

(ix) The year of jubilee

The rules about the sabbatical year are immediately followed in Leviticus by the rule about the jubilee (from the Hebrew *yobel*). In order to restrict the creation of *latifundia*, to prevent the concentration of rural properties, measures were adopted and laws promulgated in Mesopotamia and in Egypt which, although in one way very restrained, can be considered to be the antecedents of the Israelite jubilee (North 1954, 46). The hypothesis put forward by Shifman (1975, 94-100), that there are also the beginnings of the jubilee in Ugarit, seems improbable to Milano (1977, 24), who seeks to refute it. But when we come to the *Sitz im Leben* of the Israelite jubilee, a beginning is not easy to establish. At all events, by analogy with other Old Testament laws, the jubilee is not the work of a sole author, but an amalgam of different economic and seasonal practices which, according to North (1954, 212), will have been remodelled by the relevant authorities in the twelfth century, at the time of the settlement. Some scholars see this law as no more than a 'theological construction from the time of the exile'. Others regard it as a supplement to the legislation on the freeing of Hebrew slaves. In practice it was destined to give those who had been freed the chance of an autonomous existence; since it was not possible to think of restoring their properties to them every seven years, the rhythm of fifty years was adopted (Cazelles 1958, 115). This was a sabbath of sabbaths (Menes 1928, 39), so to speak, a super sabbatical year (North 1954, 129). While the sabbatical year involved occasional *ad hoc* measures, the authors of the jubilee noted that to achieve their aims they had to resort to radical transformations of the situation created by an unfair distribution of property (ibid., 187).

The questions of rest, of help for the poor, of emancipation, have already been touched on in other laws; the distinctive feature of the jubilee remains the restoration of property, a meaasure which we do not find anywhere else in the Old Testament (158). Not only will the earth rest ('A jubilee shall that fiftieth year be to you; in it you shall neither sow, nor reap what grows of itself, nor gather the grapes from the undressed vines... you shall eat what it yields out of the field', Lev.25.11f.), but the land given by Yahweh cannot be sold in perpetuity; it can only be leased temporarily (Causse 1922, 78), since what belongs to the Lord cannot be alienated, at least definitively: 'The land shall not be sold in perpetuity, for the land is mine; for you are strangers and sojourners with me. And in all the country you possess, you shall grant a redemption of the land' (Lev.25.23f.). 'In this year of jubilee, each of you shall return to his property' (Lev.25.13).

It is not certain that the law of jubilee was ever applied in Israel, but it has a twofold objective: the freedom acquired at the exodus from Egypt must be rediscovered by all the children of Israel and the property received in common on the entry into Canaan cannot be alienated for ever (ibid., 247).

Conclusion

The texts and works that I have used have shown the spread of a need for justice over the different regions of the ancient Near East from the end of the third millennium onwards. In Mesopotamia and Egypt, Canaan and Israel, we find a great many common elements in this respect. The Hebrew idea of justice can be compared to Egyptian Maat, and the biblical word-pair *mishpat-tsedeq* has distant antecedents in Babylonia and among the Western Semites. In the earliest literary and religious texts from Mesopotamia there is a distinction between the good and the bad judge and praise for the one who brings justice and protects the weak.

These tendencies also appear in the legislative texts drawing on a common Mesopotamian stock. Urukagina, the prince-pontiff of Lagash, who is considered the first social reformer in history, promulgated a series of measures aimed at protecting the poor from abuses of power and the exactions practised by the great. Something similar appears to an even greater degree in the reforms of Gudea and in the codes of Ur-Nammu, Lipit-Ishtar, Eshnunna and above all Hammurabi.

However, we must not forget that the efforts of these sovereigns tend above all to reinforce their empires and their personal power. They resorted to tried means: they used force not only to maintain order and peace, but in order to rally the masses to themselves (Sollberger 1973, 36); they sought to appear as the defenders of justice, the protectors of small folk, and for that they used almost stereotyped declarations which we find in the prologues of Mesopotamian codes (Limet 1973, 82).

Biblical law emerged in the context of a broad legal corpus which embraced the various regions of the ancient Near East. The discoveries from the beginning of the century on enabled scholars to note striking similarities of form and content between the laws of the Torah and the Mesopotamian laws. The pan-Babylonian school (headed by Winckler, Delitzsch and A. Jeremias) even thought that it could claim the complete dependence of the former on the latter. The discovery of new texts and the use of more rigorous comparative methods have led to the abandonment of this simplistic theory and have allowed more sophisticated solutions to be developed (Prevost 1976, 353).

Cuneiform laws played a very important role in the first stages of Israelite law, but the latter seems to be distinguished by an ethical side (Cazelles 1969, 197ff.) which appeared in much more attenuated form in the Babylonian, Assyrian and Hittite laws or even was lacking altogether.[1]

Since the struggle against idolatry was one of the main objectives of the Old Testament, Israelite legislation attached extremely severe penalties to idolatry, but the sanctions against other crimes derived from a more humanitarian spirit than that which prevailed in other oriental codes (de Vaux 1961, 158f.). Whereas for example the Code of Hammurabi punished with the death penalty any assistance given to a runaway slave, Deuteronomy forbids the handing over of a slave who has escaped his master and seeks refuge.

On the other hand we should recall that whereas the Babylonians above all stress the inviolable aspect of property, the Hebrews attach more importance to respect for human and even animal life (Kitchen 1966, 148) – which we do not find elsewhere and which can only be found rarely today. Moreover, the biblical laws do not contain the numerous references to social stratification which characterize the Laws of Eshnunna and above all the Code of Hammurabi (Larue 1969, 35). Another striking feature of the Israelite laws is that they emanate from God and not from the sovereign, that they are addressed far less to official authorities, judges, than to the people taken collectively or individually (Gemser 1953, 62).

The protection of those at the greatest disadvantage was as much the aim of Mesopotamian legislation as it was of Israelite; however, it is only in the latter that the most unprotected are commended as objects for care, not only out of goodness and charity, but also out of a feeling of humility which is explained by the history of the Jewish people. Israel was to remember that it, too, had been a stranger in Egypt and that there was no better way to keep this memory alive than not to oppress the stranger. This way of presenting the laws means that no blind obedience was called for but one marked by discernment, a conscious, reasoned obedience (Boecker 1976, 178). With this appeal to common sense, to the conscience of the people, these laws show their truly democratic nature (Gemser 1953, 63).

In Egypt, where the Pharaoh was the source and the master of the law (Speiser 1967, 193), almost nothing has been found so far which can compare with the Mesopotamian codes. However, Egypt has bequeathed to us a large number of writings, and as the stay of the Hebrews in the Nile valley lasted for centuries, it is not surprising that some of the statements of the prophets, some psalms and some proverbs show analogies with the writing of Egyptian wise men, hymns and stories.

The *Instructions to Merikare*, which form a mixture of political considerations and exhortations to justice, already herald what we find in the Hebrew prophets (Peet 1931, 109). There, too, as in Amos (5.22-24), it is said that God will not be deceived by any sacrifice: he prefers the virtues of the honest man to the 'ox of the sinner' (Lichtheim 1976, II, 106; Cazelles 1976, 12).

There are striking and indubitable parallels between the *Wisdom of Amenemope* and Prov.22.17-24.22, in each of which there are commands not to rob the wretched, not to remove landmarks from the edges of fields, not to falsify balances.

Among the faults which the dead person claims not to have committed and which feature in the *Book of the Dead*, called the Bible of the ancient Egyptians, the most significant relate to injustice, to the exploitation of the slave and the poor man. However, we should not forget that the *Book of the Dead* accompanying the mummy was less a code for living than a contribution to the magic of the rites. As for Maat, one of the main legacies of ancient Egypt, it corresponded to a number of notions the sense of which changed over the ages and with circumstances but which as a whole related more to the concept of order than that of justice.

There were important differences in the view of the world held in Mesopotamia and in Egypt, but as long as the Near East kept its cultural coherence, from the middle of the fourth millennium to the middle of the first, both areas seemed to be aware of the close ties which bound them to nature (Frankfort 1948, 364). In these countries people seemed not only dominated by but also supported by the great cyclical movements of nature: if at particularly painful moments they felt oppressed by insoluble contradictions, on the whole their involvement in nature had a soothing (ibid., 371), if not anaesthetic, effect on them. For example, the fertile inundations of the Nile which rarely failed and which guaranteed a minimum of prosperity gave birth to a concept of the eternal return which was represented by a desire for order and harmony and favoured the maintaining of the *status quo*.

Obviously reality was not always so simple, but it is a fact that in the Egyptian wisdom literature which occupies such an important place in the cultural life of the country, we find again the opposition between the passionate man and the peaceful silent man, and it is the latter who is regarded as being on the right road becaue he never disturbs the *status quo*. The other is judged severely because by his impetuous interventions he destroys the harmonious integration of the established order (Wright 1950, 44).

The popular uprising which marks the beginnings of the First Intermediate Period in Egypt and which is considered to be the first social revolution in antiquity lasted for a relatively short time and had relatively limited effects. The famous *Story of the Man from the Oasis*, the spirit of which is akin to the social revolt, and which has been compared to the recriminations of the great Israelite prophets, chiefly Amos, had what seems to have been an ephemeral success.

A similar situation also seems to have prevailed in Mesopotamia: in its history and literature we find many complaints and lamentations. However, the inhabitants of this region seem to have accepted their condition with fatalism as being part of the immutable ordering of things (Bottéro 1961, 163).

At the time of its settlement in Palestine in the thirteenth century, Israel was in many respects at an early stage in comparison with developments among its powerful neighbours (Saggs 1978, 183), without any political institutions and with virtually no social institutions. Having arrived in a country which occupied a central position among the civilizations of the Near East, subject to foreign influences, to powerful military, political and social pressures, the newcomers were deeply impressed and stimulated by certain aspects of life which they found there. However, they only adopted the modes of existence and thought of others to a very limited degree. With a 'morality related to the perfection of its monotheism' (Cazelles 1946, 18), and having undergone misfortunes in the first stages of its history which affected its very existence, Israel proved more intransigent than others towards evil and more fervent about good (Saggs 1978, 185). Given the survival of the practices of primitive Semitism, and given the experience of slavery in Egypt, the Israelites refused to recreate the kind of autocratic, tyrannical society to which they had been subjected. Contrary to long-established societies, the first Israelites had less respect for tradition; they rejected more easily the age-old formulae and proved more disposed to accept solutions which matched the aspirations of societies in the course of change (ibid., 187).

For the prophets who drew on the past but had their eyes fixed on the future, even the verdicts of Yahweh were not immutable. In their view there was no order established once for all, no institution which deserved to be preserved for its own sake, since the value of each depended on its capacity for being adapted to human needs.

This dynamic attitude also appeared in the Torah, where the legal and social problems are treated as changes of life (Cazelles 1980, 9); among other things that is represented by the increasing humanization of justice as one moves from the Covenant Code to the Deuteronomic Code and the Holiness Code.

The opposition and contrast between the static approach on the one hand and the dynamic approach on the other are further reinforced by the difference in ideas about God held by the societies in question. The Egyptians and Mesopotamians (according to Mowinckel, Noth, Vriezen and others) regarded the divine as being immanent in nature. The Israelites rediscovered God in history. According to Jacob, Yahweh is the God of history and that is his surest mode of revelation (Albrektson 1967, 11ff.). It was not cosmic phenomena but history itself that became a manifestation of the dynamic will of God. Man ceased to be, as in Mesopotamia, a simple servant of God or, as in Egypt, set in a predetermined position in a static universe. During the exodus, and during the rough but uplifting solitude of the desert, Yahweh transcended the phenomena of nature, and instead of contemplating him, people listened to his voice and followed his orders (Frankfort 1948, 370f.).

This totalitarian and segregated presentation of historical events as divine notions which is supposed to appear only in the Bible does not seem to correspond entirely to what we find in Amos (9.7; cf. Saggs 1978, 204) and has provoked criticism from some scholars (Hempel, Lindblom, Barr, etc.; cf. Albrektson 1967, 14). In fact it seems that outside Israel, other societies in the Near East considered their gods to be capable of controlling not only nature but also history (Paul 1971, 1171). However, Yahweh stood apart from nature in a different way from the gods of the people of Mesopotamia (Saggs 1978, 88), of whom none formulated an overall view of the universe in which history was entirely ruled by the will of a sole God according to a single global plan (Paul 1971, 1171). The God of the Yahwist has a much stronger personality than that of the other Near Eastern gods (Cazelles 1976, 79f.). The God with whom the people of Israel make a covenant is regarded as the source and foundation of justice and that is his first form of action (Gen.18.25; Ps.9.5; cf. Schwarzschild 1971, 476).

God is not only 'great, mighty and terrible', he is 'impartial and incorruptible' (Deut.10.17).

The monotheistic principle as it is formulated in the Old Testament signifies implicitly that the law of justice, like the laws of physics, must prevail without any discrimination. The Torah does not allow taking advantage of the weak or favouring the mighty (Lev.19.15); its command is not only not to exploit the stranger, but to love him as oneself (Lev.19.33-34).

However, according to one of the most significant affirmations in Judaism, God is not the only one to rule the universe and history; man also has power over the world and 'the destiny of humanity is a game which two play' (Neher 1977, 129). According to H.W.Wolff (1960, 224), the continuity of history is the act neither of an arbitrary God nor of the simple will of man, but represents the continuity of an inviolable covenant. Relations with the divine, writes Emmanuel Levinas (1963, 36), pass through relations among human beings and coincide with social justice: that is the whole spirit of the Jewish Bible.

Assuming the common experience of the group, moved by a keen sense of collective responsibility, the prophets stress the obligation not only to believe but to act. Contrary to Egyptian eschatology, where there is a cycle, an implacable succession of misery and happiness, the prophets teach the people that their fate depends above all on their own behaviour. They take the side not of theoretical formulation but of creative effort to introduce the inalienable rights of the human individual into social practice (Neher 1977, 140).

It is probably largely thanks to this dynamism that the quest for social justice, which elsewhere came sharply to a halt (Mesopotamia, cf. Jacobsen 1976, 21f.) or suffered a long eclipse (Egypt), was to be pursued by the people of the Bible almost without interruption down to our own day.

ABBREVIATIONS

AAWLMG	Abhandlungen der Akademie der Wissenschaften und der Literatur in Mainz – Geistes- und sozialwissenschaftliche Klasse
AES	Archives européennes de sociologie
AHDO	Archives d'histoire du droit oriental
AJS	American Journal of Sociology
AJSL	American Journal of Semitic Languages and Literatures
AnBib	Analecta biblica
ANET	Ancient Near Eastern Texts relating to the Old Testament
ANET.S	Ancient Near Eastern Texts relating to the Old Testament.Supplement
AnOr	Analecta orientalia
APD	Archives de philosophie du droit
ArOr	Archiv orientalni
ASoc	Annales/Année Sociologique(s)
ASRel	Archives de sociologie des religions
AStE	Annuario di studi ebraici
ASTI	Annual of the Swedish Theological Institute
ATA	Alttestamentliche Abhandlungen
AUSS	Andrews University Seminary Studies
AzTh	Arbeiten zur Theologie
BA	Biblical Archaeologist
BASOR	Bulletin of the American Schools of Oriental Research
BBB	Bonner Biblische Beiträge
BeO	Bibbia e oriente
BFCT	Beiträge zur Förderung christliche Theologie
BEvTh	Beihefte zur Evangelischen Theologie
BHH	Biblisch-historisches Handwörterbuch
Bib	Biblica
BIFAO	Bulletin de l'institut français d'archéologie orientale
Bijdr	Bijdragen. Tijdschrift voor philosophie en theologie
BJRL	Bulletin of the John Rylands Library
BJS	British Journal of Sociology

BSFE	*Bulletin (trimestriel) de la société française d'égyptologie*
BSHPF	*Bulletin de la société de l'histoire du protestantisme français*
BTB	*Bulletin de théologie biblique*
BTW	*Bibeltheologisches Wörterbuch*
BTS	*Bible et Terre sainte*
BZAW	Beihefte zur Zeitschrift für die alttestamentliche Wissenschaft
BZSF	Biblische Zeit- und Streitfragen zur Aufklärung der Gebildeten
CBQ	*Catholic Biblical Quarterly*
CEg	*Chronique d'Egypte*
CRHPR	Cahiers de la revue d'histoire et de philosophie religieuses
CSoc	Christianisme social
CSSH	Comparative Studies in Society and History
DB (H)	*Dictionary of the Bible*, ed. J. Hastings
DB (V)	*Dictionnaire de la Bible*, ed. F. Vigouroux
DB.S	*Dictionnaire de la Bible. Supplément*
Diog	*Diogenes*
DLZ	*Deutsche Literaturzeitung*
EB	*Encyclopaedia Britannica*
EJ	*Encyclopaedia Judaica*
ETL	*Ephemerides theologicae Lovanienses*
ETR	Etudes théologiques et religieuses
EvE	Evangelische Ethik
Evid	Evidences
EvTh	*Evangelische Theologie*
FuF	Forschungen und Fortschritte
GöM	Göttinger Miszellen
GOTR	*Greek Orthodox Theological Review*
HDSW	Handwörterbuch der Sozialwissenschaften
HT	*History and Theory*
HTR	*Harvard Theological Review*
HUCA	*Hebrew Union College Annual*
IDB	*Interpreter's Dictionary of the Bible*
IJPR	*International Journal for the Philosophy of Religion*
Int	*Interpretation*
ITQ	*Irish Theological Quarterly*
JAOS	*Journal of the American Oriental Society*
JAOS.S	*Journal of the American Oriental Society. Supplement*

JBL	*Journal of Biblical Literature*
JCS	*Journal of Cuneiform Studies*
Jdm	*Judaism*
JDT	*Jahrbücher für deutsche Theologie*
JEA	*Journal of Egyptian Archaeology*
JE	*Jewish Encyclopaedia*
JESHO	*Journal of (the) Economic and social History of the Orient*
JJS	*Journal of Jewish Studies*
JJSoc	*Journal of Jewish Sociology*
JNES	*Journal of Near Eastern Stuies*
JQR	*Jewish Quarterly Review*
JSocS	*Jewish Social Studies*
JTS	*Journal of Theological Studies*
Jud	*Judaica*
KuD	*Kerygma und Dogma*
Log	*Logos*
MDOG	Mitteilung der deutschen Orientgesellschaft
MGJW	*Monatschrift für Geschichte und Wissenschaft des Judentums*
NZST	*Neue Zeitschrift für systematische Theologie*
OBL	Orientalia et biblica Lovaniensia
Or	*Orientalia*
OrAnt	*Oriens Antiquus*
OTS	*Oudtestamentische Studiën*
PAAJR	*Proceedings of the American Academy for Jewish Research*
PEQ	*Palestine Exploration Quarterly*
RA	*Revue d'assyriologie et d'archéologie orientale*
RB	*Revue biblique*
RdE	*Revue d'égyptologie*
REJ	*Revue des études juives*
RHDF	*Revue historique de droit français et étranger*
RIDA	*Revue internationale des droits de l'antiquité*
RivBib	*Rivista biblica*
RSO	*Rivista degli studi orientali*
RSR	*Recherches de science religieuse*
RThom	*Revue thomiste*
RTP	*Revue de théologie et de philosophie*
RTK	*Roczniki teologiczno-kanoniczne*
RTPE	*Receuil de travaux relatifs à la philologie et à*

	l'archéologie égyptiennes et assyriennes
Saec	*Saeculum*
SAK	Studien zur altägyptischen Kultur
SBFLA	Studii biblici Franciscani liber annuus
ScEs	*Science et esprit*
ScrHie	Scripta Hierosolymitana
SDIO	Studia et documenta ad iura orientis
Sem	*Semitica*
SJT	*Scottish Journal of Theology*
Spec	*Speculum*
SR	*Studies in Religion*
StZ	*Stimmen der Zeit*
SVT	Supplements to Vetus Testamentum
TGUOS	*Transactions of the Glasgow University Oriental Society*
TLZ	*Theologische Literaturzeitung*
ThR	*Theologische Rundschau*
ThViat	*Theologia viatorum*
UF	Ugarit-Forschungen
UUÅ	Uppsala universitets årsschrift
VDI	Vestnik drewnej istorii
VF	Verkündigung und Forschung
VT	Vetus Testamentum
WMANT	Wissenschaftliche Monographien zum Alten und Neuen Testament
YLBI	*Yearbook. Leo Baeck Institute*
ZA	*Zeitschrift für Assyriologie*
ZAW	*Zeitschrift für die alttestamentliche Wissenschaft*
ZÄS	*Zeitschrift für ägyptische Sprache und Altertumskunde*
ZDPV	*Zeitschrift des Deutschen Palästina-Vereins*
ZEE	*Zeitschrift für evangelische Ethik*
ZLTK	*Zeitschrift für die (gesamte) lutherische Theologie und Kirche*

NOTES

Introduction

1. Léon Epsztein, *L'Economie et la morale aux débuts du capitalisme industriel en France et en Grande-Bretagne*, Paris 1966.

1. The Mesopotamian Laws

1. Cf. also L.Cardellini, *Die biblischen 'Sklaven'-Gesetze im Lichte des keilschriftlichen Sklavenrechts*, BBB 55, 1981. I was only made aware of this important doctoral thesis after completing the present book.

2. In fact the Code of Hammurabi is not just based on the *lex talionis*, since as we shall see it also provides for legal compromises.

2. Egyptian Maat

1. Unfortunately, Egyptian sources themselves are silent on the Code of Boccharis, which is known to us only through Diodore, who wrote in the first century of our era. Boccharis is said to have legislated on contracts and to have limited the accumulation of interest, thus protecting the debtor. There would be a certain similarity here to what we find in the Pentateuch, but in the latter the ends are more human and less poetic than in Boccharis (Cazelles 1946, 164).

2. G.Mattha and G.R.Hugues, *The Demotic Legal Code of Hermopolis West*, Cairo 1975. This demotic code is a document of prime importance for our knowledge of Egyptian law on the eve of the Macedonian conquest; it contains a series of decrees on loans, on estate, on relations between neighbours, registering documents, succession following on death, and so on (cf Melèze-Mordrezejewski 1977, 469).

3. Note that according to the author of a work which has just appeared and which came to my notice after writing this chapter 'the dispositions decreed by Horemheb would fit into a legislation which already existed and was relatively complex' (J.-M.Kruchten, *Le Décret d'Horemheb*, Brussels 1981, 225).

4. We should note here that contrary to what was believed until recently, what we see engraved on the tomb of Rekhmire, the forty *sheshemu* laid out before the vizier, are in no way the scrolls of parchment or leather on which the laws will have been written but kinds of whips, probably the insignia of judicial power (cf. Menu 1978, 478; Posener 1977, 63-6).

5. According to some writers the construction of the pyramids represents a policy of full employment.

6. This period (2270-2240) does not seem to coincide with the end of the reign of Pepi II, a period to which, as we have just seen, the revolution is dated by other historians. This shift in time would in fact call for an explanation, but it would not take us any further, and as far as this book is concerned it does not seem indispensable.

7. We should recall that this same qualification was attributed to Urukagina; the merits of these two figures cannot easily be compared, but the *ensi* of Lagash certainly seems to have the advantage of coming at least a century earlier, since his reign is to be put in the twenty-fourth century at the latest.

8. This work is about King Snefru, founder of the Fourth Dynasty, but in fact the First Intermediate Period is the only one to offer striking analogies with the picture drawn by Neferti.

9. Note, however, that according to C.Desroches-Noblecourt (1976, 15) it must not be forgotten that the experience of Akhenaten 'must have served to influence the great reforms of Rameses and to shape his behaviour'.

10. U.Bouriant, 'malheureux'; J.H.Breasted, 'poor man'; K.H.Pflüger, 'commoner'; Van de Walle, 'bourgeois'; W.Helck, 'Freier', which does not exactly mean poor but at any rate someone very low in the social hierarchy; G.Roeder, 'Bürger'; R.Hari, 'homme libre', the meaning of which is taken from Thompson 1940, 76ff. (cf.Hari 1964, 312). According to B.Menu, the *nmh* is an individual not (yet) meshed into the gearwheels of lay or religious administration.

11. But note that according to Theodorides 1975, 87, the history of Egypt does not take place entirely in a vacuum.

3. *Justice in the Old Testament as seen by Old Testament Scholars*

1. Cremer 1893, 272-80; Skinner 1902, 272-81; Hirsch 1905, 219-24; Descamps 1949, 1417-60; Koch 1962, 548; Nötscher 1962, 453-61; Achtemeier 1962, 80-5; Schwarzschild 1971, 476-7; Jacobs 1971, 180-4.

2. Ortloph 1860, 401-26; Kautzsch 1881; Wildeboer 1902, 167-9; Cramer 1907, 79-99; Fahlgren 1932; Rosenthal 1950-1951, 411-30; Koch 1953; Mach 1957; Michel 1964; Justesen 1964, 53-61; Jepsen 1965, 78-89; Rosenberg 1965; Swetnam 1965, 28-40; Read 1966, 29-36; Toaff 1968-1969, 111-22; Berkovits 1969 (esp. ch.7, 'Sedeq and S'daqah'); Scullion 1971, 335-48; Whitley 1972, 469-75; Ringgren 1972, 134-42; Bianchi 1973, 306-18; id. 1974, 89-110; Crüsemann 1976, 427-50.

3. Herzberg, 1922; Van der Ploeg 1943; Thomson 1963, 74-86; Beuken 1972, 1-30; Jeremias 1972, 31-42.

4. Diestel 1860, 196-9; Ritschl 1874, 101-6; Fuchs 1927; Dünner 1963, 71ff.; Beaucamp 1969, 205ff.

5. Fahlgren 1932, 117; von Rad 1965, 370-82 ('The Righteousness of Yahweh and Israel'); Ziesler 1972 (esp. I, 'The Old Testament – The Nature of Hebrew Justice'); Crüsemann 1976, 428,432.

6. Bauer 1837, 478; Martin 1892; Baudissin 1921; Lofthouse 1939; Jacob

1958, 94ff., 'The Righteousness of God'; Eichrodt 1961, 239ff. ('The Righteousness of God'); Vella 1964.

4. The Rationalist Study of the Bible and Justice in the Old Testament from a Sociological Perspective

1. As indicated by the title of the book, according to the author there were already people before Adam and it is wrong to attribute the main sacred texts to Moses.
2. Causse 1937, 9; D.W.Caspari 1923, 7; Liebeschütz 1964, 52; Schmueli 1968, 167-247: Momigliano 1980, 315.
3. Sonmbart 1911; Oelsner 1962, 183-212; Liebeschütz 1964, 46; Baumgarten 1964; Andreski 1969, 1-18; Liebeschütz 1967, 328.
4. Kübel 1870; Buhl 1899; Walter 1900; Kleinert 1905; Wiener 1909; Hermann 1916, 1-28: Kellermann 1917; Eberharter 1924; Balscheit and Eichrodt 1944; Weinberger 1948; Donner 1963, 229-49.
5. Lods 1950 (with a preface by André Parrot which gives some biographical information about A.Lods).
6. In the meantime there appeared the interesting book by Amitai (1905), which cites Henry George and draws attention to the importance of Galandauer 1891.
7. Kimbrough 1969, 313-20 (with a complete bibliography of Causse's publications).

5. Justice in the Old Testament and the Kindred Approach of Historical Materialism

1. Pedersen 1926, I, 375. But note that for example N.K.Gottwald stresses that the main conflict of interest in Near Eastern society at the time when Israel emerged was not between sedentarism and nomadism, agriculture and pastoralism, but between the city and the country (1977, 189; cf. also 1979).
2. It is interesting to cite here Löw 1890 (which discusses the concern for animals attested in Judaism since earliest times).

6. Nomadism and Social Justice

1. Albright 1953, 102; de Vaux, 1949: Noth 1960, 69; Weippert 1974, 279; Delcor 1973, 322.
2. Herren 1805, I, 210; Contenau 1950, 990; Leemans 1950, 125; Kupper 1957, 15.

7. Prophecy and Social Justice

1. Some bibliographical studies which give an indication of this are Fohrer 1962; 1975; Scharbert 1968; Ramlot 1968, especially VII 'Les Prophètes, les réalités sociales et le monde', 1099f.; Schmidt 1972; Jacob 1973; Limburg 1978.

2. It is hardly completely by chance that Adam Müller, the traditionalist and pillar of economic and political romanticism, was keenly interested in the history of ancient Israel and that in *Die Elemente der Staatskunst* (1809) he made an apologia for Moses (cited by Weinberger 1948, 78, 86f.).

3. Wolff 1971, 62. Note that according to some scholars it now seems that Amos 'was something like an agricultural administrator of king Hoshea, which would better explain his knowledge of the politics of the time, the traditions of the country and the vigour of his style' (Cazelles 1973, 14; cf. Vesco 1980, 483).

8. *The Social Laws of the Pentateuch*

1. De Vaux 1961, 150. To go deeper into the question it is important to take account of the review by Langlamet (1978, 277-300) of the recent works of Veijola 1977 and Birch 1976. There is also interesting information in Milgrom 1978 and Crüsemann 1978, esp. 198,217, who seeks to explain the serious criticism of the kings as a result of a whole series of economic and social factors.

2. Weinfeld 1972, 294-7; Malfroy 1965, 49-65; Schmid 1966, 200; Carmichael 1974, 18. In spite of its promising title, Gaspar 1947 is not of interest for the present study.

3. The offering of a tenth of the fruits of the earth, herds, or any other source of revenue.

4. von Rad 1966, 14. According to Lipinski 1976, 120-3, the legislator envisages the case of the purchase of a person who is free.

5. Klingenberg 1977, 23. This is the subject of an article by Weingort-Boczko (1979a, 235-45) who in the same year also had his doctoral thesis published (Weingort-Boczko 1979b). According to Weingort, despite its undoubted qualities, Klingenberg's work is open to certain criticisms. But as Weingort is chiefly interested in a later period than ours, his analyses are not of major importance for this study.

Conclusion

1. Bracker 1962, 174, cited by Boecker 1976, 11, who is more cautious on the question; McNeill and Sedlar 1968, 140.

BIBLIOGRAPHY

Mesopotamia

1. Legal, literary and religious texts

Ancient Near Eastern Texts Relating to the Old Testament, ed.J.B.Pritchard, Princeton 1950, Supplement 1969 (= *ANET*, *ANET.S*)

Barton, G.A. (1918), *Miscellaneous Babylonian Inscriptions*, New Haven

Cardascia, G. (1969), *Les Lois assyriennes*, Paris

Cruveilher, P. (1938), *Commentaire du Code d'Hammourabi*, Paris

Driver, G.R., and Miles, J.C.(1952-55), *The Babylonian Laws*, two vols, Oxford

Finet, A. (1973), *Le Code de Hammurapi*, Paris

Lambert, M. (1956), 'Les "Réformes" d'Urukagina', *RA* 50, 169-84

Seux, M.J. (1976), *Hymnes et prières aux dieux de Babylonie et d'Assyrie*, Paris

Szlechter, E. (1955), 'Le Code d'Ur-Nammu', *RA* 49, 169-77

—(1957), 'Le Code de Lipit-Ishtar', *RA* 51, 57-82, 177-96

—(1978), *'Les Lois d'Eshnunna'*, *RIDA* 25, 109-219

Thureau-Dangin, F. (1905), *Les Inscriptions de Sumer et Akkad*, Paris

Yaron, R. (1969), *The Laws of Eshnunna*, Jerusalem

2. Aids to research

Boyer, G. (1938), 'Introduction bibliographique à l'histoire du droit suméro-akkadien', *AHDO* 2, 63-110

Cardascia, G. (1966), *Droits cunéiformes, Introduction bibliographique à l'histoire du droit et à l'ethnologie juridique*, Brussels

Reallexikon der Assyriologie, 1966, 'Gesetze 3', 243-97

The Assyrian Dictionary of the Oriental Institute of the University of Chicago, Chicago and Glückstadt 1956-77

3. General works and specialist studies

Artzi, P. (1964), ' "Vox populi" in the El Amarna Tablets', *RA* 58, 159-66

Bottéro, G. (1961), 'Désordre économique et annulation des dettes en Mésopotamie à l'époque paléo-babylonienne', *JESHO* 4, 113-64

Boyer, G. (1965), *Mélanges d'histoire du droit oriental*, Toulouse

Cardascia, G. (1956), 'Les Droits cunéiformes', in R.Monier, G.Cardascia and J.Imbert, *Histoire des institutions et des faits sociaux des origines à l'aube du Moyen Age*, Paris, 17-68

—(1960), 'La Transmission des sources cunéiformes', *RIDA* 7, 31-50

—(1979), 'La Place du talion das l'histoire du droit pénal à la lumière des droits du Proche-Orient ancien', in *Mélanges Jean Dauvillier*, Toulouse, 169-83

Cuq, E. (1929), *Etudes sur le droit babylonien, les lois assyriennes et les lois hittites*, Paris

Deimel, A. (1931), 'Sumerische Tempelwirtschaft zur Zeit Urukaginas und seiner Vorgänger', *AnOr* 2, 1-113

Deshayes, J. (1969), *Les Civilisations de l'Orient ancien*, Paris

Diakonoff, I.M. (1958), 'Some Remarks on the "Reforms" of Urukagina', *RA* 52, 1-15

Diamond, A.S. (1957), 'An Eye for an Eye', *Iraq* 19, 151-5

Edzard, D.O. (1957), *Die zweite Zwischenzeit Babyloniens*, Wiesbaden

Evans, G. (1958), 'Ancient Mesopotamian Assemblies', *JAOS* 78, 1-11

Falkenstein, A. (1956), *Die neusumerischen Gerichtsurkunden*, Munich

Finkelstein, J.J. (1961), 'Ammi-saduqa's Edict and the Babylonian Law Codex', *JCS* 15, 91-104

—(1970), 'On Some Recent Studies in Cuneiform Law', *JAOS* 90, 243-53

Fish, T. (1938), 'Aspects of Sumerian Civilization in the Third Dynasty of Ur', *BJRL* 22, 160-74

Frankfort, H. and H.A., Wilson, J.A., Jacobsen, T., Irvin, W.A. (1948), *The Intellectual Adventure of Ancient Man. An Essay on Speculative Thought in the Ancient Near East*, Chicago

Garelli, P. (1969), *Le Proche-Orient asiatique – Des origines aux invasions des peuples de la mer*, Paris

Garelli, P., and Nikiprowetzky, V. (1974), *Le Proche-Orient asiatique. Les empires mésopotamiens, Israël*, Paris

Hruška, B. (1974), 'Die Reformtexte Urukaginas', in *Le Palais et la royauté. XIXe rencontre assyriologique internationale 1971*, Paris, 151-61

Jacobsen, T. (1943), 'Primitive Democracy in Ancient Mesopotamia', *JNES* 2, 1943, 159-72

—(1957), 'Early Political Development in Mesopotamia', *ZA* 52, 91-140

—(1964), 'Note sur le rôle de l'opinion publique dans l'ancienne Mésopotamie', *RA* 58, 157-8

—(1976), *The Treasures of Darkness. A History of Mesopotamian Religion*, New Haven and London

Klima, J. (1967a), 'Au sujet de nouveaux textes législatifs de la Babylonie ancienne', *ArOr* 35, 121-7

—(1967b), 'Zu einigen Problemen der altmesopotamischen Gesetzgebung', *FS für Wilhelm Eiler*, Wiesbaden, 107-21

—(1972), 'La Perspective historique des lois hamourabiennes', *CRAI*, 297-317

Korošec, V. (1961), 'Le Code de Hammurabi et les droits antérieurs', *RIDA* 8, 11-27

Kramer, S.N. (1961a), *History Begins at Sumer*, London (second edition)
—(1961b), 'Sumerian Literature', in *The Bible and the Ancient Near East*, Essays in Honor of W.F.Albright, Garden City, 249-66
—(1964a), *The Sumerians: Their History, Culture and Characters*, Chicago
—(1964b), ' "Vox populi" and the Sumerian Literary Documents', *RA* 58, 148-56
Kraus, F.R. (1973), *Vom mesopotamischen Menschen der altbabylonischen Zeit und seiner Welt*, Amsterdam and London
Lambert, M. (1964), 'Le Destin d'Ur et les routes commerciales', *RSQ* 39, 89-109
Lambert, W.G. (1970), 'The Reading of the Name Uru.Ka.gi.na', *Or* 39, 41
Larue, G.A. (1969), *Babylon and the Bible*, Grand Rapids
Leemans, W.F. (1968), 'King Hammurapi as Judge', *Symbolae Iuridicae et Historicae Martino David dedicatae*, Leiden, 107-29
Limet, H. (1973), 'Réflexions sur la nature et l'efficacité d'une opposition', in *La Voix de l'opposition en Mésopotamie*, symposium organized by the Institut des Hautes Etudes de Belgique, 66-88
McNeil, W.H., and Sedlar, J.W. (eds.) (1969), *The Ancient Near East*, New York
Malamat, A. (1963), 'Kingship and Council in Israel and Sumer: A Parallel', *JNES* 22, 247-31
Moscati, S. (1955), *Histoire et civilisation des peuples sémitiques*, Paris
Oppenheim, A.L. (1954), 'The Seafaring Merchants of Ur', *JAOS* 74, 6-17
Parrot, A. (1960), *Sumer*, London
Peet, T.E. (1931), *A Comparative Study of the Literatures of Egypt, Palestine and Mesopotamia*, London
Peters, J.P. (1921), 'Notes and Suggestions on the Early Sumerian Religion and its Expression', *JAOS* 41, 131-49
Rosen, B.-L. (1977), 'Some Notes on Eshnunna Laws 20 and 21 and a Legal Reform in the Law of Hammurapi', *RA* 71, 35-8
Rosenberg, R.A. (1965), 'The God Sedeq', *HUCA* 36, 161-77
Schmökel, H., (1966), 'Zwischen Ur und Lothal: die Seehandelsroute von Altmesopotamien zur Induskultur', *FuF* 40, 143-7
Sollberger, E. (1973), 'L'Opposition au pays de Sumer et Akkad', in *La Voix de l'opposition*, 28-36
Speiser, E.A. (1954), 'Authority and Law in Mesopotamia', *JAOS* 17, 8-15
Stephens, F.J. (1955), 'Notes on Some Economic Texts of the Time of Urukagina', *RA* 49, 129-36
Szlechter, E. (1953), 'A propos du Code d'Ur-Nammu', *RA* 47, 1-10
—(1957), 'Les Anciennes Codifications en Mésopotamie', *RIDA* 4, 73-92
—(1965), 'La Loi dans la Mésopotamie ancienne', *RIDA* 12, 55-77
Wittfogel, K. (1964), *Le Despotisme oriental* (with an introduction by P.Vidal-Naquet), Paris
Woolley, L. (1950), *Ur of the Chaldees*, Toronto (second edition)

Egypt

1. Legal, literary and religious texts

Barguet, P. (1967), *Le livre des morts des anciens Egyptiens*, Paris

Barucq, A., and Daumas, F. (1980), *Hymnes et prières de l'Egypte ancienne*, Paris

Erman, A. (1927), *The Literature of the Ancient Egyptians*, London

Helck, W. (1955), 'Das Dekret des Königs Haremheb', *ZÄS* 80, 109-36

Kruchten, J.M. (1981), *Le Décret d'Horemheb*, translation, epigraphical and institutional commentary, Brussels (doctoral thesis)

Lefebvre, G. (1949), *Romans et contes égyptiens de l'époque pharaonique*, Paris

Lichtheim, M. (1976), Ancient Egyptian Literature, two vols, Los Angeles

Mattha, G., and Hugues, G.R. (1975), *The Demotic Legal Code of Hermopolis West*, Cairo

Maystre, C. (1937), *Les Déclarations d'innocence (Livre des morts, ch.125)*, Cairo

Michaeli, F. (1961), *Textes de la Bible et de l'Ancien Orient*, Neuchâtel

Peterson, S.J. (1967), 'A New Fragment of the Wisdom of Amenemope', *JEA* 52, 120-8

Pflüger, K. (1946), 'The Edict of King Haremhab', *JNES* 5, 260-8

Posener, G. (1952), 'Le Début de l'enseignement de Hardjedef', *RdE* 9, 1952, 109-20

Roeder, G. (1961), 'Der Erlass des Königs Hor-em-Hab über die Wiederherstellung der Gerechtigkeit', in *Der Ausklang der ägyptischen Religion mit Reformation. Zauberei und Jenseitsglauben*, Die ägyptische Religion in Text und Bild IV, Zurich and Stuttgart, 90-112

Simpson, W.K. (ed.) (1972), *The Literature of Ancient Egypt: An Anthology of Stories, Instructions and Poetry*, New Haven and London

Suys, E. (1935), *La sagesse d'Ani*, AnOr 11

Thomas, D.W. (ed.) (1961), *Documents from Old Testament Times*, London and New York

Van de Walle, B. (1947), 'Le décret d'Horemheb', *CEg* 43, 230-8

Zába, Z. (1956), *Les Maximes de Ptahhotep*, Prague

2. Aids to research

Annual Egyptological Bibliography, Leiden 1948-80

Dictionnaire de la civilisation égyptienne, ed. G.Posener and J.Yoyotte, Paris 1959

Mélèze-Modrzejewski, J. (1977), 'Chronique des droits de l'Antiquité: Egypte gréco-romaine et monde héllenistique', *RHDF* 55, 468-90

Menu, B. (1977/78), 'Chronique des droits de l'Antiquité: Egypte ancienne', *RHDF* 55, 1977, 233-9; 'Egypte pharaonique', *RHDF* 56, 1978, 475-84

Pirenne, J., and Theodorides, A. (1966), *Droit égyptien. Introduction bibliographique à l'histoire du droit et à l'ethnologie juridique*, Brussels

3. *General works and specialist studies*

Aldred, C. (1968), *Akhenaten. Pharaoh of Egypt*, London
—(1975) , 'Egypt: The Amarna Period and the End of the Eighteenth Dynasty', in *The Cambridge Ancient History*, ch.XIX
Allam, S. (1973), 'De la divinité dans le droit pharaonique', *BSFE* 68, 17-30
—(1978), 'Un droit pénal existait-il *stricto sensu* en Egype pharaonique?', *JEA* 64, 65-8
Anthes, R. (1952), 'Die Maat des Echnaton von Amarna', *JAOS.S* 14, 1-36
Auffret, P. (1979), *Les Deux Grands Hymnes à Aton et à Yahvé créateurs*, Ecole pratique des hautes études, V section, mémoire
Bakir, A.E. (1953), *Slavery in Pharaonic Egypt*, Cairo
Beckerath, J.von (1978), 'Nochmals die Regierungsdauer des Haremhab', *SAK* 6, 43-9
Bolkestein, H. (1939), *Wohltätigkeit und Armenpflege im vorchristlichen Altertum*, Utrecht
Bonneau, D. (1964), *La Crue du Nil*, Paris
Bouriant, U. (1885), 'La stèle de Horemheb', *RTPE* 6, 41-51
Breasted, J.H. (1906-07), *Ancient Records of Egypt*, 5 vols, Chicago
—(1912), *The Development of Religion and Thought in Ancient Egypt*
—(1933), *The Dawn of Conscience*, New York
—(1948), *A History of Egypt from the Earliest Times to the Persian Conquest*, London , second edition
Brunner, H. (1963), 'Der freie Wille Gottes in der Ägyptischen Weisheit', in *Les Sagesses du Proche-Orient ancien, Colloque de Strasbourg 1962*, Paris, 105-20
Capart, J. (1907), *Une rue de tombeaux à Saqqarah*, Brussels
Cottrell, L. (1955), *Life under the Pharaohs*, London
Daumas, F. (1962), 'La Naissance de l'humanisme dans la littérature de l'Egypte ancienne', *OrAn* 1, 155-84
—(1965), *La Civilisation de l'Egypte pharaonique*, Paris
Della Monica, M. (1975), *La Classe ouvrière sous les pharaons*, Paris
Desroches-Noblecourt, C. (1976), 'Ramsès II, l'homme et le dieu', *BTS* 185, 13-17
Drioton, E., and Vandier, J. (1938), *L'Egypte*, Paris
Dykmans, C. (1936-37), *Histoire économique et sociale de l'Ancienne Egypte*, three vols, Paris
Edwards, I.E.S. (1961), *The Pyramids of Egypt*, London
Endelsfelder, E. (1979), 'Zur Frage der Bewässerung im Pharaonischen Ägypten', *ZÄS* 106, 37-51
Erman, A. (1936), *Der Welt am Nil*, Leipzig
Fecht, G. (1958), *Der Habgierige und die Maât in der Lehre des Ptahhotep*, Glückstadt
Fensham, F.C. (1962), 'Widow, Orphan and the Poor in Ancient Near Eastern Legal and Wisdom Literature', *JNES* 21, 1962, 129-39
Frankfort, H. (1948), *Kingship and the Gods*, Paris
Goyon, G. (1977), *Les Secrets des bâtisseurs des grandes pyramides*, Paris

Grumach, I. (1972), *Untersuchungen zur Lebenslehre des Amenemope*, Berlin

Hari, R. (1964), *Horemheb et la reine Moutnedjemet*, Geneva

Harris, J.R. (1968), 'How long was the Reign of Horemheb?', *JEA* 54, 95-9

Helck, W. (1975), *Wirtschaftsgeschichte des Alten Ägypten*, Leiden

Kanawati, N. (1978), *The Egyptian Administration in the Old Kingdom*, Warminster

Lanczkowski, C. (1960), *Altägyptischer Prophetismus*, Wiesbaden

Leclant, J. (1963), 'Publications récentes concernant les "sagesses" de l'Egypte ancienne', in *Les Sagesses du Proche-Orient ancien*, Paris, 5-26

Lurje, I.M. (1971), *Studien um altägyptischen Recht*, Weimar

Menu, B. (1982), *Recherches sur l'histoire juridique, économique et sociale de l'ancienne Egypte*, Paris

Meyer, E. (1913), *Geschichte des Altertums*, 5 vols. in 7, ³1910-39: Vol.I.2, 'Aegypten bis zum Ende der Hyksoszeit', 5-327

Montet, P. (1959), *L'Egypte et la Bible*, Neuchâtel

Morenz, S. (1977), *La religion égyptienne*, Paris

Moret, A. (1940), 'La Doctrine de Maât', *RdE* 4, 1-14

Mumford, L. (1966), 'The First Megamachine', *Diog* 55, 3-20

Newberry, P.E. (1900), *The Life of Rekhmara*, London

Peet, T.E. (1924), 'Contemporary Life and Thought in Egypt', in *The Cambridge Ancient History*, Vol.II

Philips, A.K. (1977), 'Horemheb, Founder of the XIX Dynasty?', *Or* 46, 116-21

Pirenne, J. (1938a), 'Introduction à l'histoire du droit égyptien – Les trois cycles de l'histoire juridique et sociale de l'ancienne Egypte', *AHDO* 2, 11-62

—(1938b), 'Une nouvelle interprétation des "instructions du roi Khéti à son fils Merikarê"', *RdE* 3, 1-16

—(1965), *La Religion et la morale dans l'Egypte antique*, Neuchâtel and Paris

Posener, G. (1956), *Littérature et politique dans l'Egypte de la XIIᵉ dynastie*, Paris

—(1971), 'Literature', in *The Legacy of Egypt*, ed.J.R.Harris, Oxford, 220-56

—(1973), 'Une nouvelle tablette d'Aménémope', *RdE* 25, 251-2

—(1977) 'Les quarante rouleaux de lois', *GöM* 25, 63-6

Preiser, W. (1969), 'Zur rechtlichen Natur der altorientalischen Gesetze', *FS Karl Engish*, Frankfurt am Main, 17-36

Schenkel, W. (1978), *Die Bewässerungsrevolution im Alten Ägytpen*, Mainz

Schulman, A.R. (1971), 'Egyptian Literature in the Bible', *EJ* 6, 484

Seidl, E. (1942), 'Law', in *The Legacy of Egypt*, ed. S.R.K.Glanville, Oxford, 198-217

—(1957), *Einführung in die Ägyptische Rechtsgeschichte bis zum Ende des Neuen Reiches*, Glückstadt

Spiegel, J. (1950), *Soziale und weltanschauliche Reformbewegungen im Alten Ägypten*, Heidelberg

Theorides, A. (1967), 'A propos de la loi dans l'Egypte pharaonique', *RIDA* 14, 107-52
—(1971), 'The Concept of Law in Ancient Egypt', in *The Legacy of Egypt*, ed. J.R.Harris, Oxford, 291-322
—(1973), 'Les Egyptiens anciens "citoyens" ou "sujets de Pharaon"?', *RIDA* 14, 51-112
—(1974), 'Egyptian Law', *EB* 6, 501-3
—(1975), 'Les Relations de l'Egypte pharaonique avec des voisins', *RIDA* 22, 87-140
Thompson, H. (1940), 'Two Demotic Self-Dedications', *JEA* 26, 68-78
Van Seters, J. (1964), 'A Date for Admonitions in the Second Intermediary Period', *JEA* 50, 13-23
Vercoutter, J. (1979), 'Bas-relief et peinture', in *Le Temps des pyramides*, Paris, 121-70
Volten, A. (1937-38), *Studien um Weisheitsbuch des Anii*, Copenhagen
—(1963), 'Der Begriff der Maat', in *Les Sagesses du Proche-Orient ancien*, Paris, 73-102
Westendorf, W. (1966),, 'Ursprung und Wesen der Maat der altägytischen Göttin des Rechts, der Gerechtigkeit und der Weltordnung', *Festgabe für Dr Walter Will*, 201-5
Westermann, C. (1974), 'Sacred Kingship', *EB* 16, 118-22
Williams, R.J. (1962), 'The Alleged Semitic Origin of the Wisdom of Amenemope', *JEA* 47, 100-6
Wilson, J.A. (1954), 'Authority and Law in Ancient Egypt', *JAOS.S* 17, 1-7
—(1956), *The Culture of Ancient Egypt*, Chicago
Yoyotte, J. (1953), 'Pour une civilisation du pays de IAM', *BIFAO*, 173-8
—(1960), 'Egypte ancienne', in *Encyclopédie de la Pléiade, Histoire universelle* I, Paris

Ugarit

1. Legal, literary and religious texts

Caquot, A., Sznycer, M., and Herdner, A. (1974), *Mythes et légendes, textes ougaritiques* I, Paris
Gibson, J.C.L., and Driver, G.R. (1978), *Canaanite Myths and Legends*, Edinburgh (second edition)

2. Aids to Research

Cardascia, G. (1966), 'Ougarit (Ras Shamra)', in *Droits cunéiformes. Introduction bibliographique*, 127-37
—(1979), 'Ras Shamra', *DBS* 9, 1124-1466

3. General works and specialist studies

Astour, M. (1959), 'Les Etrangers à Ugarit et le Statut juridique des Habiru', *RA* 53, 70-6

Cazelles, H. (1973), 'De l'idéologie royale orientale', *The Gaster Festschrift, The Journal of the Ancient Near Eastern Society of Columbia University* 5, 59-73

De Langhe, R. (1957), 'La Bible et la littérature ugaritique', in *L'Ancien Testament et l'Orient. Etudes présentées aux VIe journées bibliques de Louvain, 11-13 sept. 1954*, OBL 1, 65-87

Milano, L. (1977), 'Sul presunto giubileo à Ugarit (PRU V,9)', *OrAnt* 16, 23-33

Scullion, J.J. (1971), 'Sedeq-Sedaqah in Isaiah cc 40-66', *UF* 3, 335-48

Shifman, J.S. (1975), 'Ugaritskij Jubilej', *VDI* 132, 94-100

Israel

1. Legal, literary and religious texts

Buis, P. (1969), *Le Deutéronome*, Paris

—(1976), *La notion d'alliance dans l'ancien Testament*, Paris

Cazelles, H. (1946), *Etudes sur le Code de l'alliance*, Paris

—(1958), *Le Lévitique*, Paris

Merendino, R.P. (1969), *Das deuteronomische Gesetz*, Bonn

Rad, G.von (1966), *Deuteronomy*, OTL, London and Philadelphia

Reinach, T. (ed.) (1895), 'Hécatée d'Abdère', in *Textes d'auteurs grecs et romains relatifs au judaïsme*, Paris

Lehmann, M. (1963), *Sprüche der Väter*, 3 vols, Basle

Schuhl, M. (1878), *Sentences et proverbes du Talmud*, Paris

Maimonides (1928), *Guide for the Perplexed*, ed M.Friedländer, London (second edition)

Spinoza (1862), *Tractatus Theologico-Politicus*, ed. R.Willis, London

2. Aids to research

Bulletin biblique, ed. P.-E.Langevin, Quebec 1930-1978

Bulletin signalétique (527) – Histoire et sciences des religions, Paris

Elenchus Bibliographicus Biblicus, ed. P.Nober, Rome

Falz, Z.W., *Current Bibliography of Hebrew Law*, Jerusalem 1966-1968

Dictionnaire de la Bible. Supplément, ed. Letouzey & Ané, Paris 1928-81

Encyclopaedia Judaica, Jerusalem 1971-1972

Hahn, H.F. (1966), *The Old Testament in Modern Research*, Philadelphia and London

Quell, G. and Schrenck, G. (1959), *Righteousness*, Bible Key Words, London = *TDNT* II, *'dikaios'*, etc., 174-225

Wright, G.E. (1946), *The Westminster Historical Atlas to the Bible*, London

3. General works and specialist studies

Achtemeier, E.R. (1962), 'Righteousness in the OT', *IDB* 4, 80-5
Adler, C. (1897), 'Die Sozialreform im alten Israel', *HDSW* 2, 695-9
Agus, J.B. (1957), 'The Prophet in Modern Hebrew Literature', *HUCA* 28, 289-324
Albrektson, B. (1967), *History and the Gods. An Essay on the Idea of Historical Events as Divine Manifestations in the Ancient Near East and Israel*, Lund
— (1972), 'Prophecy and Politics in the Old Testament', in *The Myth of the State*, Scripta Instituti Donneriani Aboensis VI, Stockholm, 45-56
Albright, W.F. (1953), *Archeology and the Religion of Israel*, Baltimore (¹1946)
—(1968), *Yahweh and the Gods of Canaan*, London
Alt, A. (1953-59), *Kleine Schriften zur Geschichte des Volkes Israel*, three vols, Munich
Amitai, L.K. (1905), *La Sociologie juive appliquée à l'époque moderne*, Paris
Anderson, G.W. (1966), *The History and Religion of Israel*, Oxford
André, T. (1892), *L'Esclavage chez les anciens Hébreux*, Paris
Andreasen, N.E. (1971), *The Old Testament Sabbath: A Traditio-Historical Investigation*, Vanderbilt University thesis
—(1974a), 'Festival and Freedom. A Study of an Old Testament Theme', *Interp* 28, 281-97
—(1974b), 'Recent Studies of the Old Testament Sabbath', *ZAW* 86, 453-69
Andreski, S. (1964), 'Method and Substantive Theory in Max Weber', *BJS* 15, 1-18
Astour, M. (1959), Métamorphoses de Baal; les rivalités commerciales au IXᵉ siècle', *Evid* 75, 35-40; 77, 54-8
Auvray, P. (1967), 'Richard Simon et Spinoza', in *Religion, érudition et critique à la fin du XVIIᵉ siècle et au début du XVIIIᵉ*, Paris, 201-14
Bach, R. (1957), 'Gottesrecht und weltliches Recht in der Verkündigung des Propheten Amos', *FS G.Dehn*, Neukirchen, 23-34
Baeck, L. (1918), 'Die Schöpfung des Mitmenschen', in *Soziale Ethik im Judentum*, Frankfurt am Main, 9-15
—(1948), *The Essence of Judaism*, New York
—(1964), *Judaism and Christianity*, Philadelphia
Balscheit, B., and Eichrodt, W. (1944), *Die soziale Botschaft des Alten Testament für die Gegenwart*, Basle
Baltzer, K. (1968), 'Considerations regarding the Office and the Calling of the Prophet', *HTR* 61, 567-81
Bamberger, B.J. (1969), 'The Changing Image of the Prophet in Jewish Thought', in *Interpreting the Prophetic Tradition*, The Goldenson Lecture 1955-1956, ed.H.M.Orlinsky, Cincinnati and New York
Bardtke, H. (1971), 'Die Latifundien in Juda während der zweiten Hälfte des achten Jahrhunderts v.Chr.', *Hommages à André Dupont-Sommer*, Paris, 235-54

Baron, S.W. (1952), *A Social and Religious History of the Jews*, two vols, New York (second edition)

Barr, J. (1969), *Biblical Words for Time*, London

Barton, J. (1979), 'Natural Law and Poetic Justice in the Old Testament', *JTS* 30, 1-14

Baudissin, W.W. (1921), 'Der gerechte Gott in altsemitischer Religion', *FS Harnack*, Tübingen

Bauer, B. (1837), 'Der Begriff der göttlichen Gerechtigkeit im zweiten Teile des Propheten Jesaja', *Zeitschrift für spekulativen Theologie*, 487ff.

Baumgarten, E. (1964), *Max Weber, Werk und Person*, Dokumente ausgewählt und kommentiert, Tübingen

Beaucamp, E. (1969), 'La Justice in Israel', *Studi in onore del Card. A.Ottaviani* I, Rome, 201-35

Beer, G. (1911), 'Das Stehenlassen der Pe'a Lev, 19,9', *ZAW* 31, 152-4

Berkovits, E. (1969a), 'The Biblical Meaning of Justice', *JdM* 18, 188-209

—(1969b), '*Sedeq and S'daqah*', ch. 7 in *Man and God. Studies in Biblical Theology*, Detroit

Bertheau, E. (1842), *Zur Geschichte der Israeliten.* Zwei Abhandlungen: I *Ueber Gewichte, Münzen und Masse der Hebräer; II Die Bewohner Palästinas seit den ältesten Zeiten*, Göttingen

Beuken, W.A.M. (1972), 'Mishpāt, the First Servant Song and its Context', *VT* 22, 1-30

Bianchi, H. (1973), 'Tsedeka-Justice', *Bijdr* 34, 306-18

—(1974), 'Das Tsedeka-Modell als Alternative zum Konventionellen Strafrecht', *ZEE* 18, 89-110

Bible au présent (La) (1982), Actes du XXᵉ Colloque des intellectuels juifs de langue française, Paris

Birch, B.C. (1976), *The Rise of the Israelite Monarchy*, Missoula

Bizzel, W.B. (1916), *The Social Teaching of the Jewish Prophets. A Study in Biblical Sociology*, Boston

Black, J.S., and Chrystal, G. (1912), *The Life of William Robertson Smith*, London 1912

Boczko-Weingort, A. (1979a), 'L'Interdiction de l'interêt en droit juif', *RHDF* 57, 235-45

—(1979b), *Le Prêt à intérêt dans le droit talmudique* (thesis), Paris

Boecker, H.J. (1976), *Recht und Gesetz im Alten Testament und im Alten Orient*, Neukirchen

Boman, T. (1960), *Hebrew Thought Compared with Greek*, London and Philadelphia

Boyer, P. (1975), 'Le Point de la question. L'imprononçable. L'écriture nomade', *Change* 22, 41-72

Bracker, H.D. (1962), *Das Gesetz Israels verglichen mit den altorientalischen Gesetzen der Babylonier, der Hethiter und der Assyrer*, Hamburg

Bright, J. (1981), *A History of Israel*, London and Philadelphia (third edition)

Brunet, C. (1975), *Essai sur l'Isaîe de l'histoire*, Paris

Brunner, H. (1959), 'Gerechtigkeit als Fundament des Thrones', *VT* 8, 426-8

Bruppacher, H. (1924), *Die Motive der alttestamentlichen Armutsbeurteilung*, Zurich

Buber, M. (1949), *The Prophetic Faith*, New York (Hebrew original 1942)

—(1964), 'Falsche Propheten', in *Schriften zur Bibel*, 3 vols, Munich, II, 943-9

—(1920), *Der heilige Weg*, Frankfurt am Main

Buhl, F. (1899), *Die sozialen Verhältnisse der Israeliten*, Berlin

Buis, P. (1976), *La notion d'alliance dans l'Ancien Testament*, Paris

Buis, P., and Leclercq, J. (1963), *Le Deutéronome*, Paris

Caquot, A. (1959), 'Remarques sur la loi royale du Deutéronome', *SEM* 9, 21-33

—(1960), 'Remarques sur la fête de la "néoménie" dans l'ancien Israël', *RHR* 158, 1-18

—(1970), 'La Religion d'Israël des origines à la captivité de Babylone', in *Histoire des religions, Encyclopédie de la Pléiade*, 359-461

—(1977), 'Renan et la Bible hébraïque', *BSHPF* 133, 331-49

Cardascia, G. (1956), 'Le Droit hébraïque', in *Histoire des institutions*, 83-96

—(1977), 'Droits cunéiformes et droit biblique', *Proceedings of the Sixth World Congress of Jewish Studies Jerusalem 1973*, Jerusalem, 63-70

Cardellini, I. (1981), *Die biblischen 'Sklaven'- Gesetze im Lichte des keilschriftlichen Sklavenrechts*, BBB 55

Carmichael, C.M. (1974), *The Laws of Deuteronomy*, Ithaca and London

Caspari, D.W. (1923), *Die Gottesgemeinde von Sinai und das nachmalige Volk Israel: Auseinandersetzung mit Max Weber*, BFCT 27, I

Causse, A. (1900), *Le Socialisme des prophètes*, Montauban

—(1900), *Der Ursprung der jüdischen Lehre von der Auferstehung*, Cahors

—(1913), *Les Prophètes d'Israël et les religions de l'Orient. Essai sur les origines du monothéisme universaliste*, Paris

—(1919), 'La Législation sociale d'Israël et l'idéal patriarcal', *RTP* 7, 189-215, 237-56

—(1922), *Les 'Pauvres' d'Israël*, Strasbourg and Paris

—(1924), *Israël et la vision de l'humanité*, Strasbourg and Paris

—(1926), *Les Plus Vieux Chants de la Bible*, Paris

—(1937), *Du groupe ethnique à la communauté religieuse. Le problème sociologique de la religion d'Israël*, Paris

Cazelles, H. (1951), 'A propos de quelque textes difficiles relatifs à la justice de Dieu dans l'Ancien Testament', *RB* 58, 169-88

—(1957), 'Loi israëlite', *DBS* 5, 498-530

—(1966), 'Pentateuque', *DBS* 7, 687-858

—(1963), 'Les Débuts de la sagesse en Israël', in *Les Sagesses du Proche-Orient ancien*, Paris 27-40

—(1968), 'La Loi, code moral', *Studi in onore di Card. A.Ottaviani* I, Rome, 195-200

—(1971), 'Bible et politique', *RSR* 59, 497-530

—(1973-74), *Lois du Pentateuque. Structures sociales d'Israël et théologie biblique*, lecture notes, Paris (duplicated)

—(1973a), *Introduction critique à l'Ancien Testament*, Paris

—(1973b), 'Bible, histoire et sociologie du prophétisme', *Les Quatre Fleuves*. Cahiers de recherche et de réflexion religieuses 3, Paris, 6-21

—(1976), 'Le Dieu de Moïse et le dieu des Egyptiens', *BTS* 185, 11-12

—(1977a), 'Adolphe Lods et la religion d'Israël', *RHPR* 57, 327-34

—(1977b), 'Les Origines du Sabbat', *BTS* 187, 2-4

—(1978), *Le Messie de la Bible*, Paris

—(1980), 'Torah et Loi, préalables à l'étude historique d'une notion juive', *Hommage à Georges Vajda*, Louvain, 1-12

—(nd), 'Aspirations à la justice dans le monde prébiblique et la réponse de Dieu à des aspirations par la révélation biblique', 1-10 (in preparation)

Chalon, M. (1973), *Le Binome hébreu mispat-sedaqah et la notion biblique de justice*, dissertation Institut Catholique de Paris (duplicated)

Clements, R.E. (1973), *Prophecy and Covenant*, London

—(1976), *A Century of Old Testament Study*, London

Clévenot, M. (1976), *Materialist approaches to the Bible*, Maryknoll, New York

Cohen, H. (1924), 'Das soziale Ideal bei Platon und den Propheten', *Jüdische Schriften*, three vols., Berlin I, 306-30

—(1924, II), 'Der Prophetismus und die Soziologie' II, 398-401

Cohen, S. (1965), 'The Political Background of the Words of Amos', *HUCA* 36, 153-60

Cohn, H.H. (1971), 'Slavery', *EJ* 14, 1655-9

Condon, K. (1970), 'Justification in the Bible', *ITQ* 37, 265-79

Contenau, G. (1950), *La Vie quotidienne à Babylone et en Assyrie*, Paris

Cox, D. (1977), *Sedaqa and mishpat. The Concept of Righteousness in Later Wisdom*, SBFLA 27, 33-50

Craghan, J.F. (1972), 'Amos dans la nouvelle recherche', *BTB* 2, 245-62

Cramer, K. (1907), 'Der Begriff tsedaqa bei Tritojesaia', *ZAW* 27, 7-99

Cremer, H. (1893), 'Gerechtigkeit – Der alttestamentliche Begriff', *Biblisch-theologisches Wörterbuch der neutestamentlichen Gräcität*, Gotha, 272-80

—(1897), *Die Christliche Lehre von den Eigenschafen Gottes* (cf. III, 'Die Gerechtigkeit Gottes'), Gütersloh

Crenshaw, J.L. (1970), 'Popular Questioning of the Justice of God in Ancient Israel', *ZAW* 82, 1970, 380-95

Crüsemann, F. (1976), 'Jahwes Gerechtigkeit (sedāqā/sädäq) im Alten Testament', *EvTh* 36, 427-50

—(1978), *Der Widerstand gegen das Königtum*, WMANT 49

Dacquino, P. (1969), 'La formula "Giustizia di Dio" nei libri del'Antico Testamento', *RivBib* 17, 103-19

Darmesteter, J. (1892), *Les Prophètes d'Israël*, Paris

David, H. (1950), 'Hammurabi and the Law in Exodus', *OTS* 7, 149-78

Davies, E.W. (1981), *Prophecy and Ethics*, Sheffield

De Geus, C.H.J. (1976), *The Tribes of Israel*, Assen and Amsterdam

—(1977), 'Die Gesellschaftskritik des Propheten und die Archäologie', *ZDPV* 98, 50-7

Delahoutre, M. (1977), 'Actualité du shabbat', *BTS* 187

Delcor, M. (1975), 'Quelques cas de survivances du vocabulaire nomade en hébreu biblique', *VT* 25, 307-22

Descamps, A. (1949), 'Justice et justification dans l'Ancien Testament', *DBS* 4, 1417-60

Despotopoulous, C. (1969), 'Les Concepts de juste et de justice selon Aristote', *APD* 14, 283-308

De Vries, S.J. (1968), *Bible and Theology in Netherland*, Wageningen

Dhorme, E. (1957), *La Religion des Hébreux nomades*, Brussels

Diestel, L. (1860), 'Die Idee der Gerechtigkeit vorzüglich im AT biblisch-theologisch dargestellt', *JDT*, Gotha, 196-9

Dietrich, W. (1976), *Jesaja und die Politik*, Munich

—(1979), *Israel und Kanaan. Vom Ringen zweier Gesellschaftsysteme*, Stuttgart

Dijkema, F. (1943), 'Le Fond des prophéties d'Amos', *OTS* 2, 18-34

Dion, P.E. (1975), 'Le message moral du prophète Amos s'inspirait-il du "droit de l'alliance"?', *ScEs* 27, 5-34

Diringer, D. (1942), 'The Early Hebrew Weights Found at Lachish', *PEQ* 74, 82-103

Donner, H. (1963), 'Die soziale Botschaft der Propheten im Lichte der Gesellschaftsordnung in Israel', *OrAnt* 2, 329-45

Dow, J.G. (1891), 'Hebrew and Puritan', *JQR* 3, 52-84

Dubnow, S. (1925), *Weltgeschichte des jûdischen Volkes*, ten vols, Berlin

Duhm, B. (1875), *Die Theologie der Propheten als Grundlage für innere Entwicklungsgeschichte der israelitischen Religion*

Dünner, A. (1963), *Die Gerechtigkeit nach dem Alten Testament*, Bonn

Eberharter, A. (1924), *Die soziale und politische Wirksamkeit des alttestamentlichen Propheten*, Salzburg

Eichrodt, W. (1961), 'The Righteousness of God', in *Theology of the Old Testament*, London and Philadelphia, 239ff.

Eisenberg, J., and Abecassis, A. (1978), *A Bible ouverte*, Paris

Eissfeldt, O. (1951), 'The Prophetic Literature', in *The Old Testament and Modern Study*, ed. H.H.Rowley, Oxford, 115-80

Elliger, K. (1935), 'Prophet und Politik', *ZAW* 53, 3-22

Ellul, J. (1967), 'Le Droit biblique d'après l'exemple de la royauté et les cultures orientales', *Mélanges offerts à Jean Brethe de la Gressaye*, Bordeaux, 253-73

Epstein, I. (1959), *Judaism*, London

Fahlgren, K.H. (1932), *Sedākā, nahestehende und gegengesetzte Begriffe im Alten Testament*, Uppsala

Falk, Z.W. (1964), *Hebrew Law in Biblical Times*, Jerusalem

Fendler, M. (1973), 'Zur Sozial-Kritik des Amos; Versuch einer wirtschafts- und socialgeschichtlichen Interpretation alttestamentlicher Texte', *EvTh* 33, 32-53

Fenton, J. (1880), *Early Hebrew Life; A Study in Sociology*, London

Finkelstein, L. (1946), *The Pharisees. The Sociological Background of their Faith*, two vols, Philadelphia

—(1969), *New Light from the Prophets*, London

Fohrer, G. (1965), 'Das sogennante apodiktisch formulierte Recht und der Decalog', *KuD* 11, 49-74

—(1928), 'Zehn Jahre Literatur zur alttestamentlichen Prophetie (1951-1960)', *TR* 28, 1-75, 235-97

—(1967), *Studien zur alttestamentlichen Prophetie (1949-1965)*, BZAW 99, Berlin

—(1975), 'Neue Literatur zur alttestamentlichen Prophetie (1961-1970)', *TR* 40, 193-209

Fraine, J.de (1954), *L'Aspect religieux de la royauté Israëlite*, Rome

Friedmann, G. (1975), 'Le Shabbat confronté à la société industrielle en Israël', in *Le Shabbat dans la conscience juive. XIVe colloque d'intellectuels juifs de langue française*, Paris, 85-9

Fuchs, H. (1927), *Das alttestamentliche Begriffsverhältnis von Gerechtigkeit und Gnade in Prophetie und Dichtung, Christentum und Wissenschaft*, Dresden

Fuchs, K. (1955), *Die alttestamentliche Arbeitergesetzgebung*, Heidelberg

Galandauer, H. (1891), *Der Socialismus in Bibel und Talmud*, Mainz

Galin, K. (1951), 'Das Königsgesetz in Deuteronomium', *TLZ*, 134-42

Gamoran, H. (1971), 'The Biblical Law against Loans on Interest', *JNES* 30, 127-34

Gamper, A. (1966), *Gott als Richter in Mesopotamien und im Alten Testament*, Innsbruck

Gaspar, J.W. (1947), *Social Ideas in the Wisdom Literature of the Old Testament*, Washington

Gaudemet, J. (1967), *Institutions de l'Antiquité*, Paris

Gelin, A. (1953), *Les Pauvres de Yahvé*, Paris

Gemser, B. (1953), 'The Importance of the Motive Clause in Old Testament Law', *SVT* 1, 50-66

Gerstenberger, E. (1965), *Wesen und Herkunft des 'apodiktischen Rechts'*, WMANT 29

Ginzberg, E. (1931), 'Studies in the Economics of the Bible', *JQR* 22, 393-408

Glatzer, N.N. (1963), 'Buber als Interpret der Bibel', in *Martin Buber*, ed. P.A.Schilpp and M.Friedman, Stuttgart, 346-63

Glueck, N. (1946), *The River Jordan*, London

Goitein, S.D. (1955), *Jews and Arabs*, New York

Goldberg, A. (1975), 'Der einmalige Mensch: Der absolute Wert des Lebens und der Würde des Menschen im rabbinischen Judentum (1-3 Jahrhundert n.C)', *Saec* 26, 145-56

Goldberg, N.K. (1977), 'Der Gerechte ist der Grund der Welt', *Jud* 33, 147-60

Gordis, R. (1971), 'The Bible as a Cultural Monument', in *The Jews: Their Religion and Cutlure*, ed. L.Finkelstein, New York, 1-42

Gordon, C.H. (1958), 'Abraham and the Merchants of Ur', *JNES* 17, 28-31

—(1962), *Before the Bible. The Common Background of Greek and Hebrew Civilization*, New York

Gottwald, N.K. (1964), *All the Kingdoms of the Earth*, New York

—(1979), 'Sociological Method in the Study of Ancient Israel', in *Encounter with the Text, Form and History in the Hebrew Bible*, ed. J.M.Buss, Philadelphia, 69-81

—(1977), 'Were the Early Israelites Pastoral Nomads', *Proceedings of the Sixth World Congress of Jewish Studies. Jerusalem 1973*, Jerusalem, 165-89

—(1979), *The Tribes of Yahweh*, Maryknoll, NY (London 1980)

Graetz, H. (1936), *Die Konstruktion der jüdischen Geschichte*, Berlin

Graham, W.C. (1934), *The Prophets and Israel's Culture*, Chicago

Gray, J. (1962), *Archaeology and the Old Testament World*, London

Greenberg, M. (1960), 'Some Postulates of Biblical Criminal Law', *Y.Kaufmann Jubilee Volume*, Jerusalem, 5-28

Gressmann, H. (1924), 'Josia und das Deuteronomium', *ZAW* 42, 313-37

Grieshammer, R. (1982), 'Maat und Sädäq. Zum Kulturzusammenhang zwischen Ägypten und Kanaan', *GöM* 55, 35-42

Gunkel, H. (1906), 'Die Grundprobleme der Israelitische Literaturgeschichte', *DLZ* 27, 1798-9, 1862-6

Gunneweg, A. (1959), *Mündliche und schriftliche Tradition der vorexilischen Prophetenbücher*, Göttingen

Guttmann, J. (1925), 'Max Webers Sociologie des antiken Judentums', *MGWJ* 69, 193-223

Halladay, W.L. (1973), review of G.E.Mendenhall, *The Tenth Generation*, *Interp.* 27, 469-74

Hallo, W.W. (1977), 'New Moons and Sabbaths: A Case Study in the Contrastive Approach', *HUCA* 48, 1-18

Hammershaimb, E. (1966), *Some Aspects of the Old Testament Prophecy from Isaiah to Malachi*, Rosekild og Bagger

Hansel, G. (1975), 'Le Shabbat dans la loi juive', in *Le Shabbat dans la conscience juive*, Paris, 29-35

Haran, M. (1972), 'La Recherche biblique en hébreu', *ETR* 47, 145-59

Harari, I. (1971), 'Differences in the Concept of Law Between the Ancient Egyptians and the Hebrews', in *Proceedings of the Twenty-seventh International Congress of Orientalists. Ann Arbor 1967*, Wiesbaden, 52f.

Harrelson, W. (1977), 'Karl Barth on the Decalogue', *SR* 6, 229-40

Hentschke, R. (1965-66), 'Erwägungen zur israelitischen Rechtsgeschichte', *ThViat* 10

Hermann, J. (1911), 'Die soziale Predigt der Propheten', BZSF, Berlin

Herrmann, S. (1963), 'Prophetie in Israel und Ägypten. Recht und Grenze eines Vergleiches', *SVT* 9, 47-65

—(1965), *Die prophetischen Heilserwartungen im Alten Testament*, Stuttgart 1965

—(1967), 'Prophetie und Wirklichkeit in der Epoche des Babylonischen Exils', *AzTh* 32

Herren, A.H.L. (1805), *Ideen über die Politik, den Verkehr und den Handel der vornehmsten Völker*, Göttingen

Hertzberg, H.W. (1922), 'Die Entwicklung des Begriffes mishpat im AT', *ZAW* 40, 256-87

Hertzler, J.O. (1936), *The Social Thought of Ancient Civilization*, New York

Heschel, A. (1962), *Les Bâtisseurs du temps*, Paris

—(1962), *The Prophets* (original, Cracow 1936), New York

Hirsch, E.G. (1905), 'Right and Righteousness', *JE* 10, 419-24

Holstein, J.A. (1975), 'Max Weber and Biblical Scholarship', *HUCA* 46, 159-79

Homerski, J. (1972), 'Rola proroków w zyciu politycznym Izraels w ocenie wspólzesnych egzegetów', *RTK* 19, 35-43

Horst, F. (1972), 'Recht und Religion im Bereich des Alten Testaments', in *Um das Prinzip der Vergeltung im Religion und Recht des Alten Testaments*, ed.K.Koch, Darmstadt, 181-212

Hulst, A.R. (1966), 'Bemerkungen zum Sabbathgebot', *FS T.C.Vriezen*, Wageningen, 152-64

Huppenbauer, H.W. (1962), 'Auferstehung', *BHH* 1, 149-52

Issermann, E.M. (1933), *Rebels and Saints. The Social Message of Prophets of Israel*, St Louis

Jackson, B.S. (1971), 'Liability for Mere Intention in Early Jewish Law', *HUCA* 42, 197-225

—(1973), 'Reflections on Biblical Criminal Law', *JJS* 224, 8-38

Jacob, E. (1958), 'The Righteousness of God', in *Theology of the Old Testament*, London, 94ff.

—(1963), 'Les Prophètes bibliques sont-ils des révolutionnaires ou des conservateurs?', *CSoc* 71, 287-97

—(1969), 'L'Etat actuel des études vétérotestamentaires en Allemagne', *ETR* 4, 289-305

—(1973), 'Quelques travaux récentes sur le prophétisme', *RHPR* 53, 415-25

—(1980), 'La Dimension du prophétisme d'après Martin Buber et Abraham J.Heschel', in *Prophecy. Essays presented to Georg Fohrer*, Berlin and New York, 26-34

Jacobs, L. (1964), *Principles of the Jewish Faith*, London

—(1971), 'Righteousness', *EJ* 14, 180-4

Jacobson, D. (1942), *The Social Background of the Old Testament*, Cincinnati

Jepsen, A. (1927), *Untersuchungen zum Bundesbuch*, Stuttgart

—(1965), 'Tsdq und tsedaqa im Alten Testament', in *Gottes Wort und Gottes Land, FS Herzberg*, Göttingen, 78-89

Jeremias, J. (1972), 'Mishpat im ersten Gottesknechtslied', *VT* 22, 31-42

Johnson, B. (1977-78), 'Der Bedeutungunterschied zwischen *sädäq* und *sedaqa*', *ASTI* 11, 31-9

Justesen, J.P. (1963), 'On the Meaning of Sädaq', *AUSS* 2, 53-61

Kahn, Z. (1867), *L'Esclavage selon la Bible et le Talmud*, Paris

Kaiser, O. (1969), 'Gerechtigkeit und israelitischen Propheten und griechischen Denkern des 8-6 Jahrhunderts', *NZS* 11, 327

—(1965), 'Dike und Sedaqa. Zur Frage nach der sittlichen Weltordnung', *NZST* 7, 251-73

Kapelrud, A.S. (1966), 'New Ideas in Amos', *SVT* 15, 193-206

Kaufmann, U. (1960), *The Religion of Israel* (Hebrew 1937), Chicago and London

Kautsky, K. (1910), *Der Ursprung des Christentums*, Stuttgart

Kautzsch, E. (1881), *Die Derivative des Stammes* tsdq *im alttestamentlichen Sprachgebrauch*, Tübingen

Keel, O. (ed.) (1980), *Monotheismus im Alten Israel und seiner Umwelt*, Biblische Beitrage 14, Fribourg

Keller, E.B. (1974), 'Hebrew Thoughts on Immortality and Resurrection', *IJPR* 5, 16-44

Kellermann, B. (1917), *Die ethische Monotheismus der Propheten und seine sociologische Würdigung*, Berlin

Kessler, C. (1977), 'Le Shabbat dans la tradition juive', *BTS* 187, 4-15

Kimbrough, S.T. (1969), 'Une conception sociologique de la religion d'Israël: l'oeuvre d'Antonin Causse', *RHPR* 49, 313-20

Kitchen, K.A. (1966), *Ancient Orient and Old Testament*, London

Kleinert, P. (1905), *Die Propheten Israels in sozialer Beziehung*, Leipzig

Klima, J. (1953), 'Einige Bemerkungen zum Sklavenrecht nach der vorham-murapischen Gesetzesfragmenten', *ArOr* 21, 143-52

Klingenberg, E. (1977), *Das israelitische Zinsverbot in Torah, Mishnah und Talmud*, AAWLN.G. 7, 5-102

Koch, K. (1953), *Sdq im Alten Testament. Eine traditionsgeschichtliche Untersu-chung*, Heidelberg Dissertation (typescript)

—(1962), 'Gerechtigkeit im Alten Testament', *BHH*, 548

—(1971), 'Die Entstehung der soziale Kritik bei den Propheten', in *Probleme biblischer Theologie. Gerhard von Rad zum 70.Geburtstag*, Munich 1971, 236-58

—(1976), 'Die drei Gerechtigkeiten. Die Umformung einer hebräischen Idee in aramäischen Denken nach dem Jesajatargum', in *Rechtfertigung. FS Käsemann*, Tübingen 245-67

—I (1982), II (1983), *The Prophets*, London and Philadelphia (two vols)

Kohn, H. (1956), *The Idea of Nationalism. A Study in its Origin and Background*, New York.

Koigen, D. (1934), *Das Haus Israel*, Berlin

Kraus, H.J. (1966), *Worship in Israel*, Oxford

—(1969), *Geschichte der historisch-kritischen Erforschung des Alten Testaments*, Neukirchen

Kübel, F.E. (1870), *Die soziale und volkswirtschaftliche Gesetzsgebung des Alten Testaments unter Berücksichtigung moderner Anschauungen dargestellt*, Wiesbaden

Kupper, J.R. (1957), *Les Nomades en Mésopotamie au temps des rois de Mari*, bibliothèque de la faculté de philosophie de l'université de Liège CXLL, Paris

Kuyper, L.J. (1977), 'Righteousness and Salvation', *SJT* 30, 233-52

Larès, M.M. (1974), *Bible et civilisation anglaise. Naissance d'une tradition (Ancien Testament)*, Paris

Lauterbach, W. (1936), *Der Arbeiter im Recht und Rechtpraxis des Alten Testaments und des Alten Orients*, Heidelberg (thesis with an important bibliography)

Leemans, W.F. (1950), *The Old Babylonian Merchant – His Business and his Social Position*, SDIO 3

Lehmann, M. (1963), *Sprüche der Väter*, Basle (three vols.)

Lehmann, M.R. (1953), 'Abraham's Purchase of Machpelah and Hittite Law', *BASOR* 129, 15-20

Lemaire, A. (1973), 'Le Sabbat à l'epoque royale israélite', *RB* 80, 161-85 (important bibliography)

Lemche, N.P. (1976), 'The Manumission of Slaves – The Fallow Year – The Sabbatical Year – The Yobel Year', *VT* 26, 38-59

Lesètre, H. (1926), 'Dîme', *DB (V)*, 1431-5

Levinas, E. (1963), *Difficile liberté*, Paris

Lewy, I. (1957), 'Dating of Covenant Code Sections on Humaneness and Righteousness (Ex.XII, 20-26; XXIII, 1-9)', *VT* 7, 322-6

L'Hour, J. (1963), 'Une législation criminelle dans le Deutéronome', *Bib* 44, 1-15

Liebeschütz, H. (1964), 'Max Weber's Historical Interpretation of Judaism', *YLBI* 9, 41-68

—(1967), *Das Judentum im deutschen Geschichtsbild von Hegel bis Max Weber*, Tübingen

Limburg, J. (1978), 'The Prophets in Recent Study: 1967-77', *Interp* 32, 56-68

Lindblom, J. (1924), *Die literarische Gattung der prophetischen Literatur*, UUÅ, Theol., 1

—(1963), *Prophecy in Ancient Israel*, Oxford

Lipinski, E. (1976),'L'Esclave hébreu', *VT* 26, 120-3

Locher, C. (1982), 'Wie einzigartig war das altisraelitische Recht?', *Jud* 38, 132ff.

Lods, A. (1906), *Le Croyance à la vie future et le culte des morts dans l'antiquité israélite*, Paris

—(1922), 'Les "Pauvres" d'Israel d'après un ouvrage récent', *RHR* 85, 190-201

—(1924), 'Jean Astruc et la critique biblique au XVIIIᵉ siècle', *RHPR* 11, 57-60

—(1932), *Israel from its Beginnings to the Middle of the Eighth Century*, London

—(1937), *The Prophets and the Rise of Judaism*, London

—(1950), *Histoire de la littérature hébraïque et juive*, Paris

Loewe, R. (1961), 'Jewish Scholarship in England', in *Three Centuries of Anglo-Jewish History*, ed. V.D.Lipman, Cambridge, 125-48

Lofthouse, W.F. (1938), *The Righteousness of Jahweh*, London

Lohfink, N. (1976), 'Die Sabbatruhe und die Freizeit', *StZ* 194, 395-407

Löw, A. (1890), *Thierschutz im Judenthume nach Bibel und Talmud*, Budapest

Lurje, M. (1927), *Studien zur Geschichte der wirtschaftlichen und sozialen Verhältnisse in israelitisch-jüdischen Exil*, BZAW 45, Giessen

Lutaud, O. (1977), *Winstanley. Son oeuvre et le radicalisme 'digger' (Puritanisme révolutionnaire et utopie sociale)*, Lille thesis

Maarsingh, B. (1961), *Onderzoek naar de ethiek van de wetten in Deuteronomium (Inquiry into the Ethics of the Laws in Deuteronomy)*, Dutch with an English summary, Winterswigh

Mach, R. (1957), *Der Zaddik im Talmud und Midrash*, Leiden

Macholz, G.C. (1972a), 'Die Stellung des Königs in der israelitischen Gerichtsverfassung', *ZAW* 84, 157-82

—(1972b), 'Zur Geschichte der Justizorganisation in Juda', *ZAW* 84, 314-40

Maier, J., (1972) *Geschichte der Jüdischen Religion*, Berlin and New York (with an important bibliography)

Malchow, B.V. (1982), 'Social Justice in the Wisdom Literature', *Biblical Theology Bulletin* 12, 120-4

Malfroy, J. (1965), 'Sagesse et loi dans le Deutéronome', *VT* 15, 49-65

Maloney, R.P. (1974), 'Usury and Restrictions on Interest-Taking in the Ancient Near East', *CBQ* 36, 1-20

Mark, M. (1936), *Le People juif à la poursuite d'un équilibre économique*, Geneva

Martin, J. (1892), *La Notion de justice de Dieu dans l'Ancien Testament*, Montauban

Martin-Achard, R. (1956), *De la mort à la résurrection. L'origine et le développement d'une croyance dans le cadre de l'Ancien Testament*, Paris

Marx, K. (1843), 'On the Jewish Question', *Karl Marx: Early Texts*, ed. D.McLellan, Oxford 1971, 85-114

Mauss, M. (1923-24), 'Essai sur le don. Forme et raison de l'échange dans les sociétés archaïques', *ASoc* 1, 30-186

May, B. (1923), *Soziale Leben in Israel zur Zeit der Propheten*, Frankfurt am Main

May, H.G. (1932), 'The Fertility Cult in Hosea', *AJSL* 48, 73-98

May, H.G., and Graham, W.C. (1936), *Culture and Conscience: An Archaeological Study of the New Religious Past in Ancient Palestine*, Chicago

Meislin, B.J., and Cohen, M.L. (1964), 'Backgrounds of the Biblical Law against Usury', *CSSH* 6, 250-67

Mendelssohn, I. (1940), *Slavery in the Ancient Near East*, Oxford

Mendenhall, C.E. (1954), 'Ancient Oriental and Biblical Law', *BA* 17, 26-46

—(1962), 'The Hebrew Conquest of Palestine', *BA* 25, 66f.

—(1969), review of M.Weippert (1971), *Bib* 50, 432-6

—(1973), *The Tenth Generation. The Origins of Biblical Tradition*, Baltimore and London 1973

Menes, A. (1928), *Die vorexilischen Gesetze Israels*, BZAW 50

Meyer, M.A., (ed.) (1974), *Ideas of Jewish History*, New York

Michel, D. (1964), *Begriffsuntersuchung über šadāq-sedaqa und ämät-ämuna*, Heidelberg Habilitationsschrift (duplicated)

Milgrom, J. (1978), 'Priestly Terminology and the Political and Social Structure of Pre-Monarchic Israel', *JQR* 59, 65-81

Momigliano, A. (1978), 'Greek Historiography', *HTh* 17, 1-28
—(1980), 'A Note on Max Weber's Definition of Judaism as a Pariah-Religion', *HTh* 19, 313-18
Monnier, J. (1878), *La Justice de Dieu d'après la Bible*, Paris
Moret, A. (1941), *Histoire de l'Orient*, Paris
Müller, A. (1809), *Die Elemente der Staatskunst*, Dresden
Munk, E. (1947), *La Justice sociale en Israël*, Neuchâtel
Nahmani, H.S. (1964), *Human Rights in the Old Testament*, Tel Aviv
Negretti, N. (1973), *Il settimo giorno. Indagine critico-teologico delle tradizione presacerdotali e sacerdotali circa sabato biblico*, AnBib 55
Neher, A. (1956), *La Justice dans l'Ancien Testament*, Discours de rentrée à l'audience solennelle du 16 Sept.1955 à la cour d'appel de Colmar, Besançon
— (1948), 'Fonction du prophète dans la société hébraïque', *RHP* 28, 30-42
—(1950), *Amos. Contribution à l'étude du prophétisme*, Paris
—(1955), *L'Essence du prophétisme*, Paris
—(1966), *Le Puits de l'exil. La théologie dialectique du Maharal de Prague (1512-1609)*, Paris
—(1977), *Clefs pour le judaïsme*, Paris
Neher, A.et R. (1974), *Histoire biblique du peuple d'Israel*, 2 vols., Paris
Neufeld, E. (1955), 'The Prohibitions against Loans and Interest in the Ancient Hebrew Laws', *HUCA* 26, 255-412
—(1958), 'Socio-economic Background of *Yōbel* and *Shemitta*', *RSO* 33, 53-124
—(1960), 'The Emergence of Royal-Urban Society in Ancient Israel', *HUCA* 31, 31-53
Nicholson, E.W. (1967), *Deuteronomy and Tradition*, Oxford
North, R.G. (1954), *Sociology of the Biblical Jubilee*, AnBib 4
—(1982), 'Social Dynamics from Saul to Jehu', *Biblical Theology Bulletin* 12, 109-19 (with an interesting bibliography)
Noth, M. (1943), *Überlieferungsgeschichtliche Studien*, Halle
—(1960), *A History of Israel*, London and New York (second edition)
Nötscher, F. (1915), *Die Gerechtigkeit Gottes bei den vorexilischen Propheten*, ATA 6
—(1962), 'Gerechtigkeit im Alten Testament', *BTW*, 453-61
Nyström, S. (1946), *Beduinentum und Jahwismus. Eine sociologisch-religionsgeschichtliche Untersuchung zum Alten Testament*, Lund
Oelsner, T. (1962), 'The Place of Jews in Economic History as Viewed by German Scholars', *YLBI* 7, 183-212
Orlinsky, H.M. (1971), 'Whither Biblical Research', *JBL* 90, 1-14
Ortloph, A. (1860), 'Ueber den Begriff von *tsdq* und den wurzelverwandten Wörtern im zweiten Theile des Propheten Jesaja', *ZLTK* 21, 201-46
Parkes, J. (1961), 'Jewish-Christian Relations in England', in *Three Centuries of Anglo-Jewish History*, ed. V.D.Lipman, Cambridge, 149-67
—(1969), *The Foundations of Judaism and Christianity*, London
—(1961), *Whose Land? A History of the Peoples of Palestine*, Harmondsworth

Paul, S.M. (1970), 'Studies in the Book of the Covenant in the Light of Cuneiform and Biblical Law', *SVT* 18

—(1971), 'Prophets and Prophecy', *EJ* 13, 1150-75

Pedersen, J. (1926), *Israel, its Life and Culture*, two vols, London and Copenhagen

Petitjean, A. (1976), 'Les conceptions vétérotestamentaires du temps. Acquisitions, crises et programme de la recherche', *RHPR* 56, 383-400

Phillips, A. (1970), *Ancient Israel's Criminal Law. A New Approach to the Decalogue*, Oxford

Popkin, R. (1969-72), 'Bible Criticism and Social Science', *Boston Studies in the Philosophy of Science* 14, 339-55

Porteous, N.W. (1967), 'The Basis of the Ethical Teaching of the Prophets' (1950), in *Living the Mystery*, 47-60

Porter, J.R. (1965), 'The Legal Aspects of the Concept of "Corporate Personality" in the Old Testament', *VT* 15, 360-80

Prévost, M.-H. (1976), 'Formulation casuistique et formulation apodictique dans les lois bibliques', *RHDF* 54, 340-60

Procksch, O. (1950), *Theologie des Alten Testaments*, Gütersloh

Rad, G.von (1966), ' "Righteousness" and "Life" in the Cultic Language of the Psalms', in *The Problem of the Hexateuch and Other Essays*, Edinburgh, 243-66

—(1962), 'The Righteousness of Jahweh and of Israel', *Old Testament Theology* I, Edinburgh, 370-82

Ramlot, L. (1968), 'Histoire et mentalité symbolique', in *Mélanges J.Coppens* 3, Gembloux-Paris, 82-90

—(1970), 'Prophétisme', *DBS* 8, 811-1222

Raphaël, F. (1970), 'Max Weber et le judäisme antique', *AES* 11, 297-36

—(1982), *Judaisme et capitalisme. Essai sur la controverse entre Max Weber et Werner Sombart*, Paris

Rathjens, C. (1962), 'Die alten Welthandelstrassen und die Offenbarungsreligionen', *Oriens* 15, 115-29

Read, W.E. (1966), 'Further Observations on Sädäq', *AUSS* 4, 29-36

Renan, E. (1887-97), *Histoire du peuple d'Israël*, five vols, Paris

Reventlow. (1962), H., *Das Amt des Propheten bei Amos*, Göttingen

Ringgren, H. (1971), 'Les Recherches d'Ancien Testament en Scandinavie', *ETR* 46, 419-28

— (1972), 'The root SDQ in Poetry and the Koran', *FS G.Widengren*, II, Leiden, 134-42

Ritschl, A. (1874), *Die christliche Lehre von der Rechtfertigung und Versöhnung II: Der biblische Stoff der Lehre*, Bonn

Rivkin, E. (1971), *The Shaping of Jewish History. A Radical New Interpretation*, New York

Rogerson, J.W. (1978), *Anthropology and the Old Testament*, Oxford

Rosenthal, F. (1950-51), 'Sedaka, Charity', *HUCA* 23, 411-30

Rosenzweig, F. (1921), *Der Stern der Erlösung*, Frankfurt am Main

Rotenstreich, N. (1972), *Tradition and Reality*, New York

Rowley, H.H. (1938), 'The History of Israel: Political and Economic', in *Record and Revelation, Essays in the Old Testament*, ed. H.W.Robinson, Oxford

—(1951), 'Trends in Old Testament Study', in *The Old Testament and Modern Study*, ed. H.H.Rowley, Oxford, XV-XXXI

—(1956), *Prophecy and Religion in Ancient China and Israel*, London

—(1967), *Worship in Ancient Israel: Its Forms and Meaning*, London

Runes, D.D. (1959), *Pictorial History of Philosophy*, New York

Safran, A. (1977), 'Le Sabbat dans la tradition juive', *RTP*, 136-49

Saggs, H.W.F. (1978), *The Encounter with the Divine in Mesopotamia and Israel*, London

Salomon, R. (1932), *Le Prêt à intérêt en législation juive*, Paris

Sarna, N. (1972), 'Zedekiah's Emancipation of Slaves and Sabbatical Year', in *Orient and Occident. Essays presented to Cyrus H.Gordon (1972), Alter Orient und Altes Testament*, Neukirchen 22, 143-9

Scharbert, J.M. (1968), 'Die prophetische Literatur. Der Stand der Forschung', *ETL* 44, 346-406

Schiper, I. (1959), 'Max Weber on the Sociological Basis of the Jewish Religion', *JJSoc* I, 250-60

Schluchter, W. (ed.) (1981), *Max Webers Studien über das antike Judentum*, Frankfurt am Main

Schmid, H.H. (1966), *Wesen und Geschichte der Weisheit. Eine Untersuchung zur altorientalischer und israelitischer Weisheitsliteratur*, BZAW 101, Berlin

—(1968), *Gerechtigkeit als Weltordnung. Hintergrund und Geschichte des alttestamentliches Gerechtigkeitsbegriffes*, Tübingen

Schmidt, J.M. (1972), 'Probleme der Prophetenforschung', *Verkündigung und Forschung*, BhEvTh 17, 37-81

Schofield, J.N. (1969), *Law, Prophets and Writings*, London

Schottroff, W. (1977), 'Zum alttestamentlichen Recht', *VF* 22, 3-29

Schultz, H. (1862), 'Die Lehre von der Gerechtigkeit aus dem Glauben im alten und neuen Bunde', *JDT*, Gotha, 510-72

Schwarzschild, S.S. (1971), 'Justice', *EJ* 10, 476f.

Séguy, J. (1972), 'Max Weber et la sociologie historique des religions', *AsRel* 33, 71-103

Sekine, M. (1963), 'Erwägungen zur hebräischen Zeitauffassung', *SVT* 66-82

Sérouya, H. (1964), *Maimonide, sa vie, son oeuvre*, Paris

Shaskolsky, R.L. (1970), 'Protest and Dissent in Jewish Tradition. The Prophets as Dissenters', *Jdm* 19, 15-29

Scmueli, E. (1968), 'The "Pariah-People" and its "Charismatic Leadership". A Re-evaluation of Max Weber's *Ancient Judaism*', *PAAJR* 36, 167-247

Silver, A.H. (1928), *The Democratic Impulse in Jewish History*, New York

Skinner, J. (1902), 'Righteousness in OT', *DB(H)* 4, 272-81

Smith, M. (1969), 'The Present State of Old Testament Studies', *JBL* 88, 19-35

Smith, J.M.Powis (1918), 'Southern Influence upon Hebrew Prophecy', *AJSL* 35, 1-19
—(1931), *The Origins and History of Hebrew Law*, Chicago
Smith, W.R. (1881), *The Prophets of Israel and their Place in History*, Edinburgh
Soares, T.G. (1915), *The Social Institutions and Ideals of the Bible*, New York
Soden, W.von (1965), 'Die Frage nach der Gerechtigkeit Gottes im Alten Orient', *MDOG* 96, 41-59
—(1982), 'The Sabbath is for Ever – A Symposium', *Jdm* 31, 3-98
Sombart, W. (1911), *Die Juden und das Wirtschaftsleben*, Leipzig
Speiser, E.A. (1960), 'Leviticus and the Critics', *Y.Kaufmann Jubilee Volume*, Jerusalem, 29-45
—(1967), *Oriental and Biblical Studies*, Philadelphia
Steinmann, J. (1954), *Les Plus Anciennes Traditions du Pentateuque*, Paris
—(1959), *Le Prophétisme biblique des origines à Osée*, Paris
—(1960), *Richard Simon et les origines de l'exégèse biblique*, Paris
Swetnam, J. (1965), 'Some Observations on the Background of *tsdyq* in Jeremias 23:5a', *Bib* 46, 28-40
Szlechter, E. (1955), 'Le Prêt dans l'Ancien Testament et dans les codes mésopotamiens d'avant Hammurabi', *RHPR* 35, 16-25
Tanner, R. (1967), 'Zur Rechtsideologie im pharaonischen Ägypten', *FuF* 41, 247-50
Thomson, H.C. (1963), 'Shopet and mishpāt in the Book of Judges', *TGUOS* 19, 74-85
—(1970), 'Old Testament Ideas on the Life after Death', *TGUOS* 22, 46-55
Toaff, E. (1968-69), 'Evoluzione del concetto ebraico di zedāka', *AStE*, 111-22
Tresmontant, C. (1982), *Le Prophétisme hébreu*, Paris
Troeltsch, E. (1913), Review of Louis Wallis, *Sociological Study of the Bible*, *TLZ* 15, 454-8
—(1916), 'Das Ethos der hebräischen Propheten', *Logos* 6, 1-28
Türck, U. (1935), *Die sittliche Forderung der israelitischen Propheten des 8.Jahrhunderts*, Göttingen
Urbach, E.E. (1964), 'The Laws regarding Slavery as a Source for Social History in the period of the Second Temple, the Mishnah and Talmud', *Annual of Jewish Studies*, London, 1-94
Vajda, G. (1947), *Introduction à la pensée juive du Moyen Age*, Paris
Van der Ploeg, J. (1940), 'Sociale en economische vraagstukken uit de geschiedenis van Israel tijd der Koningen', *JEOL* 7, 390-9
—(1943), '*Shāpat* et *mishpāt*', *OTS* 2, 144-55
—(1950), 'Les Pauvres d'Israël et leur piété', *OTS* 7, 1950, 236-70
—(1950), 'Studies in Hebrew Law', *CBQ* 12, 248-59
—(1951), 'Studies in Hebrew Law', *CBQ* 13, 1; 28-43, 3, 296-307
—(1969), 'Le Pouvoir exécutif en Israël', *Studi in onore del Card. Ottaviani*, I, Rome, 509-19
Van Leeuwen, C. (1955), *Le développement du sens social en Israël avant l'ère chrétienne*, Assen

Vaux, R. de (1949), 'Les Patriarches hébreux et les découverts modernes', *RB* 56, 5-36

—(1965), 'Les Patriarches hébreux et l'histoire', *RB* 72, 18

—(1961), *Ancient Israel*, London and New York

— (1962), Review of M.Weippert (1971), *RB* 76, 272-6

Vawter, B. (1972), 'Intimations of Immortality and the Old Testament', *JBL* 91, 158-71

Veijola, T. (1977), *Das Königtum in der Beurteilung der deuteronomischen Historiographie*, Helsinki

Vella, J. (1964), *La giustizia forense di Dio*, Supplementi alla Rivista Biblica, Brescia

Vellas, V.M. (1964), 'The Spiritual Man according to the Old Testament', *GOTR* 10, 107-20

Vesco, J.-L. (1968), 'Les Lois sociales du Livre de l'alliance (Exode XX,22 – XXIII, 19)', *RThom* 68, 241-64

—(1980), 'Amos de Teqoa, défenseur de l'homme, *RB* 87, 481-513

Virgulin, S. (1972), 'La risurrezione dai morti in Is.26.14-19', *BeO* 14, 49-60

Vlastos, G. (1972), 'Justice and Happiness in the Republic', in *Plato II: Ethics, Politics and Philosophy of Art and Religion. A Collection of Critical Essays*, ed. id., London

—(1974), 'Equality and Justice in Early Greek Cosmologies', *CP* 42, 156-78

Vogt, J. (1971), *Bibliographie zur antiken Sklaverei*, Bochum

Wagner, G. (1977), *La Justice dans l'Ancien Testament et le Coran*, Neuchâtel

Waldow, H.E. von (1978), 'Social Responsibility and Social Structure in Early Israel', *CBQ* 32, 182-204

Wallis, L. (1902), 'The Capitalization of Social Development', *AJS* 7, 763-96

—(1905), *Egoism: A Study in the Social Premises of Religion*, Chicago

—(1922), *Sociological Study of the Bible*, Chicago (fourth edition)

—(1935), *God and the Social Process*, Chicago

—(1942), *The Bible is Human. A Study in Secular History*, New York

—(1949), *The Bible and Modern Belief*, Durham NC

—(1953), *Young People's Hebrew History*, New York

Walter, F. (1900), *Die Propheten in ihren sozialen Beruf und das Wirtschaftsleben ihrer Zeit*, Freiburg im Breisgau

Weber, M. (1967), *Ancient Judaism*, London (paperback ed.)

Weil, P. (1975), 'Le Shabbat comme institution et comme expérience', in *Le Shabbat dans la conscience juive*, Paris, 11-18

Weiler, I. (1980), 'Zum Schicksal der Witwen und Waisen bei den Völkern der Alten Welt', *Saec* 31, 157-93 (with an important bibliography)

Weinberger, O. (1948), *Die Wirtschaftsphilosophie des Alten Testament*, Vienna

Weinfeld, M. (1972), *Deuteronomy and the Deuteronomic School*, Oxford

—(1973), 'The Origin of the Apodictic Law', *VT* 23, 63-75

Weinrich, F. (1932), *Der religiös-utopische Charakter der prophetischen Politik*, Giessen

Weippert, M. (1971), *The Settlement of the Israelite Tribes in Palestine*, London

—(1974), 'Semitische Nomaden des zweiten Jahrtausends', *Bib* 55, 25-80

Welch, A.C. (1912), *The Religion of Israel under the Kingdom*, Edinburgh

—(1936), *Prophet and Priest in Old Israel*, London

Whitley, C.F. (1972), 'Deutero-Isaiah's Interpretation of *Sedeq*', *VT* 22, 469-75

Wicksteed, P.W. (1892), 'Abraham Kuenen', *JQR* 4, 571-605

—(1912), *Die Religion der Propheten*, in Volksschriften über die jüdische Religion, Frankfurt am Main

Wildeberger, H. (1963), 'Jesajas Verständnis der Geschichte', *SVT* 9, 83-117

Wildeboer, G. (1902), 'Die älteste Bedeutung des Stammes *tsdq*', *ZAW* 22, 1902, 167-9

Wilson, R.R. (1978), 'Early Isarelite Prophecy', *Interp* 32, 1978, 3-16

—(1980), *Prophecy and Society in Ancient Israel*, Philadelphia (with an important bibliography)

Wolff, H.W. (1960), 'Das Geschichtsverständnis der alttestamentlichen Prophetie', *EvTh* 20, 218-35

—(1964), *Gesammelte Studien zum Alten Testament*, Munich

—(1971), *Die Stunde des Amos. Prophetie und Protest*, Munich

—(1975), 'Prophecy from the Eighth through the Fifth Century', *Interp* 32, 17-30

Wolfson, H.A. (1934), *The Philosophy of Spinoza*, Harvard

Woolley, L. (1935), *Abraham*, London

Wright, G.E. (1950), *The Old Testament against its Environment*, London

Yadin, Y. (1961), 'Ancient Judean Weights and the Date of the Samaria Ostraca', *ScrHie* 8, 9-25

Yardeni, M. (1970), 'La Vision des Juifs et du judaîsme dans l'oeuvre de Richard Simon', *REJ* 79, 178-203

Yeivin, S. (1962), 'The Origin and Disappearance of the Khab/piru', *Actes du XXVᵉ congrès international des Orientalistes, Moscou 1960*, I, Moscow 439-41

Zeitlin, S. (1974), 'The Need for a Jewish Translation and Interpretation of the Hebrew Bible, *JQR* 65, 269-88

Ziesler, J.A. (1972), *The Meaning of Righteousness in Paul* (Ch.1, 'The Old Testament – The Nature of Hebrew Justice'), Cambridge 1972

INDEX

The ideas (e.g., right, law, justice) which form the very substance of the present work hardly appear at all in the index: rather, it contains essentially specific minor topics and proper names, including those of writers whose work is discussed in the text.